ACCESS

THE GUIDE TO A BETTER LIFE FOR DISABLED AMERICANS

Preface by BETTY FURNESS
Introduction by FRANK G. BOWE

DAVID OBST BOOKS
RANDOM HOUSE NEW YORK

LILLY BRUCK

ACCESS

THE GUIDE TO A BETTER LIFE FOR DISABLED AMERICANS

Grateful acknowledgment is made to the following for
permission to reprint previously published material:
Accent On Living Magazine; For the cartoon on page 172.
Copyright © 1977 by Accent On Living, Inc., Bloomington, Ill.

Library of Congress Cataloging in Publication Data

Bruck, Lilly.
Access.
Includes index.
1. Handicapped—Law and legislation—United States.
2. Handicapped as consumers—United States.   I. Title.
KF3738.B78   346′.73′013   77-90308
ISBN 0-394-73445-6 (pbk.)
          0-394-50133-0

Manufactured in the United States of America
9 8 7 6 5 4 3 2
First Edition

TO SANDRA SCHNUR,
who became my friend
and inspiration

ACKNOWLEDGMENTS

Special thanks are due several people:

Dr. Joseph Fenton, Chief, Special Centers, Rehabilitation Services Administration, and Mr. Bernard Posner, Executive Director, President's Committee on Employment of the Handicapped for their significant support of my work

My husband, Sandor, and my daughter, Sandy, whose moral support and graceful tolerance make my work possible

My editor, Kathy Matthews, who first approached me about this book and whose superb competence is equaled by her unlimited patience

David Obst, who had the vision and confidence that this book was needed

CONTENTS

IV. RECREATION

8. Arts, Libraries, Sports

9. Barrier-Free Travel

PREFACE

The consumer movement has grown over the last forty years from a good idea to an impressive fact of national life. From humble beginnings, principally in the trade unions, it has led to the passage of laws at all levels of government, which go a long way toward giving individual consumers a fairer shake in the marketplace.

A decade ago, when I became involved in consumerism, many of the rights that are now written into law—the right to know exactly how much it costs to borrow money, the right to have labels on clothing that tell the buyer how to care for it, the right to know just what is in our food—were merely ideas, spread by enthusiasts who were usually very much on the defensive against hostile business lobbyists. We still have a long way to go, but at least there has been progress toward a fairer give-and-take between buyer and seller.

That is good news for those of us who are physically able to deal with the everyday problems of the marketplace. But what about the special problems faced by those who have some disability which makes it more difficult for them to obtain goods and services?

In today's complicated marketplace, consumer education is a necessary tool for all consumers. People with disabilities have to learn even more: they must know that they have the right to assert themselves as customers, and to demand that the barriers of environment and attitude be removed from the marketplace and give them equal access to goods and services for which they spend their consumer dollars.

Most of us haven't had to cope with trying to enter a store in a wheelchair, only to find steps or revolving doors barring entrance, aisles, check-out lanes and fitting-room doors too narrow, rest rooms inaccessible, public telephones and water fountains out of reach.

Deaf and blind persons are constantly frustrated by the barriers in communication, physical barriers and, perhaps worst of all, barriers of attitude. How do you know if the elevator goes up or down if you don't see the red or green signals? Why should you miss out on some desirable purchase on the next counter because you can't see the counter or can't hear the sale announced on the store's public address system? Do you get the information you need if you must comparison-shop by telephone? Do you know what to do if mail-order merchandise does not arrive? Do you hesitate to complain about unsatisfactory goods or services because store personnel have not yet learned how to communicate properly with disabled customers?

Lilly Bruck, bless her, has taken up the cause of those who must endure these problems. She doesn't weep with pity; she gets right into the task of trying to ease the frustration of disabled consumers with some great advice. She suggests a host of solutions that are sound and practical. It is a remarkable treasury of information. Much of it can be of use to all of us. Best of all, it will help disabled consumers to be more able in the marketplace.

– BETTY FURNESS

INTRODUCTION

When Dr. Bruck first shared with me her plans for this book, I was immediately enthusiastic and urged her to avail herself of the resources of the American Coalition of Citizens with Disabilities (ACCD), the national advocacy organization I direct. Later, when she had completed the extensive research and careful writing that was required, she showed me the final product and I realized that she had reached all of the goals she had set for herself. Accordingly, I am pleased to contribute this brief introduction.

This is, to my knowledge, the first book on the topic ever published by a major American publishing house. Some books, such as my own *Handicapping America,* have focused upon the ways this country handicaps disabled people, but none I have seen explains to disabled individuals how they can better make use of their resources to obtain needed goods and services in the marketplace.

Dr. Bruck is, in my estimation, the nation's premier authority on consumer education for disabled people. She became a leader in this area long before other experts on consumer education even understood that disabled people encounter tremendous obstacles in purchasing and using goods and services they desire and need. As Director of Consumer Education for the Department of Consumer Affairs of the City of New York, she established close working relations with Ms. Eunice Fiorito, the blind Director of the Mayor's Office for the Handicapped, and together they mounted an impressive campaign to make the city, and eventually the nation, aware of the consumer needs of disabled people.

The concerns Dr. Bruck addresses in this book are enormously important. Most of America's 36 million disabled citizens are seriously undereducated and underemployed. Few have had the benefit of preparation in consumer affairs. As a result, they are seldom able to secure the products they need, both to alleviate the effects of their disabilities and to resolve the everyday consumer problems they share with most other Americans. Equally tragic, few disabled people have acquired the skills needed to make community businesses remove architectural, communication and attitudinal barriers that confront people with physical, sensory, mental and emotional impairments. Dr. Bruck explains these problems in her book and proposes pragmatic solutions of proven effectiveness that should help millions of disabled people to become more sophisticated consumers. For this great service, we are all in her debt.

— FRANK BOWE, Ph. D.

AUTHOR'S FOREWORD

Dear Reader:

As a consumer of goods and services, you are one of 240 million Americans. The goal of the consumer movement called "consumerism" is to protect your interests in the marketplace.

As a consumer with a disability, you are one of America's largest minority—36 million strong—consuming services provided by agencies, who, by tradition, also made decisions affecting your lives. Today, you want to share in these decisions, as surely you know best what is good for you. Your concern about sharing in these decisions is forcing you to become militant activists, the next minority, fighting for your equal rights as citizens.

In this book, the terms *consumer* and *consumerism* have two meanings. First, people with disabilities face not only the need to be intelligent buyers and users of goods and services, but also the challenge of advocating for long overdue improvements in production and service delivery. Essential goods are lacking altogether in many instances; in others, they may be unreliable or exorbitantly expensive. Needed services are often unavailable or grossly inferior in quality.

Second, people with disabilities must be consumers in the activist, civil rights sense, in order to become effective consumers in the market sense.

"In the past, the handicapped have sat back and let others speak for them. Now there is increasing militancy on the part of the handicapped themselves," wrote David Webb, a thirty-eight-year-old quadruplegic

Atlanta attorney in a *Newsweek* article (December 21, 1976) entitled "The Next Minority." "The physically handicapped are emerging as the nation's newest civil rights movement. And they are demanding what the majority of Americans take for granted: the ability to get on and off a bus or subway, to get in and out of a building, to attend the schools of their choice, to take full part in the community and to live independent lives with dignity."

I hope that as one of that minority, you are asserting your rights. As the disabled activist consumer, you must learn about laws that now are on the books, in order to make them realities in your life. And you must join in the fight to implement existing laws and create new laws that could change your future.

As a consumer of goods and services, you must see to it that you get the best value for your dollar in the marketplace.

As a disabled American, you must make your voice heard. You can't afford not to!

The disabled audience in this country is a large and potentially powerful one. "Eighteen percent of the population," estimated President Jimmy Carter in his address to the White House Conference on Handicapped Individuals, in May 1977. That is one American in six. There are 332,000 veterans of World War II, Korea and Vietnam; 2 million children with orthopedic handicaps; 250,000 Americans of all ages use wheelchairs; 13.4 million are hearing impaired, 750,000 of them deaf; 6.5 million are vision impaired, 1 million of them blind; 6.5 million mentally retarded; 100,000 babies each year are born with congenital impairments; 22 million people a year are injured in home accidents: disabling injuries occur at the rate of 1.2 million a year. Every day, 1,000 Americans pass their 65th birthday, entering the sphere of geriatric diseases, arthritis, heart disease, problems with vision and hearing.

Added to the number of disabled individuals those concerned with or about them, relatives, friends and professionals, the estimated number is 120 million people, more than half the entire American population. That is a potentially powerful group of people. If these people have accurate information and work together toward common goals, they can accomplish a great deal. They can make it possible for America's 36 million citizens with disabilities to obtain goods and services they need and want, under conditions that are fair and equitable.

There is more. The disabled minority is not a closed society. While nobody will ever change his color of skin or place of birth, anyone can join this minority by accident, illness or advancing age. Disability does not respect age, sex, religion or social status. Every American should consider himself an ally for disabled people seeking a fair deal.

The changes that will help disabled persons obtain products and assistance are changes that in many instances assist all Americans to obtain needed goods and services. Architectural modifications that help people using wheelchairs to gain access into stores also help mothers pushing baby carriages, elderly citizens and temporarily injured people. Communication devices and techniques that help deaf and blind individuals to get facts they need make acquisition of information easier for all consumers.

Disabled people often start the consumer game at a triple disadvantage. Because of undereducation, they may be relatively unsophisticated in the marketplace. Undereducation and unemployment may mean they have reduced buying power. Barriers in the marketplace—architectural, attitudinal, communication and transportation obstacles—may restrict their roles as consumers.

This book is about overcoming those barriers, so that you as a disabled American may obtain full equality as a citizen and as a consumer.

—Lilly Bruck

I. INTO THE MAINSTREAM

1. CONSUMER MOVEMENTS

CONSUMERISM FOR ALL CONSUMERS

Is it realistic for consumers who are disabled to expect, even to demand, equality in the marketplace? The answer is: Yes!

You are a consumer of goods and services because you spend money. The term *consumer* means anyone who purchases goods such as food, clothing, shelter, devices, instruments and vehicles, and who uses services, including maintenance and repair of products purchased, insurance and other intangibles. As consumers, people are concerned with securing maximum value, saving money, obtaining protection from fraudulent practices, and attaining guarantees that products and services live up to advertised claims.

Beginning in 1906 with the publication of Upton Sinclair's exposé of Chicago stockyards, *The Jungle,* America has moved, slowly but surely, in the direction of greater public regulation of private industry. It was not until John F. Kennedy proclaimed four rights of consumers in 1962, however, that the movement known as "consumerism" really began. Kennedy's declaration, "The Consumer Bill of Rights," enumerated these basic prerogatives of consumers: the right to choose, the right to safety, the right to be informed, and the right to be heard.

The first right related to unfair monopolies and stated that consumers had a right to have equivalent alternatives available in goods and services. The second concerned the right of consumers to product safety standards, including warnings in understandable language and adequate precautionary measures. The third right addresses the consumer's need for comprehensive and accurate descriptions of goods and services before making a decision to purchase or to use. The fourth involved the right of consumers to complain, to petition government and industry, and to have these complaints and petitions attended to and resolved.

Gerald R. Ford added the right to consumer education in 1975. Consumer education refers to public and private, formal and informal efforts to increase people's sophistication about how they spend their money. It focuses upon such areas as legislation, government regulation, advertising, consumer protection agencies, insurance, housing, education and transportation.

Consumerism, then, is the movement in America today that stresses these five consumer rights and seeks to enhance the realization of full benefits under these rights for all Americans. In recent years, consumerism has become a world-wide phenomenon, particularly as the communications media increased public awareness of the advantages and disadvantages of modern goods and services.

In America, however, yet another meaning of the term consumerism has evolved. Though the term was seldom used to describe the efforts of women and minority groups to obtain equality of opportunity, in the mid-1970s, as people with disabilities began to advocate for improved services, the term was applied to disabled activists and their movement.

The origin of this use of the word "consumerism" lies in the traditional service-delivery dichotomy of providers and consumers. Services and products needed by people with disabilities, particularly those used in education and rehabilitation, were provided by people who typically were not themselves disabled. Following a centuries-old tradition, these people spoke for or represented disabled individuals, making decisions on their behalf.

Consumers, on the other hand, were disabled people seeking to speak for themselves. Increasingly, discontent with their historically subservient role as recipients, they began in the 1970s to press for greater consumer involvement, in the making of decisions, the production of goods, and the delivery of services that vitally affected their lives.

DECADE OF DISABILITY

The 1970s will likely emerge as the Decade of Disability, for it is in this decade that historic civil and human rights advances by disabled people were dramatically achieved. These monumental gains produce a firm foundation for new achievements in the marketplace.

The 1973 Rehabilitation Act (Public Law 93-112), as amended in 1974 (PL 93-516), offered perhaps the single most significant landmark to date in the struggle of disabled people to end nearly two hundred years of second-class citizenship. Section 504 of the act, entitled "Nondiscrimination Under Federal Grants," stated in forty sweeping words that:

> *No otherwise qualified handicapped individual in the United States shall, solely on the basis of his handicap, be excluded from participation in, be denied the benefits of, or be subjected to discrimination under any program or activity receiving Federal assistance.*

Regulations did not come into being at the same time that the Rehabilitation Act of 1973 became law. This part of the act was turned over to the Secretary of Health, Education and Welfare so that he could write the regulations pertaining to Section 504, because HEW is the agency which administers the bulk of federal programs serving people with disabilities.

This job was put off for more than three years by the former Secretaries of HEW while the disabled of this country waited. When President Jimmy Carter appointed Joseph A. Califano Secretary of HEW, consumer groups again went to HEW and urged that these regulations be signed. Mr. Califano wanted more time to reconsider them.

On April 5, 1977, disabled consumer activists lost their patience. Demonstrations took place in Washington and at all regional offices of HEW across the United States, involving over five thousand people. Sitters-in at San Francisco and Washington endured three weeks of discomfort and hardships.

On April 28, 1977, Secretary Califano signed Section 504, making this date a landmark in the quest of disabled citizens for equal treatment, inaugurating a new era of civil rights for the handicapped.

George T. Stone, president of the National Association OF [sic] the Physically Handicapped, Inc., writes in the Summer 1977 issue of the NAPH *National Newsletter:*

What does all this mean to you and me?

- All new facilities must be barrier-free.
- Programs or activities in existing facilities must be made accessible to the handicapped within 60 days.
- Employers may not refuse to hire handicapped persons, if reasonable accommodations can be made by them to an individual's handicap, and if the handicap does not impair the ability of the applicant or employer to do the specific job.

■ Employers may not require pre-employment physical examinations.

■ Every handicapped child will be entitled to free public education according to his or her individual needs. Handicapped children must not be
segregated in the public schools. They must be educated with the nonhandicapped in regular classrooms.

These are just a few of the requirements of the Act. This act applies
to housing, transportation and other services offered to the general
public that are supported by Federal Funds. HEW's Office of Civil Rights
has the responsibility of enforcing these regulations . . .

Braille and recorded copies of the 504 regulations have been prepared
and distributed so that handicapped citizens can learn firsthand of their
rights.

A major public awareness program about Section 504 will be under-
taken so that the handicapped will be informed of their rights under this
new law, and also, so the non-handicapped of the land will be well
informed on the subject.

What all this means is that you and I as handicapped consumers
have to do our part to see that this law is enforced. It will be up to us to
help keep the public informed. HEW can not do the job alone; they will
need the help of the many consumer groups across the country.

Within one month of the signing of Section 504, disabled Americans
had achieved three other historic advances:

On May 19, Brock Adams, the Secretary of Transportation, announced
a decision to require all new standard-size buses purchased with federal funds
to be fully accessible.

On May 23, President Jimmy Carter declared: "The time of discrimination against the handicapped is over."

On May 25, Patricia Roberts Harris, the Secretary of Housing and Urban
Development, announced that 5 percent of all new family-unit housing built
with federal financial assistance would be constructed for full accessibility.

Monumental as these gains are, they are paralleled in importance by the
maturing of disabled Americans as a potential political force. The April
demonstration brought these people together across the historical schisms of
age, sex, race, religion and national origin to forge a united body capable of
advocating for improved services and enhanced opportunities.

This newly emerging sophistication and unity will be greatly needed in
the years to come. The advances achieved in April and May of 1977 apply
only to programs and activities receiving federal financial assistance. Virtually untouched is the vast private sector which does not depend upon

federal funds. It is here that consumerism in the market sense comes into play and it is here that disabled Americans must now focus the lion's share of their attention.

A FAIR DEAL

A Harris public-opinion poll published early in 1977 indicated that the average American consumer desired above all else a fair deal in the marketplace. Consumer confidence in industry was low, with suspicion about price gouging and unethical business practices high. Disabled consumers echoed these feelings, but with greater than average force. For the consumer who is disabled, access to stores and facilities is often severely restricted by environmental and transportation barriers. Attitudinal obstacles prevent many disabled consumers from obtaining quality services. Products needed by these individuals to overcome the effects of their disabilities are expensive and often notoriously unreliable.

The disabled population of this country has never received a fair deal in the marketplace. It is now the task of consumers who are disabled to direct their energies toward achieving this goal. The job will be a difficult, time-consuming one, and will require that disabled Americans become knowledgeable, discerning and alert consumers. Equally vital will be a cooperative endeavor involving a natural alliance of disabled people with other consumers to force private industry to respond to their demands.

SOME DEFINITIONS

I have described two meanings of the words *consumer* and *consumerism*, noting that in this book a special denotation is given that recognizes the need for disabled people to be advocates as well as purchasers and users. Some other terms must also be defined to prevent misunderstanding.

Disability and *handicap* are not identical in meaning. Except where it is unavoidable, I will use the term *disabled* and not *handicapped* to refer to physical, mental, sensory and emotional impairments that interfere with major tasks of daily living. The word *handicap* will be reserved for a unique use: to denote an interaction between a disability and an environment in which the design of the environment erects obstacles or barriers to disabled people. Thus, iron gates outside supermarkets and narrow checkout lanes within, designed to prevent shopping-cart theft, handicap people in wheelchairs by denying them convenient exit. Remove the gates, widen the lanes, eliminate the confining environment—and the customer in a wheelchair, though still disabled, is no longer handicapped in access to the store.

Access refers to more than physical accessibility. Deaf people may be denied access by auditory-based warning and announcement systems, for example. They may thus miss out on special, impromptu sales or may miss scheduled departures of transportation. Similarly, blind individuals may be denied access if messages are not offered in raised letters, Braille or other, auditory-based, communications systems.

Access is achieved by removing handicapping barriers to disabled consumers. The goal may be stated as

A DISABLED CONSUMERS' BILL OF RIGHTS

The right to ACCESS for mobility-impaired individuals
The right to INFORMATION for visually impaired persons
The right to COMMUNICATION for hearing-impaired people
The right to CONSIDERATION for mentally and emotionally impaired individuals

People who have mobility limitations include paraplegic and quadruplegic individuals, persons who have had polio, people who have lost one or more limbs in an accident or through disease, and elderly citizens whose chronic health problems reduce their mobility. These people have the right to ACCESS to all marketplaces in America.

Individuals who are blind or severely visually impaired have the right to INFORMATION that is available to sighted persons.

Deaf and seriously hearing-impaired people have the right to COMMUNICATION with all sales and other personnel. Through printed announcements, captions on television commercials, addresses and directions in print in advertisements (rather than just phone numbers to call), teletypewriters in stores and offices, and sign-language interpreters, this right may be realized.

Individuals who have general or specific learning disabilities and those who are emotionally or mentally impaired, have a right to CONSIDERATION by educated, sensitive and polite personnel.

But, and this is central to the entire book, consumers who are disabled also have the five rights enumerated earlier: to choose from among compet-

ing alternatives, to receive safe products, to be informed about character-
istics of goods and services, to be heard and to be offered consumer education. For to focus only on the disabilities of people is to miss what is so
uniquely human about them: their abilities, likes and dislikes, tastes and
preferences.

These nine rights must be more than just abstract goals or principles.
They must be real. The profit potential of 36 million disabled people,
together with their families, friends and interested neighbors, is a potent
change agent. Properly channeled, this profit potential will succeed where
the altruistic motives of businessmen have not: in changing the very face of
America's marketplaces so that every consumer will have equality.

2. IMAGES

MEDIA AND ADVERTISING

During the month of April 1977, television, radio, newspapers and magazines suddenly exploded with dramatically different stories about people with disabilities. Headlines used words like *activists, radicals, demand* and *protest* to describe the nationwide demonstration by thousands of disabled Americans for equality of opportunity. The stories had shock value because disabled persons had never before exhibited such assertiveness.

The new image was astonishingly successful in helping 36 million citizens gain unprecedented civil rights protection: a rule was made guaranteeing enforcement of rights in education, health and social services, and a spate of new legislation providing voting rights, employment security, housing and transportation privileges followed shortly thereafter.

This image—of independent, aware, intelligent and self-confident persons—fits the reality much better than does the traditional portrait of dependent, withdrawing and needy individuals. Decades of telethons and other programs had portrayed disabled people as victims, unable to control their own lives, incapable of speaking on their own behalf. This image fattened the chests of a few agencies but did little to advance the human and civil rights—or to enhance the lives—of people with disabilities.

Yet it is the old image of dependence, not the new one of independence, that continues to dominate the media. Consider these facts:

- Disabled people are never chosen to advertise products. Even devices for disabled individuals typically are demonstrated by nondisabled actors.

- Talk shows and game programs almost never feature disabled guests. TV situation comedies and dramas portray disabled characters as helpless victims of fate—and the characters are portrayed by nondisabled actors.
- Newspaper feature stories about people with disabilities focus either on superhuman achievements or on subhuman failures.

The effect is devastating. Employers faced with applications from disabled job seekers reject them out of hand. "I admire your courage," they often say, "but I'm in business to make a profit, not to dispense charity." Families of disabled children are ashamed to admit to having less than perfect children, hide them from view by society and see their counterparts on TV only as poster children in appeals. Most devastated are disabled people themselves. According to the media, these people either do not exist or are subhumans to be hidden, pitied and ignored.

Ironside, the wheelchair-bound supersleuth, who is no longer on the air, and Linda, the deaf character on the children's show *Sesame Street,* are lonely oases in the desert of neglect.

In the latter half of 1977 and early in 1978, this trend of denial in the media changed. Documentaries discuss the topic. In the NBC series *James at 15,* a dramatic episode showed the engaging young man's struggle to help his deaf friend transfer from a school for the deaf to his own public school. The friends' communication in sign language made the viewer enter into their relationship. "My eyes are my ears and my hands are my speech," the deaf boy, portrayed by a deaf actor, tells his classmates. A bigoted coach and a thoughtless date confirm Scott's mother's fears that her deaf son would get hurt in the hearing world. In the end, the supportive acceptance of his peers and Scott's triumph in sports strengthen his self-image and accomplish his integration.

"One small step for TV, one huge step for the disabled" wrote the author on the following day to NBC's vice president for programming. Paraphrased, but not quite true. Because this episode was also a huge step for television and a fine contribution to the education of nondisabled viewers.

Next time you see programs of this kind, why don't you write to the station and express your appreciation? Public approval keeps innovative programs on the air and creates more of them.

Of course, it would be asking for the moon to suggest that this particular program could have been captioned for the benefit of deaf audiences. Producers claim that visible captions disturb hearing audiences. All the more reason to work toward use of Line 21, transmitting captions visible only to deaf viewers whose TV sets are equipped with decoding devices. (See p. 26.)

When the 1964 Civil Rights Act was passed, black Americans were seldom seen in advertisements, feature stories or TV programs. The situation was similar to what it is now for disabled people. Gradually, under considerable pressure from civil rights groups, producers and advertisers began including token blacks. At the outset, only very handsome and beautiful actors and actresses were used and usually these people had prominent white features—light skin, for example, and straight hair. In commercials, black models appeared mostly in group scenes, sometimes even slightly out of focus, and black actors never handled the product. If the show was a drama or comedy, they were supportive characters, never leads.

Civil rights leaders were not satisfied. They demanded—and got—more. A report in the February 1977 issue of the *Journal of Advertising Research* states that in the 1974–75 season (the one studied), about 13 percent of all commercials showed black persons, compared with 5 percent in a 1967 study. And they do handle the product. Movies and TV shows feature black leads, and all black casts propel TV shows into the top ratings. Entire new industries have emerged to serve the black population.

The lessons are clear. Disabled people must demand fair and balanced portrayals in the media—and use of actors who are themselves disabled. Feature stories about disabilities and disabled people should be written in consultation with these people or by them, not just for and about them. Recently metropolitan newspapers report almost daily on rights and lives of disabled adults and on the education of handicapped children. Sometimes articles criticize the anticipated cost of adaptations—as could be expected.

If your local paper does not yet report or does not report fairly, put pen (or typewriter) to paper and make your voice heard.

Every disabled American can play a role. When a newspaper magazine story appears that presents a biased picture of disabled persons, write a letter to the editor, demanding an apology, and insisting that future stories be prepared with more concern for accuracy.

Here's an example of how to word your letter of protest:

TO THE EDITOR:

I am writing to applaud you on your decision to publish an article about disabled people ("Paraplegic Starts Own Business," May 23). We need more stories that bring disabilities to the attention of the public. But not this kind of a story.

Your article on John James, a 39-year-old veteran of service to his country in time of war, was demeaning and inaccurate. The use of terms like *victim* (which appeared five times in three paragraphs) and *helpless* to describe a self-employed, independent individual, creates in the readers' minds distorted pictures of what paraplegia is and means.

I demand (1) an immediate, written apology from you; (2) an insert in your next edition, publicly apologizing for the distortion, and (3) a commitment from you to consult with at least one disabled person before any subsequent stories about people with disabilities appear. I, for one, will be pleased to help.

Sincerely yours,
SAM BROWN

If you are not the demanding type, and think the editor may react to a somewhat softer reprimand—you know your local paper best. But remember, "a man's reach should exceed his grasp, or what's a heaven for?"

Send copies of your letter to the author of the story in question, to local education and citizen-advocacy groups, and to other individuals who are disabled, urging them to join you in your attempts to improve the public image of disabled people.

With radio and television programs and commercials, you can do more. Food and food products have become the first $1 billion advertiser in television. Procter & Gamble was again number one in the top 100 national advertisers in 1976, with advertising expenditures of $357 million. (The total spending for the top 100 advertisers was $4.8 billion, reports *Advertising Age*, May 16, 1977.) General Mills spent $20 million on Wheaties advertising alone, and the Dr Pepper Company spent $125,000 to make just one television commercial. Yet did you ever see a child in a wheelchair eat breakfast cereal or a teen-ager on crutches sip a soft drink?

The ages-two-to-eleven market gets a lion's share of advertisers' attention. By the time an average child is ready for kindergarten, he or she has seen 4,000 hours of televison, and 70,000 thirty-second food commercials.* Children aged six to eleven watch an average of 27 hours a week. If your child is orthopedically or otherwise disabled and more home-bound than his or her peers, the TV viewing hours may top these averages. The majority of the ads are for sweetened cereals and foods and candies, followed by other foods and toys. Don't even the telethons' poster children ever eat snack foods or play with toys? Not on TV they don't!

* Report by the Office of Research and Analysis for the New York State Assembly, March 1977.

You can do something about it. Follow the example of ACT, "Action for Children's Television." From a small group of Boston mothers who decided to do something about what glued their children to the TV sets, ACT has become a respected and influential citizens' action group. Forced by Federal Communications Commission regulations and by public opinion, networks have, among other concessions, reduced the minutes per hour devoted to commercials on children's programs and prohibited the leading character of a program, for instance Bugs Bunny or Superman to step out of the program and advertise a product, strongly influencing impressionable young minds who trust the words of their heroes.

☞ **Write to ACT, 46 Austin Street, Newtonville, Mass. 02160, to ask them for some guidelines for your action.**

A similar campaign began in 1977, protesting the excessive violence on TV programs, arguing that it may contribute to the violence shown on the newscasts. "OD'ing on the Tube," an article in *Science News* (July 1977), reports:

> After extensive hearings on TV violence, the House Interstate and Foreign Commerce Committee has issued a report summarizing the information that was gained. The report notes, among other, that: by age 18, the average TV viewer will have witnessed 18,000 murders, and seen 640,000 commercials; the American high school graduate will have spent about 15,000 hours in front of a TV set, compared with 11,000 hours in the classroom; Saturday morning's children's shows, while said to be improving in quality, still present 16.2 violent incidents per broadcast hour, compared with only 3.8 per hour during "family shows."

TV violence itself was on trial in the fall of 1977 when a fifteen-year-old boy, accused of having murdered an eighty-three-year-old woman, pleaded insanity caused by the violence he had watched on the tube. The jury ignored the plea and sentenced the boy to life in prison, but former FCC Commissioner Nicholas Johnson, now chairman of the National Citizens Committee for Broadcasting, said in a statement following the verdict: "The boy has been found guilty of a senseless murder. Television is guilty of something worse. The boy didn't profit from his crime. Television does. Network executives who know full well what they are doing are using violence in shows as a cheap dramatic device to increase corporate profits.

"They know it encourages violence in society. They know televised crimes are copied by criminals. They know televiolence desensitizes us to real life violence. They know it encourages confrontation rather than conciliation as a solution to human problems. And yet they go on using it. TV is *guilty as charged.*"

With more and more citizens voicing their protests against mainly profit-oriented TV fare, it is time for 36 million disabled Americans and their families and friends to form their own TV lobby:

- Write letters to the producers.
- Demand equal time to correct misrepresentations.
- Write to the Federal Communications Commission (FCC) demanding investigations: FCC, Broadcast Bureau, 1919 M Street, N.W., Washington, D.C. 20554.
- Write to advertisers who sponsor shows or commercials of which you disapprove.

The National Advertising Council of the Better Business Bureau, 845 Third Avenue, New York, N.Y. 10022, suggests you write to them with complaints about tasteless commercials or offensive advertising. "You can also refuse to buy the product advertised," they advise, "then write the president of the company manufacturing the product (your local library will have the address) and tell him you bought another brand because of the offensive commercial. You can also call the local station and say you will no longer watch their station because of the tasteless commercials. Complain— not only to your neighbor—but to the people who economically depend on you."

You can go beyond the negative to the positive. And you should. Write to editors, producers and advertisers with ideas for programs and ads.

- Insist that captioning be used so deaf people can understand what is being said.
- Letters to the Editor of major city newspapers provide another forum for presenting new ideas.
- You may be able to interest advertisers in the idea of using disabled actors to demonstrate products. Remind them that like other men and women, black and white, disabled people use toothpaste, shampoo their hair, wear fashionable clothes, drive fancy cars and want their laundry whiter than white, with no ring around the collar.

"Hurrah for Ex-Lax" wrote the author in a letter to Robert C. Howell, president of the company, who for the first time used an interpreter for the deaf on TV using sign language as well as lip movement in a segment occupying about one sixth of the screen while the featured actress makes a soft-sell pitch for the product. "Congratulations on acknowledging that deaf people too may sometimes suffer from irregularity. It's easy to see which brand they will choose . . ." A copy of the letter went to Ogilvy & Mather, the advertising agency that created the commercial. Mr. Howell gives credit for the idea to R. A. Peterson, senior vice president of marketing, who in turn says he was inspired by a segment on Gallaudet College for the Deaf on *60 Minutes* on CBS-TV network that he saw twice.

Write to sponsors of advertising that pleases you. Tell them that you will choose their brands from among competing products. If there is no reaction from the public, innovations may disappear; with approval, they will proliferate. It is good business to reach, not ignore, a population as large as that of 36 million disabled Americans and twice as many members of their families and friends.

There are other kinds of advertising to consider. Stores having display posters might include the symbol of accessibility to show that their facilities are easily entered and used by people with mobility limitations. Signs indicating that staff members have some knowledge of finger spelling and sign language can be used just as easily as "Se habla español" now is. In the classified section of telephone directories, restaurants can indicate the availability of Brailled menus. Movie theaters could indicate captioned films by a symbolic ear.

The aim is to make disabilities visible, common and comprehensible, to remove the strangeness and the fear that strangeness creates.

If you read this book, chances are you have seen copies of any of the magazines directed at readers with physical disabilities. You'll have seen plenty of advertisements for hydraulic van lifts, wheelchairs, ramps, urinary devices, telecommunications systems, sign-language educational toys and special trips to places all around the globe. You'll have yet to see ads for the latest best seller, a rejuvenating face cream, a masculine after-shave lotion, crunchy new cereal and miracle floor polish. Are disabled people blissfully protected from common colds, splitting headaches, upset stomachs or occasional sleeplessness that need to be relieved by well-known over-the-counter remedies?

Major advertisers seem to be unaware, or choose to ignore, the existence of inexpensive advertising space in magazines, newspapers and newsletters targeted at these special readerships. Compare some of the rates per advertising page:

Accent on Living	$510	*Time*	$34,320
Paraplegia News	190	*Good Housekeeping*	27,300
The Deaf American	150	*Money*	10,110
Handy Cap Horizons	100	*Glamour*	6,650

Of course you know that advertising rates are based on circulation. (Why do you think you get so bombarded with invitations to subscribe? It's not your subscription money they're after—it's your head count for the advertising rates. This is the equal to the *ratings,* the numbers of viewers, that TV networks fight for.) True, *per thousand of readership* on which advertising rates are based, pages in the specialty magazines for disabled readers may even cost more *per thousand* than in the multimillion-circulation magazines.

BUT in the multimillion-dollar budgets of advertisers (remember, $20 million alone for Wheaties), what percentage would a few thousand dollars constitute for advertising in your magazines?

Write to the advertisers in the multimillion-readers magazines that you will buy their products if and when you'll see their ads in your magazines!

You can also tell them that these magazines are read not only by the physically disabled themselves but by their families, by professional and lay people working with them, vocational counselors, physical and occupational therapists, physicians and technicians. And the physically disabled themselves, professionals, workers, students or home-bound, presumably read the magazines directed to their interests and needs with greater attention than those of general interest. "For this reason," writes one of the publishers, "our advertisers report a per reader response greatly exceeding publications with a more diversified circulation."

You can start your own campaign at the cost of a few postage stamps:

- Find the address of manufacturers on the wrapping of any advertised product. Write. Tell them about the market they could tap by advertising in magazines directed at special audiences.
- Write to companies that do make efforts to reach these audiences and buy their products whenever feasible.
- Suggest to members of your club, organization, church, family, friends to join in your campaign.

Individually and collectively, you just may start something!

All this can lead to better lives for disabled people, but chances are, it won't be nearly enough. Americans are deluged with information from programs and advertising. To make an impact, disabled people and their allies need to go one step further. The critical point is that one cannot sell respect for the abilities of disabled people the way cars or soap or clothes are sold.

People concerned about improving employment of disabled people have believed that public education was the answer. They prepared radio spots, TV announcements, brochures and feature stories, stressing the abilities of disabled workers, the low absenteeism rates of such workers, and the assistance available to enable employers to find qualified disabled applicants. Even the Internal Revenue Service made its contribution by permitting up to $25,000 as an immediate tax write-off to an employer who reconstructs his premises to make them accessible to mobility-impaired employees.

But what happened? Available evidence suggests that overall employment of disabled people was little changed by these promotions. Here and there an employer hired a disabled worker . . . but only here and there. Research revealed a startling fact. Most likely to hire disabled persons were employers who had already hired disabled people. The key was personal contact, personal experience.

This is why disabled people and their allies must mount campaigns that stress personal interaction.

- Follow up that letter to the editor with a personal visit.
- Go to meetings where decisions are being made by public agencies and private companies. Make yourselves visible and get to know the decision makers personally.

Some things you may want to try:

- Organize a trip to a major automobile manufacturer. Have people who had to make expensive alterations on their vehicles drive these cars and vans to the company headquarters. Demonstrate the problems . . . and ask for cooperation.
- Hold a special demonstration in front of an inaccessible store. Invite the press, of course, but talk to customers too.
- Display barrier-free buses and trolleys in action.
- Hold "public hearings" of your own, with debates and speeches about key issues.
- Publicize a "Best Stores" list . . . and a "Worst Stores" list. Take the press to examples of both.

- Mount mail and phone campaigns, urging people to patronize some facilities and not others.
- On election day, hold a press conference in front of an inaccessible polling booth . . . and talk to voters as they enter and leave. Even if and when Congress passes a law to require all polling places for national elections to be accessible, there'll be plenty of local elections and primaries not bound by such a (not yet existing) law.

The point is to be visible and to make disabilities and disabled people part of the personal experience of community residents. Go beyond using the media to involve people themselves. You'll be able to think of many more ways to do this. But remember—to many people, disabilities are feared because they are strange and unknown. Your objective is to make them familiar and known.

One disabled individual summed up the message I tried to convey in this chapter better than I can. He's Bruce Hillam, writing in the April 1977 issue of *New World,* a magazine published by the California Association of the Physically Handicapped, Inc.:

Ten years ago, another large minority, the Blacks, didn't have any problems either, according to Madison Avenue. As I watch TV now, I am amazed to learn that Blacks have all sorts of problems. They have body odor, they make terrible coffee, their cars need rebuilt transmissions, and they use the wrong dishwasher detergent.

When I can watch TV and see a crip move next door to Archie (Gloria will be divorced by then and start dating a handsome paraplegic, who will indeed be a paraplegic), or laugh to the new hit comedy Charlie and the Man (Charlie will be a misunderstood blind mechanic played by Stevie Wonder), or watch a one armed magician on Johnny Carson, I'll know things are "looking good."

If it's pointed out during the commercial breaks that every stutterer drinks milk, that I should use Texaco and let the man with the star adjust my hand controls, whether I need it or not, or that wheelchair tires will not scuff Johnson's J Wax, I'll know I have arrived. We will have a public identity as people, not objects of a Telethon.

3. ACCESS

DESIGN FOR A BARRIER-FREE MAN-MADE ENVIRONMENT

Segregation of an entire group of people does not necessarily have to be deliberate. It can, in fact, occur through thoughtlessness or inaction. Inaccessible buildings and lack of communication segregate the walking, hearing, seeing population from people with disabilities as effectively as "White Only" separated races in days now past in the United States.

Discrimination against disabled citizens is now illegal—on the books. True integration, however, can only take place when attitudes change through education, visibility, participation and integration of disabled individuals into the mainstream.

"Access America" is the trademark of a public-awareness campaign launched in May 1977 by the Architectural and Transportation Compliance Board, created by Congress in 1973, primarily to ensure compliance with standards prescribed under federal laws. The campaign intends to draw attention to architectural, transportation and attitudinal barriers affecting millions of people, and to promote barrier-free design in the man-made environment.

Man-made environmental barriers generally fall into two categories: architectural barriers and lack of communication. People in wheelchairs not only find curbs, stairs, inaccessible transportation and narrow rest-room doors insurmountable obstacles, they also spend their lives only four feet high in an environment geared to people five feet or taller. They must always look up when conversing with standing adults; they also find shelves in stores, counters in banks and fast-food eateries too high, elevator buttons, public telephones and drinking fountains out of reach, and physicians' examining tables designed for people who can climb up on them. Clearly, inaccessibility means more than forbidding stairs to occupants of wheelchairs.

Braille signs on doors and elevator buttons, tactile maps of college campuses, voice announcements in transportation systems can give to the blind access and mobility. The printed word can reach them in Brailled or taped forms. Part 138 of the *Postal Service Manual* provides for free mailing of certain matter "for the use of the blind or other persons who cannot use or read conventionally printed material because of a physical impairment and are certified by competent authority as unable to read normal reading material."

Telecommunications systems and sign-language interpreters can assist deaf people to communicate with each other and with the hearing world.

All of these measures contribute to *access*, and people with disabilities must insist that they be applied so that users may join the mainstream. "I am not a shut in, I am a shut out," wrote a Connecticut resident in a survey conducted by the author. Two things will help: laws on the books; citizens' action in the field.

ACCESSIBILITY

Public Law 90-480, the Architectural Barriers Act of 1968, seeks to make barrier-free any facility built or supported by federal funds:

■ Any building constructed or leased in whole or in part with federal funds must be made accessible to and usable by the physically handicapped.

   This law applies to any building designed, constructed or altered after standards of accessibility were developed by the General Services Administration, the Department of Housing and Urban Development, and the Department of Defense.

—U.S. Code, Title 42, Section 4151-56

Public Law 93-87, the Federal Highway Act of 1973, mandates the easy movement of people in wheelchairs across curbs on public roadways:

■ The Secretary of Transportation may not approve any State highway program which does not provide for adequate and reasonable access for the safe and easy movement of the physically handicapped across curbs.

- *Physically handicapped* specifically includes those individuals confined to wheelchairs.
- This curb cut requirement applies to all curbs constructed or replaced at pedestrian crosswalks on or after July 1, 1976.

—U.S. Code, Title 23, Section 402

The key thrust for making accessibility mandatory is the *use of federal funds.* This is also true in state laws in fifty states. Where state and local public funds are involved, accessibility is a must.

This legislation leaves a great many types of buildings outside its scope— that is, all buildings built by private capital, without government contributions. Disabled people themselves must lead the fight to make all buildings and roadways used by the public accessible to everybody, and they must involve the community in their efforts.

Made aware of their responsibilities, members of the community will work toward making accessible churches, libraries, museums, parks, theaters, any place of public assembly. As businessmen, store owners will make their buildings accessible to the man or woman in a wheelchair, the person on crutches, the blind and the hearing-impaired—all potential customers with latent purchasing power.

What you do, as a handicapped or able-bodied concerned citizen in your community, spells the difference between status quo and the gradual elimination of barriers. There are many associations of and for citizens with disabilities that will be glad to supply you with literature and counsel.

The National Easter Seal Society publishes a complete blueprint for action: *Architectural Barriers Guides,* containing guidelines for community action. In order to continue full cooperation between interested groups and overall coordination of the program—nationally, statewide and locally— they ask that you notify their Architectural Barriers Project, 2023 W. Ogden Avenue, Chicago, Ill. 60612.

Here are some more organizations that will gladly supply you with information. You may write to their national headquarters or contact their local chapters in your area:

American Institute of Architects, 1735 New York Avenue, Washington, D.C. 20006.

Architectural and Transportation Barriers Compliance Board, Washington, D.C. 20201.

National Center for a Barrier-Free Environment, 8401 Connecticut Avenue, N.W., Washington, D.C. 20015.

Paralyzed Veterans of America, Inc., 7315 Wisconsin Avenue, Washington, D.C. 20014.

President's Committee on Employment of the Handicapped, Washington, D.C. 20036.

Your state's Governor's Committee on Employment of the Handicapped.

Rehabilitation Services Administration, 330 C Street, S.W., Washington, D.C. 20201.

Publications and bibliographies, yours for the asking:

Resource Guide to Literature on Barrier-Free Environments, with selected annotations (1977). Architectural and Transportation Barriers Compliance Board, Washington, D.C. 20201.

Guilty Buildings. The President's Committee on Employment of the Handicapped, Washington, D.C. 20036.

Current Materials on Barrier-Free Design. A Clearinghouse Service of the National Easter Seal Society.

Publications available from National Center for a Barrier-Free Environment, Information Clearinghouse.

Architectural Barriers: A selected bibliography of recent materials on barriers in libraries, schools and institutions. Reference Services, Library of Congress for the Blind and Physically Handicapped, Washington, D.C. 20542.

Barrier-Free Site Design. A comprehensive study, including walks, lighting, recreation and vegetation considerations, and many human, legislative and cost factors, conducted by the American Society of Landscape Architects Foundation. U.S. Government Printing Office, Washington, D.C. 20402. $2.30.

Many cities and towns, large and small, publish "Access" booklets, listing information about all types of buildings, including commercial establishments. Before you travel to another city in the United States, you may wish to secure such a guide. (See Chapter 9, "Barrier-Free Travel," p. 225.)

Here are some examples:

Access Chicago. A Resource Guide for the Physically Handicapped of Chicago. Rehabilitation Institute of Chicago, 345 E. Superior Street, Chicago, Ill. 60611. $1.

Access Michigan. Educational and display materials; laws; building code, design rules and graphics. Michigan Center for a Barrier-Free Environment, 22646 Woodward Avenue, Ferndale, Mich. 48220.

Accessible Places in White Plains. A Handy Guide for the Handicapped. Westchester County Office for the Handicapped, 950 County Office Building, White Plains, N.Y. 10601.

If your hometown does not yet have such an access guide, how about YOU organizing a group to start one? The data can be compiled by volunteers, and a foundation may underwrite the cost of publication.

COMMUNICATIONS

Rushing into a taxi on the way to Gallaudet College in Washington, D.C., I called the address to the driver. He did not understand. I repeated it.

"Oh," he said, catching on, "the College for the Deaf and Dumb."

I winced. "Just Deaf, please!"

The average American does not yet realize that old expressions like *dumb* or *mute* equal racial slurs—they are crude and offensive. Because deafness is often an invisible disability, it is also the most misunderstood. If put to a horrible choice, as, for instance, *Roots'* Kunta Kinte, who had to choose between the loss of his foot and his manhood, the average American would hold on to eyesight and mobility over hearing. But few people are aware that deafness means much more than absence of sound. They do not realize the difficulties of pre-lingually deaf children in "doing what comes naturally" to hearing children, learning language, their *"mother tongue,"* from mother and their surroundings. "Because of my deafness, I misunderstand and am misunderstood," says Ruth Brown, teacher of communications at the New York Society for the Deaf. "The world judges my intelligence by the quality of my speech, not by its content."

Access to 13.4 million hearing-impaired Americans means breaking through the wall of silence and isolation into the world of sound and companionship. Ameslan, the American Sign Language, is the third most used language in the United States. The appearance of sign-language interpreters at public functions is no mere courtesy—it's the law, spelled out in the newly signed (April 28, 1977) regulations of Section 504 of the Rehabilitation Act of 1973. Interpreters make programs accessible to the hearing-impaired. (For use of interpreter services, see Chapter 7, "Purchase of Goods and Services," p. 198.)

TELEPHONE AND DISTANCE COMMUNICATION DEVICES

Today there are devices which can assist speech- or hearing-impaired persons in their telephone communications with others. In order to communicate, both the sender and the receiver require equipment of a similar class or kind. TTY, teletypewriter systems and their public use are described on p. 194. A comprehensive listing of additional systems and devices is published in the June 1977 issue of the *Deaf American*.

Request a copy of the list from: The "Deaf American," Official Publication of the National Association of the Deaf, Editorial Office, 5125 Radner Road, Indianapolis, Ind. 46226.

TV FOR THE HEARING-IMPAIRED

Effective as of February 1, 1977, the Federal Communications Commission makes it mandatory for television stations to transmit all emergency notifications visually as well as aurally so that persons with impaired hearing may be made aware of emergency situations. The FCC stated that television licensees could employ any method of visual presentation that results in the simultaneous and legible display of the essential information in the aural bulletin.

Emergencies, fortunately, happen rarely. But how about access for the hearing-impaired to information and entertainment the rest of society enjoys every day on television? Hearing-impaired people need to have the same opportunities as everybody else to hear what is going on in the environment. They need to hear consumer news, current events and financial news. One reason the deaf score poorly on some testing is because they are denied information. When appropriately tested, hearing-impaired people have the same IQ results as hearing people.

A powerful friend is on their side. On February 18, 1977, President Jimmy Carter sent to all television networks a letter asking for suggestions on providing 13 to 14 million deaf and hearing-impaired Americans with a full range of television services. The response of the major commercial networks was unenthusiastic, to say the least. The Public Broadcasting System had pioneered working with open captions and experimenting with closed captions for years. Letters from Lawrence K. Grossman, president of PBS, to President Carter and to the president of CBS are reprinted in the April 1977 issue of the *Deaf American.* You will find them eyeopeners.

WHAT ARE OPEN CAPTIONS?

Open captions appear as printed words that can be seen on any television set. In the past three years, PBS has distributed an average of five hours per week of programs with open captions, including a weeknight repeat of ABC's Evening News captioned at WGBH, Boston—and aired at midnight! Other major PBS series, like *Masterpiece Theatre* and *The Adams Chronicles* have been distributed in captioned versions. PBS has also provided captioned repeats of major special events, including the four presidential campaign debates.

Since viewers with normal hearing ability find open captions disruptive, they must be used with discretion.

LINE 21 AND CLOSED CAPTIONS

Closed Captioning Service, refined and tested by PBS since 1972, is a system whereby visual subtitles are imposed on line 21, a portion of the screen that does not ordinarily contain a televised picture. The encoded caption material is transmitted by the television station along with the rest of a program. It only becomes visible when decoded by a special device incorporated into the viewers' home TV receiver.

The Federal Communications Commission has given its approval to use line 21 for closed captioning. As of March 1, 1977, television networks or channels are legally able to broadcast coded captions, and decoders making the closed captions visible can be manufactured and sold. In tests conducted by PBS and Gallaudet College, 90 percent of the hearing-impaired viewers surveyed would not have been able to understand the programs under normal viewing circumstances. Some 95 percent of the test subjects indicated a strong desire to have a decoder in their homes, cost-estimated at $100.

However, the FCC regulation does not mean that networks or channels will begin broadcasting closed captions. It simply means that they have legal permission to do so. PBS is working with commercial manufacturers to encourage development of off-the-shelf home decoders. Eventually PBS will expand its program captioning ability so that most PBS-distributed programs will be captioned. PBS is encouraging all broadcasters to adopt captioning as a standard program service. But the commercial networks (ABC, CBS and NBC) oppose closed captioning, quoting cost figures which PBS President Grossman calls "off-the-wall."

"One big cop-out," the editor of the *Deaf American* calls the network excuses for resisting the idea of closed captioning of their programs. It is becoming apparent that the networks are waiting to be convinced that the deaf audience is large enough and interested enough to make it commercially practical for them to add closed captions.

Advertisers will be more approachable—to the extent that they will tell the networks to give viewers (or customers) what they ask for.

What are you waiting for?

If you are a member of the deaf community, ask family, friends, neighbors and other civic-minded citizens to contact their TV stations and request closed captioning. Tell them that they fail to realize the potential advertising revenue they are missing.

- Write to sponsors and advertising agencies, telling them that they will be able to reach many millions of additional viewers through closed captions.
- Write to your senator and congressmen asking them to help this campaign.
- Tell the people who make the sets, and the people who run the stations, and the legislators who influence public opinion, that you want TV captioning for the deaf.
- And write to President Carter thanking him for being on your side. He'll be glad to hear from you.

INFORMATION

Are you one of the more than 6.5 million people in the United States who suffer some form of severe visual impairment? Or, perhaps, you are an older person experiencing difficulty in reading normal-sized type, even with corrective lenses?

MIRACLE-TECHNOLOGY READING DEVICES

There are mechanical innovations that are working for you. You may slide this page under a lens and read it, *magnified up to sixty times* its original size, on a monitor screen in front of you.

The Optacon, a portable electronic reading aid, works by converting regular ink print into a readable, vibrating tactile form. To read, you move a miniature camera across a line of print with one hand, while the index finger of the other hand feels the enlarged letter reproduced in miniature vibrating rods on a tactile screen, approximately one inch long and one half inch wide.

Not too good at touch? A *print-to-speech machine* will read to you. It has the capacity to read nearly 200 type styles, slowly or fast and at various pitches; it will repeat words, spell words, back up a line at a time or jump back to the top of the page; it can manage pages with two or three columns; it will read or omit punctuation. The speech is easy to understand almost immediately; it can read almost any type style used in books or typewriters (not handwriting); and a capacity for skimming (skipping ahead a paragraph at a time or ahead to the next bold-print heading) is hoped to be made part of its talents.

Want to be a speed-reader? You can be a speed-listener, without high-pitched Donald Duck or dying basso-profundo sounds coming from your tape recorder. *Variable speech control systems* allow you to play any ordinary cassette speech tape up to five times its recorded speed without altering the pitch. According to the nature of the material or your familiarity with the subject, you can listen at your own rate—speed-listening over areas of limited interest or high comprehension, and selectively slowing down during important sections, the same way speed-reading is practiced.

BRAILLE AND TALKING CALCULATORS AND COMPUTERS

Man does not live by words alone, and doing mathematics in one's head or on paper is going out of style. Choose between a Braille calculator that converts signals to a Braille output by raising small pins which you can feel, or have a hand-held calculator talk to you. It's hard to think of such a talking machine as an *it;* you may want to think of *him,* by the masculine pitch of the voice as you listen to a seven-digit result of a multiplication.

Are computers your bag? You can communicate in Braille, input or output, with existing systems. Entire computer print-outs can be received in Braille, and computer programming and data processing may become your chosen profession.

Still a student or a student forever? Engage the talking computer as a private tutor. Called project VOCAB, in use now in North Carolina and eventually to serve over fifty universities, the student calls the computer over the telephone, and with a special typewriter-like keyboard, identifies himself and the lesson he needs. The computer then reads a section of the lesson. After the lesson, the student is asked a multiple-choice question about what he just reviewed. The computer then transmits new information or repeats the lesson based upon the student's response. Because the instructional material is presented in a one-to-one fashion, the student can proceed systematically at his own pace.

For names and descriptions of these devices, contact your local Associations for the Blind, or write to the Library of Congress, Division for the Blind and Physically Handicapped, Washington, D.C. 20542. See listing of Reference Circulars published by the Library of Congress, DBPH, in Chapter 8, "Arts, Libraries, Sports," p. 218.

RADIO NETWORKS FOR THE BLIND

"Talking" newspapers, magazines, consumer information, interview programs, poetry readings, reports on the arts and other events can come to you on the airwaves. They alert consumers to their rights, warn against frauds, report on new consumer protective legislation and discuss proposed bills and regulations. Politics? Let local politicians know that you like to be wooed on your special networks. Some broadcast at certain hours over FM stations, others work on full-time schedules on closed-circuit subchannels which require a special receiver.

If such a service does not yet exist in your listening area, there's work cut out for you. You can get advice from In Touch Networks, Inc., 322 West 48th Street, New York, N.Y. 10036.

The In Touch Networks was founded by Jim Jones, a former stock-market analyst who had lost his sight. A human dynamo, champion bowler, expert fund raiser and master at making volunteers work for him, he put together a fine organization and outstanding programs. Tragically, Jim died suddenly in July 1977, at the age of thirty-nine. Characteristically, he was stricken while in full action, swimming, with his wife near him, and died a few days later. The work he started so brilliantly is being continued by the two Mrs. Jones, Jim's mother and his widow.

Regular, local radio stations will give you scheduled half-hour programs if you present them with ideas. Eunice Fiorito, blind former director of New York City's Office for the Handicapped, called her program *One out of Nine*, a talk show on the municipal radio station that features interviews on topics of interest to all people with disabilities.

Ask the Mayor's Office for the Handicapped, 250 Broadway, New York, N.Y. 10007, to send you past program schedules to get ideas for a local show on your airwaves.

In pursuit of a hobby? The Handicapped Air Program, a private, voluntary, nonprofit organization, thinks that shortwave listening broadens the horizons of those confined in their homes. "It affords them an opportunity to participate in an organized activity which requires no technical know-how and no license," says Lawrence I. Cotariu, public relations director of HAP, who will be glad to send you additional information. Handicapped Air Program, 8041 N. Hamlin Avenue, Skokie, Ill. 60076.

For "Talking Books" and other services of the Library of Congress, Division for the Blind and Physically Disabled, see Chapter 8, "Arts, Libraries, Sports," p. 216.

"BRAILLEGRAM" FOR PRIVACY

Is Grandma's ninety-ninth birthday coming up or did a couple of blind friends of yours have a new baby? Western Union will deliver your good wishes in large print or in Braille. The cost for each message is $2 for the first 25 words of text, and $1 for an additional 25 words. "Western Union's new services will enable blind people to be more independent in time of need, and to participate more fully in time of joy. For the first time, someone with a visual impairment has the option of sharing a communication or not. This is something sighted people take for granted," says Joseph E. Wiedenmayer of the American Council of the Blind. Legally blind and deaf, Mr. Wiedenmayer conceived the idea late in 1974, passed the suggestion to Senator

Jennings Randolph's Subcommittee on the Handicapped, and the senator asked Western Union to explore the feasibility of the idea.

Call the Western Union toll-free telephone number in your area; say "Braillegram or Large-Print Message." The message will be delivered in large envelopes on which "Braillegram" or "Large-Print" appears in Braille and printed type.

Hope all your messages will be happy ones!

II. TOWARD FIRST-CLASS CITIZENSHIP

4. CIVIL RIGHTS

THE RIGHT TO EDUCATION

For disabled people, education was always more a privilege than a right. But now the Education for All Handicapped Children Act (Public Law 94-142) requires a free, appropriate public education for all handicapped children in the United States. No one may be refused admission to school solely on the basis of disability.

Signed November 29, 1975, the new law requires that all handicapped children between the ages of 3 to 18 be served by September 1, 1978, and that all those 3 to 21 be served by September 1, 1980, in order for the states to qualify for federal funds. The education of handicapped children 3 to 5 years old and those 18 to 21 is not mandatory in states where this requirement is inconsistent with state law or practice.

Strong incentives for the states to implement the requirements of the act are built into the law, through the millions of federal dollars available to states who comply, and the loss of millions for states who do not comply. The U.S. Commissioner may order the state education agency to cut off the federal funds to any school district found in substantial noncompliance.

School districts must locate and identify all handicapped children—Operation Find—in need of special education and related services.

Whenever appropriate, handicapped children will be "mainstreamed," that is, educated with children who are not handicapped. Special classes and separate schooling will be provided only when the nature or severity of the handicap prevents achievement of a satisfactory education program.

Mainstreaming will change the future of disabled children. In addition, their nondisabled classmates will learn understanding of individuals with disabilities. Twenty years from now, when today's schoolchildren are tomorrow's professionals, employers and employees, the strangeness of the unknown in relation to the handicapped, will, hopefully, be replaced by familiarity and recognition of individual abilities.

Mainstreaming as a law alone is not enough. Publishers will have to include handicapped individuals in their textbooks. Dick and Jane will have to play with a blind child and one in a wheelchair. Basic elements of sign language can become natural expressions of all children. Disabled people will have to come to schools and tell about their jobs so that disabled children can have role models of people who succeeded in spite of their handicaps.

Appropriate education must take place in the *least restrictive environment,* one where the child is most comfortable, so that he can develop to his fullest potential. Where mainstreaming is inappropriate, special classes, instruction in institutions or the child's home must be provided.

In any decision affecting a child's education, including placement procedures, the parents must be contacted and consulted first. They have the right to appeal the decision. The child's special education program must be developed with the participation of parents, teacher and local education agency, and the child himself, whenever appropriate. The plan must include an analysis of the child's current level of functioning, short-range and annual goals, specific services that will be provided and when, and a schedule for updating the plan as needed.

Special education services must be provided at no cost to parents. Depending upon need, special services may include transportation to and from school, payment of tuition to special schools, home instruction, special classes, special teachers and resource rooms. In special classes for handicapped students, educational needs and abilities, not disabilities, set the guidelines.

Special educational services may also involve related services such as speech pathology and audiology, psychological services, physical and occupational therapy, recreation, counseling and medical services for evaluation and diagnostic purposes.

Parents have, at long last, a single agency to hold accountable for enforcing the law. The individual state education agency is responsible for all educational programs for disabled children in the state, including those run by other agencies, such as a state hospital or a welfare department. This is important because, historically, parents were shuttled from agency to agency and school to school, without being able to pin down anyone for a final decision.

The measures are urgently needed. In 1975–76, for example, fully 42 percent, or 2 million of the 6.7 million disabled children of school age in this country did not receive an appropriate education. For the 40,000 multiple-handicapped children in this country, 60 percent were not being served. Today, of all disabled children and youths, 45 percent are unserved. In 1969–70, the figure was 60 percent, and twenty years before that, it was 90 percent. This is progress, but it's far too limited.

Parent groups have played a large role in bringing about change and in providing the stimulus for the new law. Using publicity, personal contacts with influential individuals, public meetings and mass mailings, parent groups forced state legislatures to listen to them, took unwilling school administrators to court and lobbied in Washington for the passage of PL 94-142.

That law has no expiration date. Congress intended for it to be permanent. Disabled children have earned, at least, the right—not the privilege, but the right—to an education. And with a good education, they'll get good jobs.

If you or a disabled child are denied an education, file a complaint with your local school superintendent.
For more information, write to: The Bureau, Education for the Handicapped, U.S. Office of Education, Washington, D.C. 20202, and the Office for Civil Rights, Department of Health, Education and Welfare, Washington, D.C. 20201.

Many school districts, large or small, have outstanding programs for educating children with handicaps, utilizing media, materials and educational technology resources. Children with handicaps in other localities, however, do not have access to the same number of resources, or the resources may not be of the same quality. To assist local districts in their search for appropriate educational material, a nationally funded Resource Center is available, the National Information Center of Special Education Materials (NICSEM).

NICSEM has developed a master catalog and six cross-reference indexes divided among Learning Disabilities, Mental Retardation, Speech and Hearing, Emotionally Disturbed, Physically Handicapped/Health Impaired and Visually Handicapped.

Contact your local State Education Agency. They will advise you where and how you may avail yourself of NICSEM resources.

Other resources for research on available learning materials are:

Handicapped Learner Materials Distribution Center, Audio-visual Center, Indiana University, Bloomington, Indiana 47401

Production Center for Hearing Impaired, University of Nebraska, 301 Barkley Center, Lincoln, Nebraska 68583

Head Start

Head Start now includes disabled children; in fact, 10 percent of its participants must be disabled students. Last year about 33,000 children were served. Fourteen experimental projects have been funded to develop a variety of models for serving disabled children in an integrated preschool setting.

If you need advice or assistance, write to: Office of Child Development, Office for Human Development Services, Department of Health, Education and Welfare, Washington, D.C. 20201.

Higher Education

In colleges and universities, disabled students must be admitted, placed, housed, taught and otherwise treated in a nondiscriminatory manner under Section 504. If interpreters are needed, the deaf student can get them from the Office of Vocational Rehabilitation or demand that the college supply them at no cost to him or her. If recordings or Brailled materials are needed, the blind student has a right to them. Students with mobility limitations have a right to get to classes and around the campus.

Many colleges are already accessible. To find out which ones, write for:
Some Colleges and Universities with Special Facilities to Accommodate Handicapped Students, National Easter Seal Society for Crippled Children and Adults, 2023 W. Ogden Avenue, Chicago, Ill. 60612.

For additional information, write to: Information Service, Rehabilitation Services Administration, Department of Health, Education and Welfare, Washington, D.C. 20201.

Look in your public library, state Vocational Rehabilitation Office or a college library for:

The College Guide for Students with Disabilities, by Elinor Gollay and Alwina Bennett. Information to assist students who have any type of disability which requires special accommodation. A building-by-building breakdown on campus accessibility, information about college policies toward students with disabilities, as well as information about specific types of support services available. $12, prepaid, for handicapped students or their families. $18.50 plus $1.50 shipping and handling, for all others. Abt Publications, 55 Wheeler Street, Cambridge, Mass. 02138.

The Section 504 rules and the Education of All Handicapped Children Act, are important also because they protect the right of disabled applicants and students to equality of opportunity in *all segments* of campus life.

- In schools, tests cannot be discriminatory.
- Disabled students must be enabled to participate in sports and other recreation opportunities.
- In colleges and universities, fraternities and sororities cannot discriminate if they receive a benefit from college funds or support.
- Student teaching assignments must be equally available to disabled and nondisabled students.
- If off-campus housing is coordinated by a college, it must be available to disabled as well as nondisabled students.

☞ **If you are not satisfied, file a written complaint with the college or university. The complaint should explain:**

- **Who was discriminated against**
- **In what way**
- **By whom of which institution**
- **When the discrimination took place**
- **Who was harmed by the discriminatory act**
- **Who can be contacted for the information**
- **Your name, address, zip code and telephone number**
- **As much background information as possible.**

If you are not satisfied with the response you get, file a written complaint with the Office for Civil Rights, Department of Health, Education and Welfare, Washington, D.C. 20201.

Read *Newsweek* (August 8, 1977): "A Campus Handicap," first case of a deaf student taking a college to court for not providing a sign-language interpreter.

Home Study

Home study courses to obtain high school or college credit or vocational advancement are offered by more than 700 educational institutions. Lesson materials are provided for home study. When assignments are completed, the finished work is mailed to the school for correction and comment.

It is important to check if the school is accredited so that you may receive credit for work done. Write for informative publications:

Careers for the Homebound—Home Study Educational Opportunities. President's Committee on Employment of the Handicapped, Washington, D.C. 20210.

Vocational and Educational Opportunities for the Disabled (1977). Insurance Company of North America and Human Resources Center, I.U. Willets Road, Albertson, N.Y. 11507.

Further Reading

Amicus, "Opening the Classrooms: Assuring the Right to an Appropriate Education," Vol. 2, No. 4 (June 1977). National Center for Law and the Handicapped, 1235 North Eddy Street, South Bend, Ind. 46617.

Your Rights under the Education for All Handicapped Children Act, PL 94-142, (March 1976). The Children's Defense Fund, 1520 New Hampshire Avenue, N.W., Washington, D.C. 20036.

PL 94-142 and Deaf Children. A special issue of the Gallaudet *Alumni Newsletter.* Alumni Office, Gallaudet College, Washington, D.C. 20002.

The Unfinished Revolution: Education for the Handicapped (1976 Annual Report). National Advisory Committee on the Handicapped, U.S. Department of Health, Education and Welfare, Washington, D.C. 20201.

Closer Look, National Information Center for the Handicapped (periodical). Office of Education, Bureau of Education for the Handicapped, Washington, D.C. 20202.

Perspectives in Education of the Deaf, Proceedings of National Forum V. Council of Organizations serving the Deaf, U.S. Government Printing Office, Washington, D.C. 20402. 95 cents.

The Art and Science of Parenting the Disabled Child. National Easter Seal
   Society, 2023 W. Ogden Avenue, Chicago, Ill. 60612. $1.25.

The Handicapped Child and the Parent in the Home, adapted from the *Christian
   Home* (October 1975) National Easter Seal Society, 2023 W. Ogden
   Avenue, Chicago, Ill. 60612.

Newsounds, "Parents and Public Law 94-142," Vol. 2, No. 5 (June 1977).
   Alexander Graham Bell Association for the Deaf, 3417 Volta Place,
   N.W., Washington, D.C. 20007.

You Can Get Your Child into School. A Guide for Parents of Handicapped
   Children. Virginia Association for Retarded Citizens, 827 E. Main
   Street, Suite 1801, Richmond, Va. 23219.

OPENING DOORS TO EMPLOYMENT

Today, a job is more than a paycheck. We expect personal gratification for
our time and effort. We attach great status to successful careers. We bend
over backwards to see that our children get the education needed to prepare
them for the work they want to do. We demand legislation to ensure that
everyone has an equal chance to compete for a job . . . and that includes
persons who have handicapping conditions.

People with disabilities have the need and desire to enter the world of
work. *Vocational rehabilitation* fits in with a program, process and philosophy
aimed at helping individuals with disabilities get into the world of work for
the first time or return to it after they have been struck by a disabling accident or illness. *Affirmative action* is a program aimed at encouraging employers
to hire more qualified handicapped people. An unstated secondary purpose
is to encourage more handicapped people to enter the labor market and
qualify for jobs.

Most employers will want qualified people; they'll welcome the addition
of men and women who happen to be handicapped, once mostly unfounded
myths and misunderstandings have been found to be false assumptions.
Assessments of actual on-the-job experience with handicapped workers
reveal a picture of average-or-better ratings in those areas which count most
with employers: job performance, safety and attendance. Affirmative action
covers all levels of employment, including executive. It also covers all kinds
of employment practices such as hiring, upgrading, transfer, demotion,
recruitment, layoff and termination.

VOCATIONAL REHABILITATION

Vocational rehabilitation is a process designed to develop, improve, restore a handicapped person's ability to work.

If you have a disability which interferes with your ability to work in a gainful occupation, or which makes it difficult for you to continue being employed, you may be eligible for services. If you are a homemaker and your disability interferes with your being able to function in this capacity, you may be eligible. In general, if you have a substantial employment handicap, you are eligible for rehabilitation services if there appears to be a reasonable possibility that you can become employable after rehabilitation. Employment may be competitive employment, self-employment, sheltered employment or homemaking.

Vocational rehabilitation services which may be provided under the Rehabilitation Act of 1973 include the delivery of goods or services necessary to render a handicapped individual employable, including:

1. Evaluation of rehabilitation potential
2. Counseling, guidance, referral, and placement services
3. Vocational and other training services
4. Physical or mental restoration services
5. Maintenance (financial assistance while training)
6. Interpreter services for deaf individuals
7. Reader services for blind individuals
8. Recruitment and training services for new employment opportunities in the fields of rehabilitation, health, welfare, public safety, and law enforcement, as well as other appropriate service employment
9. Teaching, orientation and mobility services for the blind
10. Occupational licenses, tools, equipment, and initial stocks and supplies
11. Transportation in connection with rendering of any vocational rehabilitation services
12. Telecommunications, sensory and other technological aids and devices

Vocational rehabilitation agencies are called by different names in different parts of the country. In some states there is a separate agency for the blind. You can apply for vocational rehabilitation services by telephone, by letter or in person. Check your telephone directory under the "State" listings for the agency nearest you or contact state agency headquarters located in your state capital.

Here are some helpful publications, to pick up at area offices or to write for:

Disabled? Vocational Rehabilitation Can Help; Vocational Rehabilitation for the Blind and Disabled; Services for the Visually Handicapped. The State Education Department, Office of Vocational Rehabilitation, or Social Security Administration, U.S. Department of Health, Education and Welfare, Washington, D.C. 20201.

The American Dream, Vocational Rehabilitation and the World of Work. Research and Training Center, Institute, W.Va. 25112.

Vocational and Educational Opportunities for the Disabled (1975); *The Rehabilitation Facility and Its Specialists* (1975). Insurance Company of North America and Human Resources Center, I.U. Willets Road, Albertson, N.Y. 11507.

200 Ways to Put Your Talent to Work in the Health Field. National Health Council, Inc., 1740 Broadway, New York, N.Y. 10019. Describes careers in health, and lists organizations that can provide general career information, some that also provide lists of training schools and some that can also provide financial aid information. Publication contains special free Information Coupon for Handicapped.

Information can also be obtained by writing to:

Rehabilitation Services Administration, Department of Health, Education and Welfare, Washington, D.C. 20201.

Association of Rehabilitation Facilities, 5530 Wisconsin Avenue, Suite 955, Washington, D.C. 20015.

AFFIRMATIVE ACTION

Looking for a job or a promotion to a better job?

The Rehabilitation Act of 1973 is perhaps your biggest ally. The law *forbids discrimination* on the basis of disability in employment and advancement by firms and organizations receiving federal funds. And if you're seeking a job in a company that does not benefit from federal funds, some recent laws will help you.

Affirmative action is required by Section 503 of the Rehabilitation Act of 1973. Companies receiving more than $2,500 in government contracts must *actively* recruit disabled employees. About half of all the businesses of America—some 3 million—are covered. Among them are virtually all of the industrial leaders of the United States.

Reasonable accommodation is also mandated. If you're a deaf mechanic working at a machine that signals malfunction by means of a buzzer, it is reasonable accommodation for the employer to add a flashing light so you can be alerted when something is wrong with the machine.

Businesses must also take affirmative action in job assignments, promotions, training, transfers and terminations. This means that handicapped workers must have the same opportunities to advance as their able-bodied co-workers. They also must be able to participate in employer sponsored activities, including social and recreational programs.

☞ For more information, write to the Office of Federal Contracts Compliance Programs, Department of Labor, 600 D Street, S.W., Washington, D.C. 20201.

Nondiscrimination is required by Section 501 of the Rehabilitation Act, which affects employment of disabled people by federal departments and agencies:

Each Federal Agency shall submit to the Civil Service Commission an affirmative action program for the hiring, placement and advancement of handicapped individuals.

It is also possible for disabled people to get federal jobs on a *noncompetitive* basis through what is known as the Schedule A program. These procedures have been established to meet the needs of individuals with handicapping conditions for whom the ordinary procedures will not apply fairly or accurately.

You may be able to avail yourself of special examinations that have been arranged for handicapped persons to ensure that their abilities are properly assessed and that they are not discriminated against because of their handicaps. Special services include:

For the blind—Readers or oral tests
For the deaf—Sign-language interpreters or written rather than oral tests
For the orthopedically handicapped, when required because of disability—Extra time or aid in marking answer sheets

Each federal agency has a selective placement coordinator to help you learn more. The Civil Service Commission maintains more than a hundred Federal Job Information Centers across the country to provide local job information. They are listed under "U.S. Government" in metropolitan-area phone directories.

☞ **If none is listed in your directory, you can dial 800-555-1212 for the toll-free number of a Federal Job Information Center in your state.**

Write for more information and helpful publications to:
Interagency Committee on Employment of the Handicapped, Civil Service Commission, 1900 E Street, N.W., Washington, D.C. 20415.

Working for the U.S.A.—U.S. Civil Service Commission
Federal Job Information Centers—Directory
Employment of Physically Handicapped Persons in Federal Service
Employment of the Deaf in Federal Service
Employment of the Blind in Federal Service
Employment of the Mentally Restored in Federal Service
Employment of the Mentally Retarded in Federal Service

Nondiscrimination is also required by Section 504 of the Rehabilitation Act. This section applies to almost all state and local governments, schools, hospitals, health clinics, social-service agencies, and colleges and universities. Recipients of federal funds cannot refuse to hire anyone on the basis of disability. Any questions about disability are banned until the individual has been hired. Tests and eligibility criteria must all be strictly job-related.

☞ **For more information, write to: Office for Civil Rights, Department of Health, Education and Welfare, 300 Independence Avenue, S.W., Washington, D.C. 20201.**

The State and Local Fiscal Assistance Amendments of 1976 provide that whatever is considered discrimination under Section 504 is also considered discrimination in cases of recipients of revenue-sharing funds.

State Employment Service offices can help you find a job. This public employment service has a network of over 2,400 local offices in cities and towns across the country. Many of these offices have specialists who have been trained to work with physically and mentally disabled individuals in their job search. Special placement counselors are available to help you assess your abilities and skills and to determine a realistic job goal. When needed, they can make arrangements for training or retraining, or help you obtain such aids as an artificial limb, eyeglasses or a wheelchair.

☜ Check your telephone directory for the office in your area, or write to the United States Employment Service, Department of Labor, Washington, D.C. 20213.

You can pick up a brochure that outlines services available at your local State Employment Service office, or write for:

"Seven Services—How the Employment Service Helps the Handicapped" Superintendent of Documents, U.S. Government Printing Office, Washington, D.C. 20402

"Employment Assistance for the Handicapped" The President's Committee on Employment of the Handicapped, Washington, D.C. 20210

If you are *blind* or *severely visually impaired,* the Randolph-Sheppard Act Amendments of 1974 may help you. The law is designed to promote jobs for blind vending-stand operators in federal buildings.

☜ For information, write to: Office for the Blind and Visually Handicapped, Rehabilitation Services Administration, Department of Health, Education and Welfare, Washington, D.C. 20201.

If you are a *veteran* of the Vietnam conflict, the Vietnam Era Veteran's Readjustment Assistance Act of 1974 may assist you in getting a job. Federal agencies and every employer doing business with the federal government under a contract or subcontract of $10,000 or more must exercise affirmative action in employment and advancement of qualified veterans of all wars, and all veterans of the Vietnam Era. Included are disabled veterans.

The Public Works Employment Act of 1977 also requires nondiscrimination for disabled and Vietnam Era veterans in projects funded under that law.

☜ For more information, write to: "Affirmative Action to Employ Disabled Veterans and Veterans of the Vietnam Era." The President's Committee on Employment of the Handicapped, Washington, D.C. 20210.

Complaints

If you believe you have been discriminated against in federal employment, write to The Disability Rights Center, 1346 Connecticut Avenue, Washington, D.C. 20036.

In assumed discrimination by an employer under government contract, take these steps:

- If the company has an internal review procedure, the complaint goes there first;
- if not, you or your authorized representative file a written complaint with the Office of Federal Contracts Compliance, Department of Labor, 600 D Street, S.W., Washington, D.C. 20201.
- If the Department of Labor investigation shows no violation, you can ask for a review of the case.

If the investigation does show a violation, efforts will be made to encourage the contractor to comply, and to state in writing that he or she will take corrective action. If this doesn't work, the contractor will be given an opportunity for a hearing of the case. If the decision goes against the contractor, it's possible for sanctions to be imposed by the Department of Labor. The government contract could be terminated.

There are also precedents for actions in court by individuals not satisfied with action taken by an employer or a federal agency. Complaints in court may also be filed under the Due Process and Equal Protection clauses of the Fourteenth Amendment, which calls for "equal protection of the laws" for all citizens.

Powerful protectors as these laws are of your right to equal opportunity in employment, there are two catches:

1. The law protects only *qualified* disabled job seekers and employees. To qualify, you must be trained or otherwise eligible for the job.
2. The quoted laws affect only employers receiving federal funds and government agencies themselves. Private businesses are not affected if they do not benefit from federal financial assistance.

In the private sector—defined here as employers who do not benefit from federal financial assistance—the going may be rough. Some states prohibit discrimination on the basis of disability, but these are general policy statements, with little or no enforcement power.

As an incentive, the Tax Reform Act of 1976 allows a deduction of up to $25,000 a year for costs of removals of architectural or transportation barriers necessary to permit or enhance employment of qualified disabled people. Deductions for expenses in making buildings, equipment, walks and parking lots more accessible to the handicapped may be made directly from income (maximum $25,000 per year), instead of being considered capital improvement, to be amortized more slowly. When renovating the entire facility, no part of any expenses can be deducted.

This may encourage many employers to make their facilities accessible. As an additional incentive, the Tax Reduction and Simplification Act of 1977 permits employers to deduct up to $100,000 annually based on the first 50 percent of disabled employees' wages. The law works this way: an employer can receive a tax credit of 50 percent of the first $4,200 of a new employee's earned wages. And if the new employee is handicapped and has received vocational rehabilitation services in the past, the employer is entitled to an additional 10 percent tax credit (60 percent) on the new handicapped employee's first $4,200 of earned wages.

This tax credit applies only to those new employees who exceed 102 percent of the previous year's work force. This provision is intended to protect present employees who might otherwise be dismissed and replaced by a "new employee" for tax-credit purposes only.

Disabled people themselves must work with private employers to call these benefits to their attention. More important, tell the employers about the abilities of disabled people and how these abilities can help the employer make a profit.

These publications contain important facts on employment of the handicapped:

Affirmative Action Report on Employment of the Handicapped. Kemp & Young, Inc., 6700 Squibb Road, Mission, Kan. 66202. Annual subscription: $40.

Affirmative Action . . . a Resource Catalogue. Flyers, pamphlets, books, films, tape/slide presentation. West Virginia University Foundation, Research & Training Center, 1223 Myers Avenue, Dunbar, W.Va. 25064.

Hiring the Handicapped: Facts and Myths; Your Disabled Employees, Will There Still Be a Spot for Them?; Hiring Persons with Hearing Impairments; If You're an Employer in the Recreation, Parks, Leisure or Cultural Services, then There Are Some Facts You Should Know about Hiring the Handicapped. The President's Committee on Employment of the Handicapped, Washington, D.C. 20210.

Workers with a Handicapping Condition and The Law. A Guide to Fair

Employment Laws for People with Handicaps; provisions of various federal, state and local laws pertaining to employment of Wisconsin's handicapped workers. Center for Public Representation, Inc., 520 University Avenue, Madison, Wis. 53703.

Working Together . . . The Key to Jobs for the Handicapped. An AFL-CIO Guide. AFL-CIO, 815 Sixteenth Street, N.W., Washington, D.C. 20006.

When You've Hired a Blind Person. American Foundation for the Blind, Inc., 15 W. 16th Street, New York, N.Y. 10011.

SETTING UP YOUR OWN BUSINESS

The Small Business Administration makes business loans when other financial assistance is not available on reasonable terms. These loans are given to

1. Assist any handicapped individual in establishing, acquiring or operating a small business concern.
2. Assist certain businesses which employ handicapped individuals.

Loans up to $350,000 for fifteen years at a low 3 percent interest may be arranged if you can demonstrate that you have the ability to own and operate your own small business concern successfully.

Check your telephone directory for the field office near you or write to: U.S. Small Business Administration, 1030 15th Street, N.W., Washington, D.C. 20416.

Ask for their "Fact Sheet on Handicapped Assistance Loans" and any related publications. (See also, in Chapter 5, "Information on Government Business Opportunities," p. 86.)

TAX BENEFITS

Don't forget to take advantage of the tax *credit* Uncle Sam offers you. The tax law formerly allowing a child-care and disabled-dependent-care deduction for qualifying employment-related expenses has been changed to a tax credit. A tax credit is taken off the final amount of tax you have to pay, after it has been computed. This is a greater tax benefit than a tax deduction, which is taken off your reported income before your tax liability is figured out.

If you incur and pay expenses for employment-related household services, child care, disabled-dependent care or disabled-spouse care, you may be entitled to a tax credit of 20 percent of your payments for such services. You must file Form 1040 to claim this credit.

"Your Federal Income Tax" (1977 edition) explains provisions of the Tax Reform Act of 1976. Pick up the publication at your local district office, or write to: Commissioner of Internal Revenue, 1111 Constitution Avenue, N.W., Washington, D.C. 20224.

You may be able to figure out the legalese by yourself, but if you are like most people and can't, an IRS representative at your local district office will explain the points to you. (See Chapter 5, "How to Communicate with Federal Agencies," p. 88.)

HOME SWEET HOME

Home, whether a house or an apartment, a condominium or a mobile home, a single-family unit or a group residential facility, is a very special place for all of us. Here we return each day to treasure our possessions, nourish our dreams, pursue our interests. Ideally, our homes are designed, unlike the world outside, to conform to our needs and desires. A good home is safe, comfortable, affordable, convenient to services and shopping facilities, and reflects our tastes and values.

A home is also a major investment. The typical family, whether it occupies a home or an apartment, spends 25 to 30 percent, and even more, of its take-home pay on housing. The cost alone mandates that the choice of where to live be made with great care.

For disabled Americans, the decision is often much more difficult than it is for most citizens. Says one leading authority: "[A disabled person] has but to look about him, at his own home, his neighbor's, down the street, in the next town, or to the farthest corners of America. He looks for something that doesn't exist." The authority overstates the case, but not greatly. The virtual lack of housing suitable for disabled persons is a deeply serious, even shocking fact.

Yet there is much you can do.

Most housing construction in America today is a private enterprise, without involvement of federal funds. This means that legislation has little to say about accessibility in housing. But a certain amount of housing construction is federally funded. It is in publicly supported housing that mobility-impaired individuals are most likely to find answers to their housing questions—at least until private builders become more responsive to the needs of disabled people.

There are two reasons for this. First, Section 504 of the Rehabilitation Act of 1973 forbids discrimination on the basis of disability in any federally supported program or activity. Thus, any housing development which received federal financial assistance prior to, during or even after construction, cannot discriminate against people because they are disabled. The second reason is that the Department of Housing and Urban Development (HUD), which funds most housing and urban development projects receiving federal assistance, is now committed to fully accessible housing.

HOUSING SUBSIDIES

The Housing and Community Development Act of 1974 is comprehensive legislation which encourages building and provision of housing that will meet the needs of the handicapped and elderly by providing federal dollars for this purpose to private builders. Under this Act, HUD's New Section 8 Housing Assistance Program, in effect since January 1, 1975, is designed to enable families to live in decent housing who would otherwise be unable to afford such housing. The program utilizes existing, substantially rehabilitated and newly constructed housing units. It is anticipated that in the next several years, the program will assist more than 300,000 families to obtain good housing. In a press conference on May 25, 1977, announcing the establishment of the Office of Independent Living, the Secretary of Housing and Urban Development, Patricia Roberts Harris, announced that 5 percent of all new family units constructed under the Section 8 and public housing programs will be designed for use by the handicapped. "This new housing goal," she said, "will make the first of a series of steps by HUD to provide properly designed, accessible housing for the non-elderly handicapped."

Section 202 of the act, the *Direct Loan Program*, encourages private and public concerns to meet the needs of the handicapped and the elderly by making loans. The definition of handicapped, for the purpose of loans under this act, has been broadened to include the mentally handicapped with specific mention of the developmentally disabled.

The act also directs the Secretary of HUD to ensure that projects receiving Section 202 loans provide a range of appropriate supportive services for the handicapped, including health, continuing education, welfare, informational, homemaker counseling and referral services *and* transportation to such services.

Under the *Rent Subsidy Program for Low-Income Handicapped and Elderly*, the act provides subsidies for the housing of qualified handicapped persons to owners of existing dwellings, newly constructed apartments and/or houses, substantially rehabilitated dwellings, and public housing agencies. To qualify, the family's income must fall below a certain level.

Under low-income housing provisions, a family can be defined as:

- One or more single elderly, disabled or handicapped individuals living together
- One or more such individuals living with another person determined essential to their well-being
- A family of two or more

The Housing Authorization Act of 1976 prohibits these rent subsidies from being considered income to persons receiving Supplemental Security Income. This prevents a cut in payments to SSI recipients. To determine eligibility, contact your local Public Housing Authority. Look in your telephone directory under "Housing," in your "State" and "Local Government" listings.

For assistance with your housing problems, contact HUD's Office for Independent Living for the Disabled, 7th and D streets, S.W., Washington, D.C. 20410.

This office, headed by David Williamson, himself disabled, coordinates all HUD programs affecting disabled people, including Section 504. Mr. Williamson can refer your request to regional, state and local authorities who are in a position to help you obtain suitable housing.

Write for these informative publications to U.S. Department of Housing and Urban Development, Washington, D.C. 20410, and regional and area offices:

Housing for Low-Income Families. HUD's New Section 8 Housing Assistance Payments Program.

8 Facts about Section 8, Fact Sheet. A Better Way to Aid Lower Income
Families in Obtaining Standard Housing from the Existing Housing
Stock.

HUD Programs That Can Help the Handicapped.

*Interim Report: Barrier-free Access to the Man-made Environment—A Review of
Current Literature.*

Housing for the Handicapped. HUD's Research Efforts. A descriptive list of
projects sponsored by the Office of Policy Development and Research
within HUD, resulting in tools which will help practitioners in housing
related fields such as design, construction and management provide
various types of housing and housing-related facilities which are accessible and usable by the handicapped.

PRIVATE-SECTOR HOUSING

In the private sector, there are as yet no centralized locations available to
render assistance to disabled individuals. Most states have laws forbidding
discrimination in housing against disabled persons. You may obtain information and guidance from state and local housing authorities, consumer protection agencies and vocational rehabilitation programs. HUD's Office of
Independent Living for the Disabled may help. Another good source of
assistance is that of private consumer and advocate organizations.

But be prepared: the search will most likely be a long and frustrating one
and you will probably have to make a number of expensive alterations
before your home is completely livable. (See Chapter 7, section called
"Home Improvement," p. 182.)

ARCHITECTURAL ADAPTATIONS

Most severely disabled people require at least some architectural modifications
in their homes. If you have become newly disabled, by accident, illness or
age, your most probable course of action will be to stay in your present
home and adapt it to your needs. You will find the publications listed below
helpful in planning for changes.

While there are many products on the market for special use and adapta-
tion, the consumer may save money by obtaining mail-order catalogues
from large companies and find devices in these catalogues he or she may
adapt for use. These are usually less expensive than those manufactured

especially for disabled or chronically ill persons. The Rehabilitation Services Administration (RSA) recently funded a project at Virginia Tech's College of Architecture and Urban Studies, entitled *Design of Bathrooms, Bathroom Fixtures and Controls for the Able-Bodied and the Disabled.*

The study indicates cost-beneficial approaches to modifying commercially available facilities that may be of interest to many disabled individuals.

Results of the research may be secured from RSA, 330 C Street, S.W., Washington, D.C. 20201.

Architectural or other alterations deemed "essential" for educational, homemaking and vocational purposes may be subsidized by rehabilitation agencies.

Contact your state or local vocational rehabilitation office for information on these subsidies.

Ramps, lifts, lowering of kitchen shelves, and bathroom attachments may be considered "medical expenses" by the Internal Revenue Service and, as such, deductible from your income tax.

Check with your local office of Internal Revenue or use their toll-free telephone information service. Also TTY and TV-phone service available. See p. 90.

These publications contain advice and suggestions for adaptations:

Wheelchair Interiors, by Sharon C. Olson and Diane K. Meredith (1973). National Easter Seal Society, 2023 W. Ogden Avenue, Chicago, Ill. 60612. 46 pp.; $1.50. Based on findings of a research project; designed "as a guide in helping to make a home not only functional, but also increasingly livable, and in hastening the day all types of environments will be accessible to all."

Home in a Wheelchair, by Joseph Chasin (1977), Paralyzed Veterans of America, 7315 Wisconsin Avenue, Washington, D.C. 20014. 32 pp.;

$2.50. The pooled experiences of PVA "wheelchair experts" who have designed and built houses for their special needs or modified existing houses to make them accessible and functional contributed to this handy manual for "wheelchair houses."

The Wheelchair in the Kitchen. Paralyzed Veterans of America, 7315 Wisconsin Avenue, Washington, D.C. 20014. $2.50. Planning and building a new kitchen, or remodeling an existing one. Safety factors, tips for use of ready-made helps, and a listing of sources of information and supplies.

Wheelchair Bathrooms. Paralyzed Veterans of America, 7315 Wisconsin Avenue, Washington, D.C. 20014. $1. Bathrooms can be adapted so that the disabled person can use them independently. Illustrated brochure on construction and alteration.

Adaptations and Techniques for the Disabled Homemaker. Sister Kenny Institute, 1800 Chicago Avenue, Minneapolis, Minn. 55404. 32-page manual; $1.75. Directions for constructing and purchasing adaptive devices.

How to Create Interiors for the Disabled, by Jane Randolph Cary (New York: Pantheon, 1978). $5.95.

MOBILE HOMES

A relatively inexpensive solution to a housing problem may be to purchase a specially designed mobile home. Many manufacturers of vans, travel trailers and motor homes will produce a model built to your specifications for a nominal additional charge, or you can make your own alterations. Mobile homes are an economical as well as a convenient solution to many housing needs. In fact, almost half of all single-family homes purchased in 1977 were mobile homes. Of homes selling for under $20,000, fully 95 percent are mobile homes.

The costs for energy—an important consideration in a suddenly fuel-conscious society—are minimal. Also, mobile-home parks offer conveniences at low cost that would otherwise be out of reach of most home owners: community recreation facilities, club houses, swimming pools, children's playgrounds. Since the majority of mobile-home parks are located in the country's "sun belt"—Florida, Arizona, Southern California, for instance—year-round outdoor living attracts Northerners of all ages, retirees and job holders.

The Department of Housing and Urban Development (HUD) funded a special study on the feasibility of mobile homes as a housing alternative for disabled people. Details about the project may be obtained from Dr. Rodger

Drecker, St. Andrews Presbyterian College, Laurinburg, N.C. 28352, or from HUD.

Standards developed at Syracuse University for HUD expand the American National Standards Institute 1961 specifications to cover housing, including mobile homes. Copies of the report are available from HUD. Also available:

Mobile Homes–Alternative Housing for the Handicapped; Buying and Financing a Mobile Home. Department of Housing and Urban Development, Washington, D.C. 20410.

Tips on Buying a Mobile Home. The Council of Better Business Bureaus, 1150 17th Street, N.W., Washington, D.C. 20036.

Your Dream House

Perhaps the most satisfying alternative is to design and build your own home. It is also the most expensive choice. But with a competent architect, and a helping hand from your family and friends (and a friendly banker), it may prove worth the cost. If you are a veteran, you know where to turn for assistance!

About thirty years ago, a funny book was the rage, *Mr. Blandings Builds His Dream House.* It described all the pitfalls befalling a first-time home builder. There's also a saying, "Fools build houses for wise men to buy." Yet, don't let that deter you—many happy people live in houses built for them. There is, however, one cardinal rule: never, never make any changes on the plans after building has begun. Take all the time for thinking, planning, discussing with your architect. But moving a window frame by an inch, after the structure has gone up, can cost you your shirt.

Here's some help to start your research on housing topics: Bibliographies, listing all the latest publications and articles are available from:

Architectural and Transportation Barriers Compliance Board, Washington, D.C. 20201.

National Center for a Barrier-Free Environment, Information Clearinghouse, 8401 Connecticut Avenue, Washington, D.C. 20015.

Current Materials on Barrier-Free Design. National Easter Seal Society, 2023 W. Ogden Avenue, Chicago, Ill. 60612.

Building Design Requirements for the Physically Handicapped. Eastern Paralyzed Veterans Association, 432 Park Avenue South, New York, N.Y. 10016. Drawings, useful in constructing or renovating a building for disabled accessibility. Can serve as a guide for architect, designer, engineer.

The following two books cost $20 each, so you may want to look them up in your library before placing your order:

Housing and Home Services for the Disabled, by Gini Laurie (editor of *Rehabilitation Gazette*), (New York, Harper & Row, 1977).

A New Barrier-Free Modular Home for the Handicapped—designed for Individual and Congregate Use by public and private groups. Study and Planning Manual for the "Pioneer" Model Home, 85 pp., 33 illustrations. Independent Living Systems, Inc., Princeton Station Office Park, Box 2331, Princeton, N.J. 08540. Provides detailed information on a specially adapted single-story home, manufactured almost entirely in a factory as a "turn-key" project. Cost of manual is refundable to ultimate purchasers of Pioneer Homes; write for free prospectus describing the project.

Housing for the Handicapped and Disabled: A Guide for Local Action by Marie McGuire Thompson (1977). National Association of Housing and Redevelopment Officials, 2600 Virginia Avenue, N.W., Washington, D.C. 20037.

This publication is a must reading for any disabled individual desiring to enhance community efforts on accessible housing. Mrs. Thompson is a nationally recognized authority on housing for disabled individuals. Appointed by President John F. Kennedy, she was Commissioner of the Public Housing Administration from 1961 to 1967. She is now serving as project director of a HEW study aimed at stimulating community action by bringing builders, developers and finance agencies together with organizations serving the handicapped, to (1) convince the building profession of both the need and the existence of this strongly emerging housing market, and (2) convince the organizations and individuals concerned with the well-being of handicapped persons that the living arrangement is an essential service toward attainment of the normalization goal.

"Housing? Or Housing Options ???," by Marie McGuire Thompson and Edward H. Noakes, AIA. A special article, reprinted from *Rehabilitation Literature* (April 1977) by the National Easter Seal Society, 2023 W. Ogden Avenue, Chicago, Ill. 60612.

Edward H. Noakes, AIA, heads his own architectural firm in Washington, D.C., where he specializes in the design of health facilities and housing for the aged and the handicapped.

The article summarizes papers presented by these two authorities at the 1976 Convention of the Easter Seal Society, discussing a wide range of options to resolve the problems of adequate housing for handicapped persons. The new approaches encompass efforts to de-institutionalize severely disabled people by developing group residences as well as the promotion of adaptive housing to ensure a freedom of choice in the community at large for less severely handicapped persons.

Several successful experimental projects in various parts of the country are described in newspaper and magazine articles. For lack of space, we can only refer you to them here. If you cannot locate them in your local library, write to me % Random House, 201 E. 50th Street, New York, N.Y. 10022. I'll be glad to send you copies of the articles that interest you.

"Living Centers for the Mentally Retarded," by J. Michael Jones, *HUD Challenge* (December 1975).

"Design of Handicapped Project in Minneapolis Breaks Barriers to Independent Living," by Carl C. Chancellor, *Journal of Housing* (August 1976).

"Tanya Towers, a New Residence for the Deaf," by Carter B. Horsley, New York *Times* (April 21, 1974).

"Apartment Building for the Blind Is Planned for Site in Manhattan," by Charles Kaiser, New York *Times* (April 7, 1977).

"First Anniversary of Tramway Finds Real Community on Roosevelt Island," by Laurie Johnston, New York *Times* (May 20, 1977).

"An Island World for Quadriplegics (Roosevelt Island)," by Francis X. Clines, New York *Times* (July 5, 1977).

GETTING AROUND TOWN

"It's going to be wonderful in the future," President Jimmy Carter said in his opening address at the White House Conference for Handicapped Individuals on May 23, 1977, "when these buses come off the assembly line—and all of the new ones are going to be these kinds of buses—when they will come up to you on the sidewalk and kneel down to let you get in."

"Kneeling down isn't enough," commented a listener in a wheelchair. "In the nineteen-fifties the blacks couldn't go to the front of the bus. I can't even get on the bus even if it kneels. I need that *Transbus* we were promised, with a lift or ramp for me and my wheelchair."

There are about 13 million elderly and handicapped persons in this country who find it difficult or impossible to use presently available mass-transportation services. More than 7 million of them are estimated to live in urban areas. This figure includes persons with impaired vision and hearing, those who can get around only with special aids such as wheelchairs, guide dogs, walkers and canes.

The federal government has jurisdiction over the areas of mass transportation and interstate transportation systems. However, until 1977, laws enacted by Congress concerning mobility for handicapped people were primarily statements of policy, with few mandatory provisions assuring enforcement. Here are some of them:

- Special efforts will be made in planning and design of mass transportation facilities and services so that they will be available to the elderly and handicapped, and be effectively utilized.

   Urban Mass Transportation Act of 1970

- All federally funded projects designed to improve bus and other motor mass transportation shall be planned and designed so that mass transportation facilities and services can be effectively utilized by the elderly and handicapped.

   Highway Act of 1973

- The Department of Transportation may not approve any mass transit project application for federal funds unless it includes assurances that rates charged elderly and handicapped persons during non-peak hours will not exceed ½ of the rate for other persons during peak hours.

   National Mass Transit Assistance Act of 1974

TRANSBUS

On May 19, 1977, Secretary of Transportation Brock Adams announced his decision to require all new public buses purchased with Department of Transportation grants to be designed for easy access by elderly and handicapped persons. "I am directing today," he stated, "the use of a new bus specification, requiring all buses offered for bid after September 30, 1979, to have a floor height of not more than 22 inches capable of kneeling to 18 inches above the ground and be equipped with a ramp for boarding . . . I believe it is my responsibility," he continued, "to insure to the extent feasible that no segment of our population is needlessly denied access to public transportation. This access is fundamental to the ability of such persons to lead independent and productive lives. We cannot deny them rights that so many others enjoy, when it is within our ability to accord them such rights."

The Secretary's decision is monumental in its importance because buses are the dominant means of public transit in the nation's cities. Eighty percent of the vehicles used in urban mass transit today are buses. Seventy-five percent of all mass-transit riders travel by bus. Fully 90 percent of urban residents live within two blocks of a bus stop.

The credit for forcing the government into the new design mandate goes to the disabled themselves. Even after having spent $27 million on the

Transbus design over the preceding six years, the former Urban Mass Transportation Administrator had announced the abandonment of the manufacture of these buses in July 1976. Organizations of the elderly and the disabled, lead by the Disabled in Action of Pennsylvania, Inc., joined together in a lawsuit to enforce the rights of handicapped and older Americans to use buses. Climax of their victory was Secretary Adams' quoted decision, following on the heels of HEW Secretary Califano's signing of the regulations for Section 504 of the Rehabilitation Act of 1973, prohibiting discrimination in all programs receiving federal funds.

The determined fighters for their rights deserve the recognition of everybody concerned with the rights of disabled Americans. The organizations are:

American Coalition of Citizens with Disabilities, Inc.
Disabled in Action of Baltimore
Disabled in Action of New Jersey, Inc.
Disabled in Action of New York, Ltd.
Disabled in Action of Pennsylvania, Inc.
National Capitol Area Chapter of the National Paraplegia Foundation, Inc.
National Caucus on the Black Aged
National Congress of Organizations of the Physically Handicapped, Inc.
National Council of Senior Citizens, Inc.
Paralyzed Veterans of America, Inc.
Pennsylvania Association of Older Persons, Inc.
United Cerebral Palsy Association, Inc.
United Cerebral Palsy Association of Pennsylvania

All the facts concerning the new vehicle are presented in the group's most recent, concise and informative brochure, "Transbus . . . What it can do for you," available from The Transbus Group, 1315 Walnut Street, 16th floor, Philadelphia, Pa. 19107.

Yet in spite of the victory, fully accessible buses won't be rolling in the streets before 1980. *The Bus of the Future Won't Get Him to Work Today,* states a position paper of the Eastern Paralyzed Veterans Association, an argument for the cost-effectiveness of accessible regular route bus service for the handicapped. They'd like to share it with you: 432 Park Avenue South, New York, N.Y. 10016.

How do you get around until then? Transportation by private Van and Livery services is frequently inconvenient and always expensive. Excessive charges, often paid undisputed by third parties, such as Medicaid, for transportation to and from medical appointments, inflate costs for people who must use these same services for transportation to and from work, let alone an occasional evening at a concert, theater or a social visit.

Use of adapted private cars, driver's licenses, special parking permits are discussed in Chapter 7, section called "In the Driver's Seat," p. 162.

PARATRANSIT

Between private passenger cars and standard public-transit vehicles there exists a wide range of urban vehicles, vans and taxis which are used to provide various urban transportation systems. This type of service, called paratransit, provides an alternate to individual passenger-car use and ownership, and it is of vital importance to people without ready access to regular mass transit. The Paratransit Vehicle Project by the U.S. Department of Transportation's Urban Mass Transport Administration (UMTA), provided funds for the development of a small general-purpose, well-designed, highly functional urban-transit vehicle that is more versatile than the typical taxicab, and can be boarded by a wheelchair passenger without assistance, if he or she so desires. To date, only some engineering prototypes of such vehicles have been produced under DOT contracts.

Several communities across the country provide door-to-door transportation services for elderly and handicapped individuals for medical appointments and social gatherings. Laudable as they are, such arrangements still do not solve the problems of transporting workers in wheelchairs to their places of employment without their having to spend a considerable part of their earnings on getting there.

New York City's Metropolitan Transportation Authority now plans to purchase a fleet of 100 wheelchair-accessible minibuses to transport at least some disabled people for the price of a regular bus or subway ride.

Write for "Paratransit," An All New Vehicle for Public Transportation. UMTA Office of Public Affairs, U.S. Department of Transportation, Washington, D.C. 20590.

RAPID-TRANSIT SYSTEMS

In subways, accessibility is severely limited. Only cities with new systems are accessible to mobility-impaired individuals: Atlanta's MARTA (Metropolitan Area Rapid Transit Association), San Francisco's BART (Bay Area Rapid Transit Association) and Washington's Metro. New York, Chicago and Boston systems remain almost totally inaccessible.

Even the accessible systems require disabled persons to traverse long distances between the train platforms and accessible elevators. Vision- and hearing-impaired passengers need clearly marked destination signs on the trains and audio announcements about destinations on platforms and about stations within the trains.

At Washington's Metro the elevator buttons are identified by raised printing and in Braille. Half-fare rates apply twenty-four hours a day. Routing and scheduling information is available for deaf citizens on a TTY service.

Dial Metro's TTY number, 638-3780, seven days a week, from 6 A.M. until 11:30 P.M. Write for "The Metro TTY," Washington Metropolitan Area Transit Authority, 600 5th Street, N.W., Washington, D.C. 20001.

Metro is also the first subway designed to warn deaf passengers of incoming trains. Every time a train comes, a row of lights on the edge of the platform grows brighter, warning deaf people to step away from the edge, and lights dim after the train leaves the station.

GUIDE DOGS ON COMMON CARRIERS

In several states, *White Cane Laws* mandate that the blind, visually handicapped or otherwise physically handicapped are entitled to full and equal advantages, facilities, privileges of all common carriers, such as airplanes, motor vehicles, railroad trains, motor buses, street cars, boats, any other public conveyances or modes of transportation.

Any blind person may be accompanied by a guide dog in any of the listed places without being required to pay extra for the guide dog. Though not yet specifically mentioned, it can be assumed that users of hearing guide dogs will be entitled to the same privileges. Since their need is less apparent, hearing guide dogs have been accorded exclusive use of a brilliantly orange collar, and their owner must carry an identification card, complete with the dog's photograph. (See "Man's Best Friend," p. 200.)

☞ **If your state doesn't yet have such a law, ask your legislators to work for one.**

For students, researchers and eager readers:

Summary of Urban Mass Transportation Activities to Improve Transportation for Elderly and Handicapped Persons. UMTA Office of Public Affairs, U.S. Department of Transportation, Washington, D.C. 20590.

The Disabled and the Elderly: Equal Access to Public Transportation. The President's Committee on Employment of the Handicapped, Washington, D.C. 20210.

Rural Passenger Transportation Primer. Selected Transportation Topics. Transportation Systems Center, Technology Sharing Program Office, U.S. Department of Transportation, Washington, D.C. 20590.

For out-of-town transportation by airplane, bus or train, see Chapter 9, p. 225.

DOLLARS AND SENSE

The purpose of *Social Security Disability Benefits* is to provide a continuing income when family earnings are reduced because of disability. Monthly checks may go to workers and their dependents when the worker becomes disabled.

Under the *Supplemental Security Income* for the Disabled (SSI), the federal government provides a basic cash income, in the form of monthly checks, to any blind or disabled person in financial need.

SOCIAL SECURITY DISABILITY BENEFITS

Protection against the loss of earnings because of disability became a part of Social Security benefits in 1954.

- An individual may be eligible for disability insurance benefits if he has a disability and files an application.

You can be considered disabled under Social Security if you have a physical or mental impairment which prevents you from doing any substantial gainful work, which is expected to last, or has lasted, for at least 12 months, or is expected to result in death.

If you are considered "blind" under the Social Security Law, you may be eligible for monthly benefits. You may be considered "legally blind" if your vision is no better than 20/200 even with glasses or if you have a limited visual field of 20 degrees or less.

Two kinds of Social Security benefits are available:

1. Benefits for those disabled since childhood—available through the Social Security of their parents (or grandparents, if they are the guardians)
2. Benefits for those disabled as adults—available through their own Social Security.

If you have worked and become disabled, your own work is the basis for benefits.

If you become disabled before 31 years of age, you may need 1½ years of work credit.

Monthly benefits can be paid to:

- Disabled workers under 65 and their families.
- Disabled widows, disabled dependent widowers, and (under certain conditions) disabled surviving divorced wives of workers who were insured at death. In these cases, benefits may be paid as early as age 50.
- Persons disabled before age 22 who continue to be disabled. If the disability is permanent, benefits will last a lifetime, and will continue after the parents' death. Unlike benefits for nonhandicapped children, benefits will not be terminated at the age of 18 (or 22 for those attending school full time).
- A disabled person is eligible for Medicare after he's been entitled to disability payments for 24 consecutive months. (See p. 68.)
- Each person who applies for disability benefits is considered for services by the Vocational Rehabilitation agency in his state. (See p. 42.)

You may apply by telephoning or visiting your Social Security office. To find your local office, look in your telephone directory under "U.S.

Government, Department of Health, Education and Welfare, Social Security Administration."

Many helpful publications on various aspects of the Social Security system are available, in *English* and *Spanish*. Pick them up at your local Social Security office or library, or write to U.S. Government Printing Office, Washington, D.C. 20402.

Disabled? Find Out about Social Security Benefits
If You Become Disabled
Your Disability Claims
Your Social Security Rights and Responsibilities—Retirement and Survivors Benefits (revised January 1977). Explains to beneficiaries what they can expect from Social Security and how to report changes which could affect their checks.
Pocket History of Social Security (March 1977). A compact overview of Social Security history listing effective dates of coverage and benefit types, earnings base and contribution rates, benefit formulas and the retirement test.

Basic booklets are also available in *Braille*. If your local office does not have them, request them from Washington or Baltimore.

For the legal-minded, a July 1977 publication by the Office of Program Policy and Planning, OPR Pub. No. 002:

Social Security, Rulings on Federal Old-Age, Survivors, Disability, Health Insurance, Supplemental Security Income and Minors Benefits. Social Security Administration, Baltimore, Md. 21235.

Direct Deposit

To avoid the risk of having your Social Security or SSI checks stolen from your mail box, arrange for direct deposit of checks in your bank account.

Ask for "Direct Deposit Form" SF-1199; the bank will help you complete the transaction.

Savings banks are now permitted to offer checking accounts. If your Social Security or SSI checks are sent directly to a savings bank, that same bank can now provide a checking-account service which, if provided, must be a free service. (See also "Your Friendly Banker," p. 168.)

Braille Notices

Notices from Social Security in Braille can be sent to blind people upon request. (See p. 91.) They will be accompanied by a regular letter so that a sighted person can also read the contents if the blind person wishes him or her to do so. Notices can also be requested in Spanish.

Address requests to Department of Health, Education and Welfare, Social Security Administration, Baltimore, Md. 21235.

SUPPLEMENTAL SECURITY INCOME (SSI)

- An individual who is blind or disabled, and who only has a limited amount of income and resources, may be eligible for supplemental security income benefits.

SSI came into effect January 1974 as an amendment to the Social Security Act, providing for a federal takeover of state programs of assistance to the disabled and aged 65 and over. Although administered by the U.S. Social Security Administration, SSI is not the same as Social Security. Money for SSI payments comes from general funds of the U.S. Treasury. It is designed for needy aged and for those whose disability has prevented them from gainful employment and thus from earning regular Social Security benefits which are paid from contributions of workers, employers and self-employed people.

You are considered *financially eligible* for this program if your monthly income falls below certain levels. If you have little or no regular cash income, and do not own many valuables that can be turned into cash, such as jewelry, stocks or bonds, you may qualify for SSI. You can have some income and still be eligible for SSI. But income from Social Security checks, veteran's compensation, workmen's compensation, pensions, annuities, gifts and other income generally reduces the amount of SSI payment.

Minimum income levels depend upon your living arrangements. For instance, if you are living with your family, your minimum income level is lower than if you were living alone.

SSI is available to *disabled children,* depending upon the family income. If a disabled person is under 18 years of age, not married, and not the head of a household, he or she is considered to be a child under SSI. If a disabled person is regularly attending a school on a full-time basis, then that person is considered a child, and eligible for SSI, until he or she is 22 years of age.

Vocational rehabilitation and training referral is mandatory for all applicants, for evaluation and possible vocational counseling, vocational training, and help in finding employment.

Apply to your local Social Security office. Call the office before you go to check what documents you will need to prove eligibility.

If you are not satisfied with the determination the office made on your behalf, you can appeal their ruling:

1. File a request with the local Social Security office within 60 days, for a reconsideration.
2. File a request with the local Social Security office within 60 days, for a hearing before the administrative law judge.
3. File a request with the local Social Security office within 60 days, for a hearing with the Bureau of Hearings and Appeals.
4. Final action on appeals is taken into federal court.

Pick up these and other publications at your local Social Security office or Department of Social Services, or write for them to U.S. Government Printing Office, Washington, D.C. 20402:

Supplemental Security Income for the Aged, Blind, and Disabled
Pocket Guide to Supplemental Security Income
Helping the Aged, Blind and Disabled
    Also available in Spanish.

HEALTH CARE COSTS – WHO PAYS FOR THEM?

A typical American consumer spends almost 11 percent of his income for health care. The purchase of health care differs from the usual consumer purchase in which the consumer chooses goods and services and pays the supplier or provider directly for the goods or services received. In health care transactions, the doctor usually determines the level of services required by the consumer-patient; the medical services are often not paid directly by the consumer, but rather by a system of third-party payments to providers on behalf of the consumer. These payments may be through a type of insurance or a public health program.

MEDICARE FOR THE DISABLED

This health insurance program under Social Security helps severely disabled people pay for the cost of health care. Medicare has two parts:

Part A, hospital insurance, pays for your care when you are in the hospital and for related health services after you leave the hospital. There is no monthly cost to you.

Part B, medical insurance, helps pay doctor bills and other medical services. It is voluntary and there is a monthly charge.

Who Can Get Medicare?

Practically everyone 65 or older is eligible for Medicare. Also, the following people under 65 are eligible:

- Disabled people who have been entitled to Social Security benefits or railroad disability annuities for two consecutive years or more; and
- People insured under Social Security or the railroad retirement system who need dialysis treatments or a kidney transplant because of permanent kidney failure. Wives, husbands or children of insured people may also be eligible if they need maintenance dialysis or a transplant.

Apply for Medicare to your local Social Security office or write to: **Social Security Administration, Bureau of Health Insurance, Room 700, East Highrise, Baltimore, Md. 21235.**

Pick up or write for these booklets:
"Your Medicare Handbook"
"A Brief Explanation of Medicare"

MEDICAID

Medicaid pays the medical bills, in whole or in part, of those individuals who have been found financially eligible under the Medical Assistance Program.

Medicaid cash benefits do not go directly to you, even if you qualify as a person in need of medical care. The payments are made directly to the provider of service or supplies, such as the physician, surgeon, hospital or supplier of drugs, sickroom supplies, eyeglasses and prosthetic appliances.

Who Is Eligible for Medicaid?

Eligibility is determined by the state, with general guidelines from the federal government. You may be eligible for Medicare if you are

- On welfare.
- Receiving Supplemental Security Income (SSI) benefits.
- Medically needy, and blind or disabled.
- Confined to a hospital where the hospital bills and/or physician's services rendered in the hospital exceed a given percentage of your annual income. You may then qualify for Supplemental Medical Care.

Apply for Medicaid benefits at your local Social Services Department. Look in your telephone directory under your city, town or county Department of Social Services, or write to the Medical Services Administration, Social and Rehabilitation Service, U.S. Department of Health, Education and Welfare, Washington, D.C. 20201

If you disagree with the agency's determination, you have a right to a fair hearing on your problem. Call or write Fair Hearing Section, your state Department of Social Services.

If you are still confused about Medicaid and Medicare—which is which and who pays for what—write for the illuminating publication

"Medicaid—How Your State Helps When Illness Strikes," obtainable from Medical Services Administration, Social and Rehabilitation Services, U.S. Department of Health, Education and Welfare, Washington, D.C. 20201.

Here are some excerpts:

MEDICARE

is an *insurance* program (money from trust funds pays medical bills for *insured* people);

is the same all over the United states;

is everywhere in the United States;

Medicare Hospital Insurance is financed by payroll contributions;

Medicare Medical Insurance is financed by monthly premiums paid by the insured person and the federal government;

paid medical bills in 1975 for nearly 13 million people;

is run by the federal government.

The Bureau of Health Insurance of the Social Security Administration of the United States Department of Health, Education and Welfare is responsible for Medicare.

MEDICAID

is an *assistance* program (money from federal, state and local taxes pays medical bills for *eligible* people);

is a federal-state partnership (states design their own Medicaid programs within federal guidelines);

varies from state to state;

is now in 49 states, the District of Columbia, Guam, Puerto Rico and the Virgin Islands; Arizona does not have a Medicaid program;

is financed by federal and state governments (the federal government contributes from 50 percent [to the richest states] to 78 percent [to the state with the lowest per capita income]);

paid medical bills in 1975 for more than 22 million people who were aged, blind, disabled, under 21 or members of families with dependent children;

is run by state governments with federal guidelines.

The Medical Services Administration of the Social and Rehabilitation Service of the United States Department of Health, Education and Welfare is responsible for federal aspects of Medicaid.

For other health insurance plans, see p. 176.
For purchase of prescription medications, see p. 135.

All health programs, health organizations, clinics, hospitals, physicians who accept Medicaid or Medicare, or health maintenance organizations are covered by Section 504 of the Rehabilitation Act of 1973. They may not refuse services solely on the basis of disability. Their programs and services, including such physicians' offices, must be accessible so that every disabled person is able to get the same service nondisabled people get. If a building is not accessible, you must be served in another building, and in some cases, your transportation to that building must be paid for you.

☜ **If you have any questions or complaints, write to: Office for Civil Rights, Department of HEW, Washington, D.C. 20201.**

DENTAL SERVICES

Dental services for handicapped patients are provided by clinics specializing in dental care for persons with physical and mental disabilities. Work is accomplished either in the dentist's chair or under general anesthesia in the hospital.

If you need information or help in locating a dentist who works with handicapped individuals, several groups may be of help:

Academy of Dentistry for the Handicapped, 1240 E. Main Street, Springfield, Ohio 45503, has a number of services including the *Journal of Dentistry for the Handicapped,* an extensive bibliography and a film *Preventive Dental Care for the Handicapped Child* (Contact VCI, Inc., 7601 Washington Avenue S., Minneapolis, Minn. 55435). Also, *The Dental Implications of Epilepsy,* A Monograph, 1977.

American Dental Association, 211 E. Chicago Avenue, Chicago, Ill. 60611, has a new (1977) booklet, prepared in cooperation with the Academy of Dentistry for the Handicapped: *Caring for Your Handicapped Child's Dental Health.*

American Society of Dentistry for Children, 435 N. Michigan Avenue, Chicago, Ill. 60611, has a booklet for those who work with the handicapped, *Dental Health for the Special Child.*

Dental Guidance Council for Cerebral Palsy, 122 E. 23rd Street, New York, N.Y. 10010, has a packet of information on dental care. (Send $1 to cover their costs.)

National Foundation of Dentistry for the Handicapped, 1121 Broadway, Suite 5, Boulder, Colo. 80302, is in the process of setting up referral directories in ten cities. Their brochure is *Dental Care for Handicapped Persons: An Important Health Issue.*

National Easter Seal Society, 2023 W. Ogden Avenue, Chicago, Ill. 60612: *Toothbrushing and Flossing,* A Manual of Home Dental Care for Persons Who are Handicapped. 20 pp., illustrated; $1.50.

Helping Handicapped Persons Clean Their Teeth. Leaflet, 15 cents.

EMERGENCY MEDICAL DATA

According to Medic Alert Foundation International, a voluntary, nonprofit organization, over 40 million people in the United States have hidden medical problems—diabetes, heart conditions, severe allergies and epilepsy are just a few examples.

The handicapped individual is particularly disadvantaged when subject to an accident or to a medical or health emergency. Personnel treating or attending the patient in such conditions may have no knowledge of the patient's problems and vital history. Allergies to drugs and serums are common and these post a major hazard when emergency treatment is required.

Members of Medic Alert receive an alerting emblem (bracelet or necklace), plus a wallet card. On the emblem is a phone number the attending physician can call for a complete record of updated medical information on the tag wearer. Some other services provide medical-history data in a wallet-size card carried by the patient. No thicker than a calling card, they may contain two full pages of medical history, together with a full twelve-set electrocardiogram.

Everyone with some medical history should carry such identification. The costs are very low for a service that could save your life.

 Ask your physician to recommend one of these services to you.

"CONSUMING" SOCIAL SERVICES

If you are unable to work or care for yourself because of physical or mental difficulties, you may be eligible for many services through your state Department of Social Services. You are eligible for social services if you:

- Have limited income
- Are an applicant for or are receiving Supplemental Security Income (SSI)
- Are receiving Medicaid

Types of services provided include:

- Meal planning, nutrition and shopping services
- Homemaker or housekeeper services
- Housing services
- Volunteer visiting services
- Assistance in obtaining health care services
- Referrals to agencies for help in finding a job, getting additional education or vocational training, or for help to enable you to cope with your disability

---

For information, or to apply for social services, contact your local Department of Social Services by telephone or letter, or in person. Check your telephone directory under the name of the state in which you live for the one nearest you. A relative or friend may apply for you if you are unable to do so yourself. Pick up at the agency, at your library, or write for the booklet: "Social Services for the Aged, Blind and Disabled."

A "CONSUMER," NOT A "CASE"

If you are a member of recent vintage in the largest minority, you may sympathize with the experiences and opinions of Dr. Ruth Perlman Klebaner, formerly assistant professor of education at the City University of New York, eloquently expressed in an article, "Rehabilitation and the Visually Handicapped Consumer," in the February 1977 issue of *Visual Impairment and Blindness:*

> . . . As we enter the third century of our history, we have begun to accept the view that social and educational services are not a *gift* to the helpless from practitioners possessing superior wisdom. Rather, we understand that services are of greatest worth when they are rendered in relation to values and goals of most significance from the point of view of the *consumer of such services.* . . .
>
> . . . In one very important aspect, the *supermarket consumer* has much greater power than the *consumer of services* at an educational or social agency; he has the direct power of buying or taking his business else-

where. The consumer at a social or educational agency is less knowledgeable about the services or products available to or needed by him and often services or studies are prepaid or funded in a process with which he has no connection and over which he has no control . . .

"Why," Dr. Klebaner asked, as a panelist at the New York State Women's Meeting in Albany, "am I a *student,* when I want to learn Spanish, but a *case* when I want to learn Braille? There is no educational institution I know of where a registrar asks for your life history when you seek a catalog of offerings. I am not looking for *help,* I need education which will make it possible for me to continue to be the person I have always been. I no longer teach, but I write; I rear my children and I participate in public functions, such as this one."

Dr. Klebaner's article continues:

. . . The blind become Visually Handicapped Consumers by exercising the right to accept that role. The exercising of that right is not to be confused with a surrender of all privacy and freedom of choice.

In order to determine whether or not to become a consumer, I want to know some information: What kind of a place is this agency? Can I have faith in the people who offer services here? What have other people like me accomplished here and could I talk to them about it?

If you want to read all of that intelligently assertive article, write for a reprint of "Rehabilitation and the Visually Handicapped Consumer" to: American Foundation for the Blind, 15 W. 16th Street, New York, N.Y. 10011.

This article should induce you to behave like a *consumer,* not a *case,* when you are interviewed or served by a representative of a social agency. Remember, he or she are not doing you personal favors, but are performing their jobs for which they are paid out of taxpayers' money, even if you don't pay for the services the moment you receive them. Without you and other clients, there'd be no work for agencies and their staff would be out of their jobs.

HOME ATTENDANT SERVICES

Several northeastern states provide home attendants for severely disabled individuals. Before you get annoyed because your state does not, consider some of the beneficiaries' problems. Early in 1977, a Catch-22 situation developed: if the disabled person worked and earned over a certain income, Medicaid announced that it would discontinue paying for an attendant. Since the disabled's salary would not be high enough to pay for a full-time attendant, he or she would be forced to give up the job and stay home in order to qualify for continued attendant services.

Why invest in Vocational Rehabilitation and other supportive services to get the disabled individual into the job market and then force him out of it by ill-advised economies? A test case in New York City, concerning nine employed individuals who were faced with exactly that devastating choice between work or survival, went literally to the wire of cut-off date, October 1977, before a last-minute decision avoided the impending irrational disaster, after months of appeals and personal despair.

Another point of dispute is the method of payment. Instead of supplying the disabled individual with funds to pay the attendant's wages, the check is made out to both, disabled and attendant, and requires both signatures on the check in order to be cashed. With this emphasis, the attendant considers himself employed by the government, with reduced inclination to carry out his immediate employer's instructions.

If none of the above dilemmas apply to you, because attendant's wages have to come out of your pocket, some suggestions may help.

High schools, colleges and universities are good sources of part-time help, full-time in the summer. A typical arrangement is to offer room and board, plus a small hourly wage, in return for services.

☞ **Contact the Student Employment office for referrals.**

By the way, some applicants may be on public assistance and will ask you not to report the income you pay them. To comply with their request, however, is to deny yourself an important medical deduction on your income tax, quite apart from being against the law.

Advertisements in the classified section of the local newspaper offer a relatively inexpensive avenue to obtaining needed help. Social services agencies are another alternative. An attractive solution is to provide an "independent living" setting for an individual whose needs are different from your own, by offering room and board that gets him away from his family cocoon or an institution, in exchange for services he can perform for you.

☞ **Arrangements may be made through state Vocational Rehabilitation agencies or local public assistance programs.**

If you need an attendant or a frequent assistant, exercise considerable care in selecting and training the individual. This person may be a great help to you on a daily basis and in emergencies, but may also cause serious problems and much unhappiness if duties and obligations are not carefully explained and/or if personalities don't mesh.

Action, the federal community organization agency, is an excellent source of trained personnel, particularly through their VISTA and the Foster Grandparents program.

Consult your local Department of Social Services for more information on these programs.

There is a growing trend toward employing disabled persons, particularly mentally retarded individuals, as attendants and personal assistants. Mildly retarded individuals may prove dependable and meticulous, resistant to boredom, and delightful companions.

Get recommendations for suitable individuals from your Department of Social Services, state vocational rehabilitation agencies, mental health organizations, or write to the National Association for Retarded Citizens, 1522 K Street, N.W., Washington, D.C. 20005, or contact your local chapter of that association.

People with disabilities are also people with abilities, often exactly the abilities you need.

DEVELOPMENTAL DISABILITIES PROGRAM

Throughout the country there is a growing concern for people who have lifetime conditions of mental retardation, cerebral palsy, epilepsy, autism and severe dyslexia ("loss of power to grasp the meaning of that which is read"— Webster). These are *developmental disabilities*, a term describing a group of handicapping conditions which often require services resembling those needed by retarded persons.

A developmental disability originates before age 18, continues indefinitely and constitutes a substantial handicap. It is a physical rather than a mental disorder. Most aspects of life are affected, and developmentally disabled persons must learn to live with their handicaps. With help, they will.

The Developmental Disabled Assistance and Bill of Rights Act states disabled persons' right to "appropriate treatment, services, and habilitation." The law recognizes that services should be designed to encourage maximum development of each person in a setting that is least restrictive of personal liberty. Further, it states that the program should meet standards ensuring the "most favorable possible outcome" for those served. The goal is to help persons who have developmental disabilities to realize their own developmental potentials.

The act authorizes grants for the purposes of:

- Developing and implementing a comprehensive and continuing plan for a system of services
- Providing services to developmentally disabled persons
- Construction of facilities to implement services
- Training specialized personnel for services and research
- Developing and demonstrating new or improved techniques of services
- Demonstration and training grants, and
- Renovating and modernizing university affiliated facilities for the interdisciplinary training of professional personnel

The federal government authorized up to $50 million to be spent on developmental disability programs in 1977, and an additional $60 million is authorized to be spent in 1978. Use of federal funds must not result in a decrease in the level of effort by states and local governments in providing services to persons with developmental disabilities, and the hope is that federal programs should stimulate an increase in effort.

Programs provided for in the act are administered by the Developmental Disabilities Office in HEW's Office of Human Development. Staff in ten regional offices are available to explain the provisions of this legislation. For listing of ten federal areas, see p. 94.

You can also write for information and request for publications to: Office of Human Development, Developmental Disabilities Office, Department of Health, Education and Welfare, Washington, D.C. 20201.

Publications: "Developmental Disabilities Program, The 1975 Amendments"; "What are Developmental Disabilities?"

HEW's Developmental Disabilities Office works with state developmental disabilities agencies and state planning councils to increase and strengthen services and safeguard the rights of persons who are faced with these long-range problems.

The programs also offer help to parents, who spend much of their lives caring for their handicapped children.

Specific information on local programs can be obtained through developmental disability agencies, rehabilitation agencies, city or county information and referral services, or the following organizations and their local affiliates:

National Association for Retarded Children, 2709 Avenue E East, Arlington, Tex. 76011.

United Cerebral Palsy Associations, 66 E. 34th Street, New York, N.Y. 10016.

Epilepsy Foundation of America, 1828 L Street, N.W., Washington, D.C. 20036.

National Society for Autistic Children, 169 Tampa Avenue, Albany, N.Y. 12208.

YOUR VOTE COUNTS

"It takes an act of God for Wayne to vote," writes a mother from Texas. "Some of the obstacles include steps getting into voting places; not being able to reach the lever and buttons on the voting machines, and it's a hassle to get Mom or Dad in the booth with our son."

If this evokes memories of similar experiences, don't give up. The largest minority in the country hasn't been the most voting one in the past. If you want politicians to count you in, they must know that you'll make your vote count.

ACCESSIBILITY OF POLLING PLACES

If you travel to the voting booth, someone is usually required to assist you to vote if you need any help. Many states have laws requiring polling places to be accessible. Advocates of these laws claim that absentee voters are being deprived of up-to-deadline information on candidates and issues, available to other voters.

To find out where the nearest accessible polling place is, contact your Board of Elections.

Former Congressman Edward I. Koch (Dem.-N.Y.) (since January 1, 1978, mayor of New York City) introduced legislation requiring access to polling places nationwide. The bill has been referred to the House Administration Committee.

Write to your representative to support the Koch bill (introduced April 16, 1977), and write also to the Chairman of the House Administrations Committee requesting his support: The Honorable Frank Thompson, H 326, The Capitol, Washington, D.C. 20515. Send a copy of your letter to The Honorable Edward I. Koch, City Hall, New York, N.Y. 10007. His Honor will be glad to hear from you and to learn that advocates like yourself are working toward passage of a law he introduced in the Congress of the United States.

Even with a federal mandate, it will require several years before all polling booths are accessible. And that still leaves primaries, local elections, school board elections falling between the cracks. Until such time as accessibility of all polling places is complete, use the assistance offered at the polling booth or vote by absentee ballot from home.

ABSENTEE BALLOTS

To vote from home by mail, you must have an absentee ballot form. Request one by writing to Absentee Voting, % your local Board of Elections. Allow ample time for the form to reach you and be returned in time to be counted in. State laws differ about closing dates for absentee ballots, so make sure by checking with the Board of Elections or read carefully the date indicated on the absentee ballot form.

A recently passed New York State law permits completed absentee ballots to be returned to a polling place up to 9 P.M. on the day of election. If such a progressive law does not yet exist in your state, lobby for one with your legislators.

You can also enroll in a political party as a permanently disabled voter. Then you will automatically receive your ballot in the mail.

Use it! In person or by absentee ballot—vote! It's your constitutional right and one of the best ways to get what you want—in your community, state and nation.

THE VOTER'S "RIGHT TO BE HEARD"

Legislators want to hear from their constituents. Communicate with them. Let them know your approval and your disapproval. Be polite but firm. Don't bribe or threaten with your vote. They'll get the message. A citizen who makes the effort to write is likely to be a regular voter.

When you write to your legislators to express your opinion on a bill, identify the bill in the first paragraph.

Dear Congressman Smith:

I urge you to support former Congressman Edward Koch's bill requiring accessibility to polling places.

Because I am orthopedically handicapped and my local polling places are inaccessible, I am forced to vote by absentee ballot. I would like to have the same right as my neighbors to make up my mind on candidates and issues, depending on up-to-the-last-minute information available to other voters.

Be specific: quote quotes, cite chapter and verse, say why, when, where, who, how. Write only about one bill. If you are interested in ten bills, write ten letters. Never write form letters—they are rarely read.

When your legislator does something you like, don't ignore it. Write! Thank him and ask him to watch to be sure the law is passed, implemented, enforced, and amended if necessary.

If he does something you don't like, write and demand an explanation.

To find out who represents you, call your local Board of Elections or newspaper or radio station. Good reference booklets, listing all state and local elected officials, their districts and mailing addresses, are published annually by the League of Women Voters:

They Represent You. $1. Available from your local chapter or the national office, 1730 M Street, N.W., Washington, D.C. 20036.

THE LAW ON YOUR SIDE

The law makes good reading, especially if it's law that protects your rights—as a citizen, as a consumer, as a human being. Laws in their original and full text aren't always easy reading, but because of their impact on our lives, highlights of new legislation are excerpted and reported in newspapers, magazines and on the air.

Naturally, publications addressed to specific audiences discuss in greater depth new legislation of particular interest to their readers. Thus, the implications of the signing of Regulations for Section 504 of the Rehabilitation Act of 1973 received more attention in the rehabilitation press than in fashion magazines.

Does this mean that you are less interested in removal of architectural barriers when you are hearing-impaired, don't worry about sign-language interpreters when your vision is poor, or don't care whether guide dogs are admitted to public places when you live in a wheelchair? I hope not! What happens to one group of disabled people vitally affects another, and what happens to all disabled citizens concerns all Americans. "No man is an island, entire of itself," wrote the poet John Donne in 1624, three hundred and fifty years ago; "every man is a piece of the continent, a part of the main; . . . any man's death diminishes me, because I am involved in mankind"—and any discrimination or other unlawful act against a disabled citizen diminishes all Americans.

Laws are there as guideposts. Those protected by laws should know them so that they can avail themselves of their benefits. While "ignorance of the law is no excuse" for the lawbreaker, knowledge of the law helps the law-abiding person. Take traffic laws. If you zip down the highway at 90 miles per hour, will it help if you tell the arresting state trooper that you didn't notice the "speed limit 55 miles" sign?

Of course not. But now, ask yourself these questions:

1. A store advertisement announces a pound of coffee for 89 cents. When you rush out to buy it, there's none in sight. "Sorry," says the clerk, "the delivery truck broke down and we don't know when the shipment will get here."

   Will it help you to know that this is an illegal act and what you should do about it?

2. You buy a toaster that carries a "full guarantee." After three days of correct use at home, it gives up the ghost. No toast.

   Do you know your rights in a "full guarantee"?

3. A store refuses your application for a charge account and a bank turns you down for a loan. No reason given.

Could it be that they didn't like the wart on your cheek? Can you find out the reason for their refusal?

The answers to these questions are, "Of course it will help you to know your rights and to assert yourself." You will find these, and many more consumer protection laws discussed in Part III of this book ("In the Marketplace," p. 101). It will *pay* for you to read them carefully, because what you don't know can hurt you, in the pocketbook.

And as another example, let's say that you read an announcement about a public hearing in which you are interested. Perhaps your utility company requests another rate hike from the Public Service Commission, and you should attend and protest loudly! But on arrival, you find a flight of stairs and no elevator. Or no sign-language interpreter is present, although you had notified the commission of your need for one. Is it your right to protest and demand your rights? Of course it is. It's a hearing that involves public funds, isn't it? And what does Section 504 mandate? Read it and act on it!

The main purpose of this book is to acquaint you with laws that protect you and to suggest ways in which you can make these laws work for you—first, by knowing them, and then, by applying them to your advantage. In many instances the pointing finger—it means YOU in sign language—refers you to agencies to whom you can write for more information on a topic that interests you, or it suggests actions you may want to take to achieve desired results.

Here are some more suggestions for *law-related literature* you'll find well worth reading, and *actions* you may want to take yourself in furtherance of a common goal—enactment and enforcement of laws that protect disabled citizens.

A Handbook on the Legal Rights of Handicapped People. President's Committee on Employment of the Handicapped, 1111 20th Street, N.W., Washington, D.C. 20210. Federal, Washington, D.C., Maryland and Virginia laws.

Rights of the Physically Handicapped, A Layman's Guide to the Law. Southwest State University, Marshall, Minn. 56242. Federal, Iowa, Minnesota, North Dakota, South Dakota and Wisconsin laws.

Rights Handbook for Handicapped Children and Adults. Co-ordinating Council for Handicapped Children, and Governor's Committee on the Handicapped, 160 North La Salle Street, Chicago, Ill. 60601. $2. Federal and Illinois laws.

Consumer Rights for Disabled Citizens. Department of Consumer Affairs, City of New York, 80 Lafayette Street, New York, N.Y. 10013. $2. Federal, New York State and New York City laws.

Please note: These four books are published not commercially, but by agencies, some of them under federal grants, and it is possible that limited numbers may have become exhausted. In that case, look them up in your local library and pay special attention to the local laws affecting the area where you live.

Amicus, a bimonthly publication of the National Center for Law and the Handicapped. 1235 N. Eddy Street, South Bend, Ind. 46617. Reports on legislation and court decisions. Precedent-setting cases may affect your personal situation, if applicable.

The National Center for Law and the Deaf, Gallaudet College, 7th Street and Florida Avenue, Washington, D.C. 20002. The center is a cooperative project of Gallaudet College and the National Law Center of the George Washington University. It has been established to develop and provide legal representation, services, information and education to the deaf and hearing-impaired community. Write to them for advice with specific problems, and request their general publications.

The Council for Exceptional Children, 1920 Association Drive, Reston, Va. 22202. Current descriptions of legislation relating to education are available.

Legis, House Office Building, Annex 2, 2nd and D streets, S.W., Washington, D.C. 20515. This is an organization that will inform you about the current status of a bill in the House or Senate so that you can be provided with up-to-the minute details before urging your representatives to take action for or against a bill in which you are interested.

Call (202/225-1772) or write, giving number of bill, name of sponsor, subject matter. The service is free, but you must enclose a self-addressed, stamped envelope, or better yet, send 50 cents for postage; since you don't know how bulky the material they'll send you will be, the envelope and postage you'd send them could be insufficient, and they can't afford to subsidize you with the difference.

Armed with brand-new information, you can request appropriate action from your congressional representatives and senators. Don't forget your state representatives and municipal elected officers. The more frequently people have to run for office, the more receptive they'll be to your requests for legislative and other assistance.

Local chapters or national headquarters of associations pertaining to your disability can be helpful in advising you of the latest legal developments of interest to you, and they may also assist you in organizing class action, lobbying efforts, even demonstrations, if necessary, to accomplish progress essential to improving your life and that of people with needs similar to yours. As you know, the turtle only advances when he sticks his neck out!

5. HOW TO COMMUNICATE WITH FEDERAL AGENCIES

INFORMATION CENTERS AND PUBLICATIONS

Have you ever tried to find an answer to a simple question about the federal government and ended up on a merry-go-round of referrals? Or have you ever had a problem so confusing that you didn't know where to look for help? Every citizen, at one time or another, needs information concerning a federal agency or program. All too often, he doesn't know where to turn.

GENERAL INFORMATION

Federal information centers have been established to take this confusion and runaround out of dealing with the federal government. Located in thirty-seven major cities throughout the country and with toll-free tie lines in forty additional cities, a center's personnel are equipped either to answer your question directly or to refer you to the *right* agency—usually federal, but sometimes state or local—for help with problems.

☎ Get in touch with your local Federal Information Center by telephone, by a visit, or by a letter. Look in your telephone directory under "U.S. Government, Federal Information Center," or write for the folder entitled "Federal Information Centers" to General Services Administration, Washington, D.C. 20405.

A useful publication covering the gamut of possible topics of interest is *The Consumers Guide to Federal Publications,* available from the Superintendent of Documents, Washington, D.C. 20402.

The booklet contains a listing of *Subject Bibliographies* and an order form for your choice of topics among the hundreds that are listed. Upon receipt of your filled-in card, free *Subject Bibliographies* will be mailed to you, for further selection of publications among the tens of thousands published each year by departments, offices and agencies of the federal government. Some are available free and some are for sale. "Handicapped" is one of the topics listed for which you may want to request a *Subject Bibliography* for further research.

INFORMATION ON GOVERNMENT BUSINESS OPPORTUNITIES

Do you run your own business, small or large? Did you know that one of the largest customers in the world is the federal government? The United States buys more goods and services to supply the administrative needs of the federal government than most any other government, business, industry or organization in the world. How to do business with the federal government, however, is a question that baffles many businesses—particularly small businesses.

If this includes you, write for a booklet that gives this answer and other information on the types of government procurement requirements which may provide business opportunities: *Government Business Opportunities,* available from the General Services Administration, Business Service Center, Washington, D.C. 20405.

CONSUMER INFORMATION

The Consumer Information Center

The Consumer Information Center is another part of the General Services Administration. The center was established to:

1. Encourage federal departments and agencies to develop and release relevant and useful consumer information
2. Increase public awareness of and access to federal consumer information

The center's staff works closely with more than two dozen federal agencies to determine what information is available that will be useful to consumers. The center also makes suggestions for new publications to the agencies, based on results of surveys to determine consumer interests. To inform consumers about the types of information available from the federal government, the center publishes a quarterly 16-page catalogue called *Consumer Information,* listing more than two hundred free or low-cost selected federal publications of consumer interest.

Many of these booklets provide factual advice on how to buy, use, and take care of products such as appliances, clothing and automobiles. Others cover topics such as child care, health and safety, housing, energy conservation, employment, recreation, and family finance. An annual catalog of Federal consumer publications in Spanish is available.

Copies of the catalogue, "Consumer Information," may be obtained by writing to the Consumer Information Center, Pueblo, Colo. 81009. To contact the Consumer Information Center for information or advice, write to the General Services Administration, Washington, D.C. 20405, or phone 202/566-1794 (Administration number); 202/755-8660 (Information number).

CONSUMER CONTACT WITH GOVERNMENT AGENCIES

If you want answers to such questions as

- What are the federal government's benefits and services for consumers?
- Which federal department or agency can help me?
- How do I obtain service?

write for the *Directory of Federal Consumer Offices,* Consumer Information Center, Pueblo, Colo. 81009.

This directory was compiled by the Consumer Information Center of the General Services Administration and the Office of Consumer Affairs of the Department of Health, Education and Welfare. It lists federal agencies and their functions for consumers, addresses and telephone numbers.

Under the heading HANDICAPPED it lists: Director, Division of Public Information, Office of Human Development Services, Department of Health, Education and Welfare, Washington, D.C. 20201; tel. 202/472-7257.

A value-packed directory for any activist citizen. If you wish multiple copies for distribution to your activist friends, you can obtain them free from Consumer News, Office of Consumer Affairs, 621 Reporters Bldg., Washington, D.C. 20201.

Several federal agencies are mentioned throughout this book, in connection with the areas of their concern. Most of them are not set up to deal with individual consumer problems, except to supply consumer information, in word and print, in answer to requests. Address communications to the Washington headquarters, as indicated, or write to or call the field offices in any of the ten federal regions: Atlanta, Boston, Chicago, Cleveland, Dallas, Denver, Los Angeles, New York, San Francisco, Seattle. Look in your telephone directory under "United States Government."

IRS-FDA-CPSC

One of the government agencies that definitely is set up to deal with individual consumer problems and with whom you most likely will deal, like it or not, is the Internal Revenue Service of the Department of the Treasury.

For answers to your federal tax questions, visit or call your local Internal Revenue office. Look in your telephone directory under "United States Government—Internal Revenue Service," for the office nearest you. If the call is not a local call for you, use the listed toll-free number, preceded by "800." You may wish to ask for the current edition of "Your Federal Income Tax," or other free publications to help you prepare your tax return. In the booklet you will find this surprising caveat:

> **We are happy to assist you by answering questions to help you prepare your return. But you should know that you are responsible for the accuracy of your return and for the payment of the correct tax. If we do make an error, you are still responsible for the payment of the correct tax, and we are generally required by law to charge interest.**

The buck stops where??

Two federal agencies actively invite consumers to communicate with them: the Food and Drug Administration (FDA) and the Consumer Product Safety Commission (CPSC).

Notify the FDA

If you come across a food, drug, medical device or cosmetic that you believe may be mislabeled, unsanitary or otherwise harmful, you will perform a public service by reporting it to the Food and Drug Administration. The information consumers supply to the FDA can and often does lead to detection and correction of a violation. Many products have been recalled or removed from the market because of action initiated by consumers.

Look in your telephone directory for any of the 130 offices throughout the United States. "U.S. Government, Department of Health, Education and Welfare, Food and Drug Administration," or write to Food and Drug Administration, 5600 Fishers Lane, Rockville, Md. 20852.

Communicate with the CPSC

If you feel that a product is unsafe and should be changed in design or removed from the market, make yourself heard by notifying the Consumer Product Safety Commission.

Head your communication: "Petition, filed under Section 10 of the Consumer Product Safety Act." Give your name, address, the consumer product for which you seek a ruling; personal experience; medical, engineering or injury data; specific risk of injury severity of the likely injury; possible reasons for such injury, such as product defect, design flaw, or unintentional or intentional misuse. If you are seeking an outright ban of the product, you should state why a safety standard would not be sufficient.

Send your petition by registered mail to: Office of the Secretary, U.S. Consumer Product Safety Commission, Washington, D.C. 20207. In case of urgent communication, use their toll-free hotline: 800-638-2666; Maryland residents: 800-492-2937.

The CPSC produces a great many publications, films and fact sheets on any number of consumer products. Not ONE addresses itself to any product or activity connected with any disability. Maybe some of your petitions, or just requests for examination and establishment of safety standards for the products you use, will get results.

Write for "Catalogue of Publications," Fact Sheets, Slides, Film, Radio and TV Spots. U.S. Consumer Product Safety Commission, Washington, D.C. 20207.

COMMUNICATION WITH FEDERAL AGENCIES FOR HEARING- OR VISION-IMPAIRED CITIZENS

Communication with the government is every citizen's right. For some Americans, physical limitations make such communication more difficult, but by no means impossible. Legislators and individual actions together must speed the process of removing barriers to communication. The motto should be: "The difficult we do today, the impossible we'll do tomorrow!"

TELECOMMUNICATIONS DEVICES

Several federal agencies that already have installed TTY systems for the use of deaf citizens are mentioned in Chapter 7, section called "GA Means 'Go Ahead' " on p. 194, as is Congresswoman Gladys Spellman's (Dem.-Md.) bill "to provide for the installation of telecommunications devices for the deaf in agencies of Federal, State and local governments," together with recommendations for your action to help in getting the bill out of committee and onto the floor for vote and enactment.

One of the government agencies setting a progressive example of such a service is the Internal Revenue Service, which has established a *toll-free* TTY number to give tax assistance to deaf persons.

The number for all states except Indiana is 800-428-4732; for Indiana, where the equipment is located, it is 800-382-4059.

Call Mondays through Fridays, Eastern Standard Time 8:30 A.M.–6:45 P.M.: Central Standard Time 7:30 A.M.–5:45 P.M.; Mountain Standard Time 6:30 A.M.–4:45 P.M.; Pacific Standard Time 5:30 A.M.–3:45 P.M. Some of the tax-related subjects they can help you with include:

- Dependency exemptions
- Earned income credit for some people earning less than $8,000

- Late or missing refund checks
- Free IRS publications
- Explanations of bills and notices

You can also find out whether you may claim as "Medical Deductions" such expenses as

- Cost of TTY equipment
- Cost of hearing aid
- Cost of trained "hearing ear" dog
- Cost of sending deaf children to special schools

BRAILLED CORRESPONDENCE

Ms. Ellen Logue of Brooklyn, N.Y., an intrepid fighter for her equal rights as a blind consumer, received this letter from the Social Security Administration on March 15, 1977:

> Although we do have the capability of responding in Braille to letters we receive in Braille, we have not fully explored the possibility of routinely sending beneficiary notices in Braille. Officials of our Bureau of Disability Insurance and our Bureau of Supplemental Social Security Income are studying this possibility.

On April 4, this letter followed:

> . . . the primary reason it would not be feasible to routinely send all notices to the blind beneficiaries in Braille is because the majority of blind people do not read Braille.
>
> The officials in our Bureau of Supplemental Security Income also commented that although the records for supplemental security income claimants are maintained in the claimants' local social security offices, most notices to them are generated through computers located here in Baltimore. The technical and logistic problems that would arise, should they attempt to send Braille notices, would be so expensive to overcome that they see no alternative but to continue sending printed notices.
>
> The officials in our Bureau of Disability Insurance, on the other hand, informed me that, because files on disability claimants are maintained centrally here in Baltimore, they can annotate their records so that notices can be prepared in Braille if the beneficiary requests it. Therefore,

I have had your disability claims file annotated to ensure that future notices will be sent to you in Braille.

Bravo, Ellen! In New York City, Ellen managed to have Consolidated Edison get her monthly utility bills transcribed in Braille by the Lighthouse, the New York Association for the Blind. (See p. 189.)

But Ellen is not satisfied with personal victories. She fights the good fight for all blind consumers. One of her complaints is that blind consumers are denied the right to be warned about possible side effects of drugs, when the Food and Drug Administration mandates such warnings, as it did, for instance, in contraceptive and estrogen preparations.

Inspired by Ellen, I discussed this problem with the FDA. Here are excerpts from a letter from the Division of Drug Labeling Compliance, Bureau of Drugs, dated March 29, 1977:

The Commissioner is proposing to establish a new regulation (21CFR 310.515) that would require certain information in the form of patient labeling concerning the use of estrogens to be given to the patient when the drug is dispensed (F.R.9/29/76). This patient labeling would be provided by the manufacturer, packer, or distributor as a separate printed leaflet independent of any other additional printed material. At the present time there are no requirements in the area that we discussed to provide for those patients who are sightless.

In researching the possibility of making taped versions of approved patient labeling available for use by the blind, we too contacted the Division for the Blind and Physically Handicapped, Library of Congress, and were informed that in order for such an endeavour to be feasible one must have sufficient material to effectively utilize the full 90 minutes available on each tape. It is the Director's opinion that a shorter message of 5 to 10 minutes duration, although technically possible, is not practical at this time.

Please be advised that your suggestion has merit and will be pursued . . .

. . . especially if blind people and those working with them will make themselves *heard!*

6. WHERE TO FIND OUT WHAT'S COMING TO YOU

As a disabled citizen, you are entitled to a broad range of services and protection from discrimination. But it won't come to you automatically. You have to find it, learn what the eligibility requirements are, and apply.

It can be confusing. There are time limits for applications in some areas, so by the time you find out about the service, you may no longer be eligible. Some services are available regardless of your income, while others have a requirement that your earnings must be below a certain level. New laws are passed each year that may affect your life. Some offer a new social service, others require that your rights be protected.

How to find out all you need to know? This book should help. I wrote it to help you learn what your rights are and what actions you should take to convert them from statements in print to facts in your life. But each person is different, and you may need personal advice for your specific problem.

GOVERNMENT ASSISTANCE

One good place to start to gather information is the Federal Office for Handicapped Individuals, Department of Health, Education and Welfare, 200 Independence Avenue, S.W., Room 338 D, Washington, D.C. 20201; Tel.: 202/245-1961.

OHI can send you general information about programs for disabled people. If you have a specific question, it can locate someone who can answer that question for you.

The folder describing the Office for Handicapped Individuals states:

> A national Clearinghouse in OHI seeks to improve the lives of handicapped individuals by enhancing the flow of information. The Clearinghouse on the Handicapped has two roles: (1) responding to inquiries from handicapped individuals, and (2) serving as a resource to organizations that supply information to, and about, handicapped individuals. OHI has identified more than 200 pertinent Federal programs and activities serving handicapped persons with over $22 billion dollars in annual Federal appropriations.

The concerns of the Office for Handicapped Individuals are represented in the ten regional offices of the Department of Health, Education and Welfare by staff members who act as OHI Coordinators.

Region	OHI Regional Office	States in Region
I	John F. Kennedy Federal Building, Government Center, Boston, Mass. 02203, 617/223-6820	Connecticut, Maine, Vermont, Massachusetts, Rhode Island, New Hampshire
II	Federal Building, 26 Federal Plaza, New York, N.Y. 10007, 212/264-5763	Virgin Islands, New York, Puerto Rico, New Jersey
III	P.O. Box 13716, Philadelphia, Pa. 19101, 215/596-1224	District of Columbia, Maryland, Virginia, Delaware, West Virginia, Pennsylvania
IV	50 Seventh Street, Atlanta, Ga. 30323, 404/526-3966	Alabama, Florida, Georgia, Mississippi, Tennessee, South Carolina, Kentucky
V	300 S. Wacker Drive, 15th floor, Chicago, Ill. 60606, 312/353-5194	Illinois, Indiana, Ohio, Minnesota, Michigan, Wisconsin
VI	1507 Pacific Avenue, Dallas, Tex. 75202, 214/749-3574	Arkansas, Texas, Oklahoma, New Mexico, Louisiana
VII	601 East 12th Street, Kansas City, Mo. 64106, 816/374-3667	Iowa, Kansas, Missouri, Nebraska

VIII	Federal Office Building, 1961 Stout Street, Denver, Colo., 80202, 303/837-4106	Colorado, Montana, Utah, Wyoming, North Dakota, South Dakota
IX	Federal Office Building, 50 Fulton Street, San Francisco, Calif. 94102, 415/556-0251	Arizona, California, Hawaii, Nevada, Pacific Territories (Guam and American Samoa)
X	Dexter Horton Building, 710 Second Avenue, Seattle, Wash. 98101, 206/442-5331	Alaska, Idaho, Oregon, Washington

The following are publications available from The Clearinghouse on the Handicapped, Office for Handicapped Individuals, Room 338d, South Portal Building, Washington, D.C. 20201.

Federal Assistance for Programs Serving the Handicapped (1976), 214 pp. A comprehensive listing and description of federal programs and activities which provide assistance and benefits to the handicapped and those working on their behalf, excerpted from the 1975 *Catalog of Federal Domestic Assistance* and supplemented through an OHI conducted survey. Will be updated annually.

Programs for the Handicapped (periodical; 6–8 issues per year). The publication serves the interest of professionals, paraprofessionals, administrators and others concerned with the needs of the handicapped.

Summaries of Selected Legislation relating to the Handicapped (1971), 12 pp.; 1972, 9 pp.; 1974, 38 pp.; 1975–76, 42 pp. Contain brief synopses of legislation enacted by the 91st, 92nd, 93rd, 94th Congress.

The Problem of Mental Retardation (1975), 18 pp. A booklet which discusses mental retardation, describing the symptoms and what can be done about it, in easy-to-understand language.

El Problema del Retraso Mental, 19 pp. Spanish version of the 1970 edition of *The Problem of Mental Retardation.*

Another good place to contact is your state Vocational Rehabilitation agency. Even if you are not eligible for VR assistance, a counselor can provide you with information you need.

NONGOVERNMENTAL ORGANIZATIONS

American Coalition of Citizens with Disabilities, Inc., 1346 Connecticut Avenue, N.W., Washington, D.C. 20036.

National Rehabilitation Association, 1522 K Street, N.W., Washington, D.C. 20036.

Mainstream, Inc., 1200 15th Street, N.W., Washington, D.C. 20005. "Call for Compliance" hotline: 202/833-1139 answers specific questions about compliance with the Rehabilitation Act of 1973.

Directory of Organizations Interested in the Handicapped. Committee for the Handicapped/People to People Program, La Salle Building, Connecticut Avenue and L Street, N.W., Washington, D.C. 20036.

These organizations serve all disabilities, represent the interests of disabled people before government agencies, promote acceptance of people with handicaps in employment, schools, health service agencies and other sectors of community life. They will also consult with you on individual problems. You may wish to contact them, join them as members or request to be put on their mailing lists for information about their activities on behalf of the entire disabled community.

I also recommend that you get in touch with an organization serving people who have the same disability as yours. These nonprofit organizations have had a lot of experience helping people find out what services are available. They have learned how to cut through red tape and have well-developed contacts in different agencies that can save you much time and worry. Take advantage of this experience. There's no need to reinvent the wheel by going around in the same circles thousands have before you. An organization can steer you straight to the horse's mouth. Many organizations have state and local chapters. Contact the national office to find the chapter nearest you.

Blindness and Visual Impairment

American Council of the Blind, 1211 Connecticut Avenue, N.W., Washington, D.C. 20036.

American Foundation for the Blind, 15 W. 16th Street, New York, N.Y. 10011.

National Blindness Information Center (National Federation of the Blind), 1346 Connecticut Avenue, N.W., Washington, D.C. 20036, has instituted a national information and referral telephone service. This new hotline service will make resource people available on the telephone to assist the blind with their needs as well as supply information on social, legal and educational problems. The toll-free number is 800-424-9770.

Deafness and Hearing Impairment

National Association of the Deaf, 814 Thayer Avenue, Silver Spring, Md. 20910.

American Speech and Hearing Association, 9030 Old Georgetown Road, Washington, D.C. 20014.

Developmental Disabilities

Mental retardation, cerebral palsy, epilepsy, autism. See p. 78.

Multiple Sclerosis

National Multiple Sclerosis Society, 205 E. 42nd Street, New York, N.Y. 10017.

Muscular Dystrophy

Muscular Dystrophy Association, Inc., 810 Seventh Avenue, New York, N.Y. 10019.

Physical Disabilities

National Paraplegia Foundation, 333 N. Michigan Avenue, Chicago, Ill. 60601.

National Association of the Physically Handicapped, 6473 Grandville Avenue, Detroit, Mich. 48228.

National Congress of Organizations of the Physically Handicapped, 7611 Oakland Avenue, Minneapolis, Minn. 55423.

Veterans (Disabled)

Disabled American Veterans, 3725 Alexandria Pike, Cole Spring, Ky. 41076.

Paralyzed Veterans of America, 7315 Wisconsin Avenue, N.W., Washington, D.C. 20014.

Periodicals

Subscribe to publications written for people with your disability. These magazines are often full of important information you need to know. You can get a list of such publications from an organization mentioned. Other publications you should know about include

Accent on Living
P.O. Box 700
Gillum Road and High Drive
Bloomington, Ill. 61701

Informer and
American Rehabilitation
Department of Health, Education and Welfare
Washington, D.C. 20201

Disabled USA
President's Committee on Employment of the Handicapped
1111 20th Street, N.W.
Washington, D.C. 20210

Rehabilitation Gazette
4502 Maryland Avenue
St. Louis, Mo. 63108

These magazines have feature stories that give in-depth coverage to some of the most important concerns of disabled people. You will also find summaries of current legislation, lists of new books, and "helpful hints" for better living. Even the ads are interesting, but be careful about buying anything you haven't seen and tried first. Many of the companies advertising in these magazines are well established and trustworthy, but others are small and not as good a risk. (In Chapter 2, section called "Media and Advertising," I commented on the fact that all advertisements in these magazines are for goods to alleviate disabilities, while advertisements for any other consumer goods are conspicuously absent. I also suggested actions you can take and, I hope, will take to remedy that situation.)

CONSUMER ACTION: RIGHT (WRITE) ON!

Any letter to an agency, requesting information about services or opportunities, should contain all these important details:

- Your full name, address and phone number
- Your age, sex, marital status, dependents, if any
- Your disability: when it started, what it is, how severe it is, whether it is chronic (permanent) or temporary
- Your need: what service or opportunity you are looking for

■ Your experience in looking: whom you contacted previously and what happened

It will take time, probably three weeks, before you get a reply. Usually you will be told to write to or phone someone in your area who has a responsibility for a specific program. Do so, enclosing a copy of the letter directing you to that person, and giving all important facts.

If you are not satisfied with the answer, go "over his head" to a superior with the request . . . and keep going until you get an answer, even if you have to write to the President himself. It pays to be persistent—eventually you will get your answer.

Don't forget to contact your congressman or senator if you believe you are not getting a service you deserve. Representatives in Congress are likely to be especially helpful—after all, they have to run for re-election every two years!

You can also write to me, care of Random House. I'll do everything I can to see that you know where to find out what's coming to you.

Keep copies of all your correspondence. This is important so you know whom you have contacted, who responded, when and what they said. If, after numerous letters, you are still getting a runaround and no end seems in sight, take your copies to a newspaper editor. The resulting story may make headlines—and jar the agency into giving you what you want.

You can also try to interest a Consumer Action program on your local radio or TV station. Send copies of your letters and other important information to the bureaucracy. Document your evidence that others are having the same problem and ask for an exposé in the newspaper or on the air.

If all this fails, have a lawyer do just two things:

1. Write a letter to the agency, saying that you will sue.
2. Call to say you will sue unless the service is provided immediately.

You can also go to a legal-aid clinic. They may represent you at no cost. If other people are complaining about the same problem, a class-action suit may be considered.

Remember, you are entitled to certain services as a citizen who is disabled. This is not charity; it is something you deserve. Usually your tax dollars paid for it. So don't be intimidated or buried under a pile of excuses—get what's coming to you.

If, after trying everything, you know the service you want isn't available to you, consider setting up your own organization or firm to provide it.

The Small Business Administration might give you a loan and the departments and agencies that should be offering the service but aren't might contract with you to do it. It's worth a try if you're confident there is a potential demand for the service and if you're willing to put in some hard work. After all, many large companies started with one person getting an idea and carrying it out.

III. IN THE MARKETPLACE

7. PURCHASE OF GOODS AND SERVICES

EVERYTHING EVERYBODY NEEDS

The best way to protect yourself as a consumer is to know your rights and to insist on them. You will be a better shopper if you know your rights. What you don't know can hurt you—in the pocketbook—and your most basic right is the right to get your money's worth. As a consumer with a disability, you are entitled to equality in the marketplace. Whether you are limited in mobility or impaired in sight or hearing, you are deprived of your consumer rights when environmental or attitudinal barriers deprive you of accessibility, information and communication.

This chapter will give you some hints on how to get top value for your shopping dollar. It will give you some advice on how to avoid being deceived or defrauded in the marketplace. And it tells you what YOU can and should do to remove the barriers to your consumer equality.

TEN CONSUMER COMMANDMENTS

I   Know thy budget; evaluate "wants" versus "needs."
II   Comparison-shop for goods, services and for the cost of credit.
III Read advertisements carefully, including the fine print; separate facts from puffery; see if any strings are attached to promises.
IV   Beware of impulse purchases; they can ruin your budget and may not look so good at home.
V   Never allow yourself to be rushed into immediate decisions, for cash or credit, by special sales or "one time" offers. The bargain that won't be there tomorrow may not be such a good deal today.

VI   Check carefully the manufacturer's warranty, and the seller's refund or exchange policy, before you part with your cash or signature.

VII Don't accept any verbal promises; they don't stand up in court. Demand that everything—conditions, guarantees, delivery date, refund policy—be written on a sales receipt or contract. Keep these documents in a safe place.

VIII Never sign a contract in a hurry. Read carefully every condition, including the fine print. Do not sign a contract that you do not understand, or one that has empty spaces over your signature, "to be filled in later." Before signing, show the contract to a knowledgeable friend or consultant. Always get a copy of the contract and keep it in a safe place.

IX   Do not be lured by promises of easy credit—payments are always hard.

X   If not satisfied with goods or services, do not despair—complain!

CHOICES IN RETAIL SHOPPING

Your choices in retail shopping are:

Neighborhood Stores	Discount Stores
Department Stores	Telephone Orders
Variety Stores	Mail Orders
Specialty Shops	Door-to-Door Sales

Which one is best for you?

Specialty shops usually have the most knowledgeable and helpful clerks or are operated by the owner. They may charge a little more than other retailers but often they throw in a lot of extra services at no extra cost. You should consider these services as well as the price. Check such things as delivery and installation, alterations, warranties and repair services, fashion and decorator advice, and ordering by mail or telephone.

A discount appliance outlet may be selling you last year's goods even if they are still in the factory package. That doesn't necessarily detract from them, but you should know what you are getting.

Watch out for merchandise advertised at very low prices. It can be bait to get you into the store so a smooth-talking salesman can switch you to more expensive goods.

There is nothing automatic about saving money when you shop. You have to work at it, but you can save yourself a lot of effort by using ads, catalogues and the telephone to gather facts before you start visiting stores.

You should check retailers for good management policy, reliability, courtesy, cleanliness, good-quality merchandise at a fair price, pleasant atmosphere, convenient location, available services, delivery, mailing, parking, convenient hours, available credit—installment contracts, charge accounts, credit cards.

Write for: "Where You Shop Is as Important as What You Buy" (617F). Pros and cons of shopping at different types of stores. Consumer Information Center, Pueblo, Colo. 81009.

HOW DO YOUR LOCAL STORES SERVE YOUR SPECIAL NEEDS?

In addition to the other criteria by which you judge and choose your favorite store, you should look for accommodations that make your shopping more convenient.

Rate your favorite store by the *access* test.

Access

- Does the store have at least one level or ramped entrance?
- Is there a hinged door next to a revolving-door entrance?
- Are doorways and aisles at least 32 inches wide?
- Is a try-on room accessible?
- Are rest rooms accessible and indicated by the International Symbol of Access?
- Is a passenger elevator door wide enough for a wheelchair to pass through? (A freight elevator does not provide accessibility!)
- If elevators are automatic, is at least one elevator equipped with lower floor-selector buttons, within reach of wheelchair shopper?
- Is at least one public telephone and one water fountain within reach?
- Are several parking spaces near the parking lot entrance reserved for cars of disabled drivers? Is the surface of the parking area smooth and hard (no sand, gravel, etc.)?
- Are there handrails on all stairways?
- Do the store's advertisements, in newspapers and the classified telephone directory, indicate the International Symbol of Access?
- Is it displayed in the store? On rest-room doors?

Information

When "specials" are featured in various departments, how will a blind shopper find out about them?

☞ **Suggest an in-house telephone with a taped message, announcing the day's special sales and their exact location.**

How will a blind customer know if the elevator is on its way up or down?

☞ **Suggest different signals, such as, for instance, one tone for UP, two for DOWN. Or LOW-HIGH, HIGH-LOW. It could be done!**

If elevators are automatic, do floor-selector buttons have raised numerals or Brailled designations? Is there a tape announcing by voice floors and departments?

Communication

Is there at least one public telephone that can be used by persons who have telephone pickup coils in their hearing aids? Are there amplifying controls?

Staff Assistance

Is the staff trained to assist shoppers with disabilities? During off-peak hours, can you get a staff member assigned as a shopping aide?

Special Services for Charge-Account Customers

Upon request and certification, perhaps a disabled customer's charge account could be marked for the store to extend certain privileges, such as:

1. Accept mail or phone orders when advertisement prohibits them
2. Hold sales merchandise, ordered by phone, for pickup at another time
3. Waive charges for parcel delivery if store does not customarily deliver free of charge

Suburban shopping centers, built more recently than urban stores, with few upper or lower sales floors, avoid many of the architectural barriers of downtown shopping areas. Merchants and consumers in suburban shopping centers are finding out that features designed for customers in wheelchairs, for instance curb cuts and ramps, are equally convenient for other wheelers: baby carriages, tricycles, shopping carts, delivery wagons, all have physical surface requirements similar to the person with mobility problems.

"It appears," writes Richard Hollerith, Jr., in an article entitled "Eliminating the Handicap," "that in many cases the problem of accommodating the handicapped may well have a common resolution with the need for greater safety precautions for all persons." The author predicts that a new generation of innovative products will result from a major project currently under way to update the official standards for a barrier-free environment. "Within a generation all everyday products will be designed for use by those of us with handicaps. It is my contention that products designed to be used by the little old lady, slightly hard of hearing, wearing glasses, not so very strong or steady, will be innovative in the true sense of the word and will be better products for everyone to use."*

A recent nationwide survey of disabled consumers, conducted by the author, brought a variety of responses:

MANY were satisfied with their suppliers.
SOME had complaints, mostly about repairs.
A FEW were outraged about discriminatory treatment.
MOST did not know the laws concerning mail orders.
ALL wished that sales personnel were taught to understand customers with disabilities and were trained to assist them appropriately.

Management and customer contact staff in retail establishments share with the majority of America's population ignorance about the physical and psychological needs of people with disabilities and how to behave toward them naturally, helpfully, neither ignoring them nor smothering them with oversolicitous assistance.

In years to come, when this generation of children will have grown up together with "mainstreamed" handicapped classmates, people with disabilities will no longer be treated with today's mixture of rejection and compassion born of ignorance, emotion and fear. The current generation of adults, however, is just now beginning to accept handicapped individuals as they become more visible, more militant, demanding and assuming their rightful place in society.

Salespeople are no exception. It will be management's duty to educate them—and themselves—how to communicate with disabled customers, as a regular feature in staff orientation.

* Reprinted from *Industrial Design* (May/June 1976), distributed by the National Easter Seal Society, 2023 W. Ogden Avenue, Chicago, Ill. 60612.

Why don't <u>you</u> suggest such training to your local merchants? It may be good training for <u>your</u> persuasive sales technique! Publications and audio visuals (films, slides) for training purposes are easily available. Listings, including description and prices, will gladly be sent upon request. Write to:

Sister Kenny Institute, Chicago Avenue at 27th Street, Minneapolis, Minn. 55407.

American Foundation for the Blind, 15 W. 16th Street, New York, N.Y. 10011.

National Association of the Deaf, 814 Thayer Avenue, Silver Spring, Md. 10910.

National Easter Seal Society, 2023 W. Ogden Avenue, Chicago, Ill. 60612.

An accomplished disabled person, maybe yourself, a friend or colleague, a member of your club or church could be invited as a guest speaker to a training session, to present his or her point of view.

And yet, watching films, reading books, listening to speakers *must* be supplemented by personal experience, in order to really get the message across. Suggest to your merchants' training programs the following:

1. Have the management and sales people spend a day shopping in their store in a wheelchair. Suddenly they are a little over four feet tall, finding doors too heavy or too narrow or revolving, trying to wheel over deep-pile carpets, getting to crowded counters, trying on clothes sitting down, going up and down in elevators—and no leaving the wheelchair for bathroom privileges . . . You bet some architectural barriers will be removed in a hurry.

2. Spend one day blindfolded as a shopper who wants to find his way around, learn what's on "special sale" and what labels tell. The next time a vision impaired customer asks for such information, it will be given from remembered experience.

3. Earplugs can only faintly simulate the isolation of deafness, but trying to communicate while wearing them will be a hassle. Watching television with the sound turned off could be assigned homework. The store personnel may be more patient the next time a customer apparently ignores somebody speaking to him or asks the same question twice.

SHOPPING BY TELEPHONE

To the questions "Do you shop occasionally by telephone? Do you receive what you expected?" most of our surveyed disabled consumers responded "Yes" and "Usually."

This, of course, refers to orders telephoned to merchants you know, food markets or suppliers of other goods and services. Provided you get helpful information and are billed at the same prices quoted on the phone, and have the privilege to return unsatisfactory deliveries, shopping by telephone will save you wear and tear, time and effort, and cost of transportation.

Ordering advertised merchandise by telephone demands a few safeguards. Be sure you read the ad carefully and critically. Study the factual information concerning quality, quantity, size of described articles. Designers and commercial photographers are wizards at making things look bigger, better, more enticing than they really are.

Be certain you order only from a reputable company and make sure of your return privileges.

Telephone Solicitations

Telephone solicitations are a different breed. People may call to inform you of sensational bargains, or to appeal to your sympathy by offering you goods allegedly produced by blind or retarded workers. Watch out!

Request that the offer be made to you in writing, on the organization's letterhead, and then check out if it is a legitimate cause before you let your kind heart run away with your money.

The unseen bargain may not be so sensational that it has to be purchased on a telephoned offer. Resist the temptation.

Most of all—get your defenses of suspicion and incredulity into action when an excited voice informs you about the prize you have just won or the good luck that your name has been picked in a drawing for some great opportunity. There is just the minor *condition* that the prize will have to be delivered to your home—by a supersalesman who will sell you something you don't need, want or can afford, or the lucky drawing of your name entitles you to something extra special only after you've sent in some cash to avail yourself of the fine opportunity!

Seems an obvious come-on? Not obvious enough for many people not to fall for the fake and get taken. Please, don't be one of them. A more or less polite "no" will save you cash and aggravation.

BUYING BY MAIL

If you are home-bound, live far from stores or find getting around tiresome and costly, you may be one of the millions of Americans who boosted the mail-order business into $19.2 billion in 1976! Mail-order companies also ranked number one in Formal Complaints Processed by Better Business Bureaus, followed way behind (one third) by complaints against auto dealers.

Catalogue Shopping

Buying by catalogue through the mail is an annual $15-billion business. Sears alone spent $125 million on catalogues in 1976. The boom in catalogue buying is attributed to four factors: the fact that more women are working today and so have less time to shop in stores; the retreat of shoppers from crime-plagued urban shopping areas; high gasoline prices; and the lack of sales help encountered in cost-pinched stores.

The proliferation in the kind of goods and services sold through the mails has made it a convenient way for many people to do some of their shopping. If this is comfortable for you, make sure that the catalogue-issuing company, or any other advertiser in newspapers, magazines or on the air, is a reliable firm of good reputation. You should also know the laws protecting the mail-order consumer:

> You have a right to expect the ordered merchandise within 30 days; if the seller cannot fill your order by the end of that period, he must notify you in writing, giving you the choice to cancel your order for a full refund or to agree to an extension of the delivery date. This decision must not cost you anything; the seller has to provide you with a postage paid reply card or envelope.

It is a good idea to check if the catalogue or advertisement from which you ordered states "Money-back guaranteed, if not satisfied." Keep the catalogue or ad in a safe place until the shipment arrives. If it is not to your liking, and if you had ordered from a reputable company, you will not encounter difficulties in receiving a refund for the returned merchandise. Most mail-order firms will not cover shipping charges on items that are returned.

Address complaints about mail orders, including fraudulent advertising, to: Direct Mail-Marketing Association, 6 E. 43rd Street, New York, N.Y. 10017; or your local Consumer Affairs office; or Federal Trade Commission, Washington, D.C. 20580; or your regional FTC office.

Write for free publication to: Consumer Information Center, Pueblo, Colo. 81009.

Shopping by Mail? You're Protected! (532 F). Explains the federal regulation on merchandise ordered through the mail.

It is not surprising that such a gold mine of profit possibilities will attract certain characters who would like to get in on the deal without giving you what you paid for. Watch out for companies that make spectacular claims for a product or that market only one item. Most of all, NEVER send money to a company whose advertisement shows only a P.O. Box number. If, after weeks of waiting, nothing arrives in the mail—and most likely it never will, because some character made off with your and other people's money and is plying his trade in another state—you surely will not get a reply from the P.O. Box. The name and business address of a company printed in the advertisement—even if you send the order to a stated P.O. Box—give you at least some assurance that you, or an agent acting for you, will find somebody to deal with or can trace companies that may have moved away.

Mail Frauds

One of the oldest U.S. laws to protect the consumer and others doing business through the mails is the criminal fraud statute adopted in 1972. Of the endless variety of fraudulent schemes, the most vicious is the sale of worthless medicines and therapeutic devices.

When you believe mail fraud exists, hold all letters, including envelopes and other evidence related to the questionable scheme, and bring the information to the attention of your local postmaster. Too often the average person doesn't report that he has been victimized because the amount is small or, in some cases, the victim is too embarrassed to report his losses.

Don't be embarrassed. Help the postal inspectors stop a dishonest scheme and you'll be helping others as well as yourself. Inspectors must find that you and other persons buying a product or service were cheated as a result of claims by the seller made in an intentional effort to defraud. Fraudulent mail schemes represent an annual loss to the public of over $500 million.

Unordered merchandise received by mail need not worry you. The Postal Reorganization Act of 1970 relieves the recipient of any responsibility. You do not have to pay, hold or return it. Consider it a gift.

One more warning: Do not accept C.O.D. packages, for yourself or neighbors, that neither you nor they expected. It's a trick frequently practiced at Christmas time. You may have paid for a package of old newspapers and your neighbors will tell you that they never asked you for the favor! Had they expected a C.O.D. package, they would have given you the money, wouldn't they? And your long-lost Aunt Sarah wouldn't send you a gift C.O.D., would she?

If you want to read more about mail frauds—and how to avoid them—ask or write for:

Mail Fraud Laws—Protecting Consumers, Investors, businessmen, patients, students. Available from your Local Postmaster, or from the Chief Inspector, Postal Inspection Service, Washington, D.C. 20260.

Mail Fraud Laws (531 F). How to protect yourself from mail-fraud schemes such as fake contests, unordered merchandise, work-at-home, medical cures, chain letters, etc. Consumer Information Center, Pueblo, Colo. 81009.

Unordered Merchandise (Consumer Bulletin #2, English and Spanish). Federal Trade Commission, Room 130, Washington, D.C. 20580.

DOOR-TO-DOOR SALES

That charming salesperson knocking at your door—unexpectedly or delivering that "prize" announced to you on the telephone earlier in the day—isn't all sweetness and light. He or she may be a graduate of an "aggressiveness training" course, ready to high-pressure you, the unwary consumer, into buying something you had not planned on and don't even need. In 1975 the direct-selling industry accounted for more than $6 billion worth of goods sold at retail by some 2 million salespersons. Even if the merchandise is legitimate—vacuum cleaners, pots and pans, brushes, cosmetics—it may be overpriced. The sales technique exploits loneliness, desire for company, susceptibility to temptation.

Has it happened to you at some time in the past? Cheer up. Now the law mandates a cooling-off period to protect consumers from their own impetuousness:

■ Within 72 hours of purchase, all door-to-door sales over $25, by cash or installment contracts, are cancelable for no other reason than the buyer's change of mind; deposit must be refunded.

■ By law, the seller must supply a cancellation postcard, which only needs to be posted within 72 hours.

It is advisable to have someone witness your dropping that card into the mail box. Failing to supply such a cancellation card can break your contract and subject the seller to a fine.

A door-to-door sale is not always defined as one taking place in your home: your place of work or any other place away from the seller's premises is subject to the same legal protection.

☞ Write for publication to Federal Trade Commission, Room 130, Washington, D.C. 20580: "Three Days to Cancel: Door-to-Door Sales." Buyer's Guide #15.

MAGAZINE SUBSCRIPTIONS

Did you ever help a "student working his way through college" by subscribing to magazines you didn't really care for or wouldn't get around to reading when they arrived? If the contract is over $25, see above. Then, before the year is up, you get bombarded with cleverly written promotion letters asking renewal of your annual subscription and offering discounts for subscribing NOW for years to come—if you act at once . . . while the offer lasts!

Doesn't seem a whole year since your first subscription started? It may not be. Many of these renewal invitations arrive long before the expiration date of your current subscription. How do you know when the renewal will begin? You don't, unless you look for the expiration date on the mailing label. It's there, but could be hidden in a code of numbers and letters. Whether you find it or not, don't rush with the renewal. You can be sure you'll get more letters later on.

A June 1977 New York State bill requires clear and conspicuous notice of expiration date of magazine or newspaper subscription date on every mailing label and in any written invitation to renew. This same law also prohibits commencement of renewal until current subscription has actually expired.

☞ If you find that such a law does not exist in your state, suggest it to your legislators.

You can also request that your name NOT be "sold" to lists if you want to be spared unwanted junk mail, including pornographic material. You can write to the Direct Mail-Marketing Association, 6 E. 43rd Street, New York, N.Y. 10017, requesting its Mail Preference Service form. When you fill in and return the form, your name will be removed from lists used by 400 cooperating mailers, who account for 70 percent of consumer third-class mail.

Got a Magazine Subscription Problem?

Help is available in the form of Magazine Action Line (MAL). Publishers Clearing House, a magazine subscription sales agency, established MAL as a free consumer service. MAL handles all consumer complaints for magazine subscriptions no matter where the subscriptions were ordered originally.

First, try to settle your problem directly with the company with whom you placed the order. If that fails, drop a line explaining the problem to: Publishers Clearing House, Attention: Magazine Action Line, 382 Channel Drive, Port Washington, N.Y. 11050.

CHARGE IT!

Magic Carpet or Time Bomb—this all-American game is played with small plastic cards. Players are advised to observe the rules created for their protection. If cards are used wisely, players will arrive at goal safely. Overuse of cards can cause time bomb to explode, injuring players and their families.

Though you'll never read this ad, you are most likely playing the game. It is estimated that eight out of every ten adults carry at least one card. Stores, oil companies, airlines, banks (Master Charge, BankAmericard, or Visa), travel and entertainment businesses (American Express, Diner's Club) are circulating about 500 million credit cards in the United States.

Sellers like credit cards because they build up customer loyalty. Buyers enjoy the ease of shopping without having to carry large amounts of cash, return privileges and the free use of the lender's money from the time of charge up to receipt of the monthly statement and the grace period to pay that statement, which can be 10 to 30 days.

Watch out! That's the trap of the game. You DO get free use of the lender's money for a short time when you pay statements in full, upon receipt. The moment you pay only part of the statement, you transform the "free" charge account into a "revolving credit" account, and wham!—you are slammed with 12 or 18 percent interests. Don't get misled by printed numbers 1 and 1½ percent per month—it means 12 or 18 percent per year.

Unless you buy no more during the month than you can afford to pay at the end of the month, charge accounts and credit cards cater more to your weakness than to your convenience.

Some banks now claim that they lose money on their prompt-paying customers and want to charge monthly fees for the service. Before you commiserate with the poor banks, remember that the service is not as "free" as they'd like you to believe. The bank takes 2 to 6 percent of the amount it pays the seller for your charged purchase. The more you buy, the greater the bank's profit.

The merchant must include these costs in the price of his merchandise if he wants to stay in business. As a result, it is actually you and the cash-paying customer who pay for the cost of your credit. Cash payers are getting wise (and Consumers Union brought a suit on their behalf), and some stores and restaurants now will give you a discount if you pay cash. They are not required to make this offer on their own, but you may ask for it.

Before charging a purchase or a meal, offer to pay cash, provided you get a discount.

If your card gets lost or stolen, notify the issuer at once. According to federal law, $50 is the limit of your liability for unauthorized use of a lost or stolen card, but your notice terminates your liability for unauthorized use altogether. This, however, still means as many notices as you have charge cards, and in the excitement of loss you may forget to cancel one or the other. You can avail yourself of a service where you can register all your credit cards, for an annual service fee. In case of loss, you make only one call to their national, toll-free, 24-hour-service phone number. They will cancel all your cards for you and arrange for replacements. You get documented proof of notification which ends your potential liability of $50 per individual card.

Hot-Line Credit Card Bureau of America
Post Office Box 7316
Fort Lauderdale, Fl. 33338

Installment buying of major items—appliances, TV sets, furniture, automobiles—is another way of enjoying now what you will pay for later. The credit offered to you by the seller—furniture store, automobile dealer—may be the costliest way to finance your purchase.

Do not be misled by low monthly payments. They last a long time and add up to much more than what you expect the item to cost you. A loan taken from a bank, credit union or insurance company to pay for merchandise, emergency or any other immediate cash needs may offer you the most reasonable conditions.

Comparison-shop for credit as you do for merchandise.

Because credit plays such an important part in our country's economy and in the lives of its citizens, recent years have produced many laws to regulate lenders and protect borrowers. They are administered by the Federal Trade Commission, to whom you can write for detailed information and to report violations. Contact the FTC in Washington (Bureau of Consumer Protection, Washington, D.C. 20580) or the nearest regional office in the following cities:

Atlanta, Ga. 30309, Room 800,
   730 Peachtree Street
Boston, Mass. 02114, Room 1301,
   150 Causeway Street
Chicago, Ill. 60603, Suite 1437,
   55 E. Monroe Street
Cleveland, Ohio 44199, Room
   1339, Fed. Office Bldg., 1240 E.
   9th Street
Dallas, Tex. 75201, Suite 2665,
   2001 Bryan Street
Denver, Colo. 80202, Suite 2900,
   1405 Curtis Street

Los Angeles, Calif. 90024, Fed.
   Bldg. Room 13209, 11000
   Wilshire Blvd.
New York, N.Y. 10007, Fed. Bldg.
   2243-EB, 26 Federal Plaza
San Francisco, Calif. 94102, 450
   Golden Gate Ave., Box 36005
Honolulu, Hawaii 98613, Room
   605, Melim Bldg., 333 Queen
   Street
Seattle, Wash. 98174, Fed. Bldg.,
   28th Floor, 915 Second Ave.
Washington, D.C. 20037, Gelman
   Bldg., 2120 L St., N.W.

The Truth in Lending Law and Regulation Z are designed to ensure that every customer who has a need for consumer credit is given meaningful information with respect to the cost of that credit. This law makes it easier for qualified applicants to compare various interest rates and to shop around for credit if they take the time to do so.

The Fair Credit Billing Act amends Regulation Z to protect consumers against inaccurate and unfair credit billing practices. During the period of time that a bill is being disputed because of a billing error, the creditor cannot charge interest on that disputed amount and cannot report the consumer to a credit reporting agency as being in default.

The Fair Credit Reporting Act regulates both credit and investigative agencies which issue consumer reports, and it also regulates the users of these reports. The primary reason for this act is to protect consumers against false or inaccurate reports about them, against results of such reports, and against the use of any reports by firms or individuals with no legitimate interests.

The Equal.Credit Opportunity Act makes it unlawful for any creditor to discriminate against any applicant for credit on the basis of sex, marital status, race, color, religion, national origin, age, or because any or all of the applicant's income is derived from public assistance.

☞ **If you are denied credit, you have the right to ask the company for the reasons in writing.**

- If the denial is due to a negative credit report on you, make an appointment with the credit reporting agency and check your record.
- If its entry of a default payment is erroneous, the agency must correct it.
- If you have an explanation for a justified default, such as that you are in dispute with the reporting merchant, submit a statement of 100 words or less; the credit reporting agency must report your explanation together with the report on default of payment so that a prospective lender may make his own judgment on your credit worthiness to him.

No negative credit report on you, and yet you were denied credit, with no reason given? Do you suspect discrimination because of your disability? No one contends that a citizen has the *right* to credit; but the right to be judged for credit worthiness—that is, ability and willingness to repay—on a nondiscriminatory basis is now a matter of law.

Regrettably, the law does not mandate that a written statement of reasons for the denial of credit be *automatically* furnished to rejected applicants. Such a procedure would serve as an effective deterrent. Creditors who know they would have to furnish a written statement to *all* rejected applicants, not only to those who know their right to ask for one, would be less likely to discriminate.

The burden should not be placed on the consumer to request the reasons in writing, particularly when those who are in categories traditionally discriminated against, lack education about their rights, are passive, suffer from a poor self-image and are easily intimidated especially in the context of seeking credit.

At present, you too may be subject to the prejudice of a loan officer who assumes that your disability may make you a poorer risk for repayment of the loan, or with whom you have difficulties in communicating orally.

☛ **Do not accept one person's negative judgment on a loan application if your personal record justifies your credit worthiness. Ask to see the loan officer's superior, or try another bank. Remember, the Equal Credit Opportunity Act protects ALL Americans.**

Holder in Due Course preserves the consumer's rights against the seller under a legally sufficient claim or defense (e.g., defective merchandise or unsatisfactory services), even if the seller had sold the installment contract to a third party (finance company). Before the enactment of this FTC Trade Regulation in May 1976, the third party had no responsibility toward the consumer, since they had bought only the credit paper and were only interested in collecting payments. The consumer had no recourse. Now the consumer has the same recourse toward a third party, such as Master Charge or BankAmericard (Visa), in case of legitimate complaint against a seller, even if that third party has already paid the seller in full for the purchase.

HARD FACTS ON EASY CREDIT

DO

shop for credit as carefully as you do for merchandise. Compare! The price of credit varies as much as the price of goods.

find out the different sources of available credit. Compare the costs of borrowing from banks, credit unions, finance companies, with the costs of installment buying.

find out what it is costing you to buy the article on time, by comparing the deferred-payment price with the cash price.

study the price tag on merchandise you're planning to buy on the installment plan. It must tell you the cash price and the de-

DON'T

believe there is an *easy* credit. Only getting it may be easy—paying back is always hard.

buy on installment credit until you have looked into all the other possibilities. With cash from a loan, you can drive a harder bargain or buy at a discount house.

be seduced by "buy now, pay later" offers. All too fast, *later* becomes *now,* and you may be in trouble.

forget that the *Truth in Lending Law* demands that you have this information so that you know the total price you'll end up paying.

DO

ferred-payment price; it must tell you all finance charges and interests; it must give you the annual percentage rate, which sets forth in % the total cost of credit (*Truth in Lending*)

make as large a down payment as possible if you do buy on the installment plan. Make your periodic payments as large as you can, to pay back as fast as you can.

read the contract carefully.

make sure it reflects your entire agreement with the seller.

demand a copy of the signed contract. Take it with you and keep it in a safe place.

know what the penalties are if you can't make your payments.

inform the bank, finance company or credit-card issuer if you have a justified dispute with a merchant and want to suspend your payments while it's in progress.

know that if a lawsuit is brought against you for default of payments, it must be brought in the county where you live or where the purchase was made.

be sure that you get your charge account statement in the mail 15 days before any finance charges take effect so that you have time to pay your bill in full, if this is your practice.

DON'T

be misled into thinking that many small payments will be easier. They will cost you more in the long run.

sign it if it contains any unauthorized blank spaces.

rely on any verbal statements or promises of salesmen.

let them "mail the copy later," and don't misplace it. It's a vital document in a dispute.

despair! In an emergency, you may be able to work out an arrangement.

let them tell you they are not responsible, and you must pay, no matter what. The law permits you to "fight first, and pay later." (*Holder in Due Course*)

believe that the seller can arbitrarily pick a distant court, just to make it hard for you to appear.

pay a penalty in finance charges because the store failed to send its bill on time. It's their fault, not yours.

DO

notify the store in writing if you believe the statement contains an error; the store must acknowledge receipt within 30 days; investigate; correct error or state reasons it believes the bill to be correct. During resolution process, store may not close account or report to credit agency. (*Fair Credit Billing Act*)

return to the seller or bank if you cannot meet payments because of unforeseen events, such as unemployment or illness. Try to make arrangements for delayed payments.

report to your state consumer protection agency if you are harassed by abusive debt collectors making obscene phone calls, threatening use of violence. Collection agencies are subject to state regulations.

get advice from trained professional counselors if you are in financial distress from overuse of credit. You can get help in debt management and future, more prudent budgeting; slowed payments may be arranged with your current creditors.

DON'T

hold up payment of your entire bill; just withhold the disputed amount and pay the balance promptly, or the store will be entitled to finance charges on the undisputed amount of the bill.

just stop payments. The balance of the entire loan could become due at once; your wages can be garnisheed; an almost fully paid up item can be repossessed; and your credit report will give you problems for years to come.

get intimidated. Congress is considering legislation to control the country's 5,000 collection agencies. Write to your congressman to support such legislation.

despair. For a directory of recognized consumer credit counseling services in your area, write to: National Foundation for Consumer Credit 1819 H Street, Washington, D.C. 20006.

These publications are yours for the asking. You'll find them good reading:

Give Yourself Credit, Guide to Consumer Credit Laws (1977). Subcommittee on Consumer Affairs, House Annex No. 1, Room 212, Washington, D.C. 20515. A simple and quick reference to the consumer credit laws passed to date, including Truth in Lending, Fair Credit Billing, Fair Credit Reporting, Consumer Leasing Act, Equal Credit Opportunity Act, and a discussion of the proposed Truth in Savings Bill. Explains the consumer's rights in a clear and understandable manner.

Consumer Information, for your protection; *Equal Credit Opportunity for Women,* your rights; *Truth in Lending,* what it means to you. Federal Deposit Insurance Corporation, 550 17th Street, N.W., Washington, D.C. 20429.

A Money Saving Offer—Truth in Lending Takes the Wraps Off Credit (Buyer's Guide #12); *Equal Credit Opportunity Act* (pamphlet and full text); *Fair Credit Billing Act; Fair Credit Reporting Act,* know your rights under—A Checklist for Consumers (Buyer's Guide #7; *Truth in Lending,* what it means to you (Federal Reserve Board) (English/Spanish). Bureau of Consumer Protection, Federal Trade Commission, Washington, D.C. 20580.

Equal Credit Opportunity Act (526 F) 1977—your right to credit and what to do if you've been denied credit on the basis of sex, marital status, race, color, religion, national origin, or age; *Fair Credit Reporting Act* (527 F) 1972—the right to learn one's own credit rating, and how to dispute incorrect information and have it removed; *Shopping for Credit Can Save You Cash* (615 F) 1974—how to compare the costs of buying with loans, credit cards, and revolving charge plans. Consumer Information Center, Pueblo, Colo. 81009.

Borrowing Basics for Women. Citibank, Public Affairs Department, 399 Park Avenue, New York, N.Y. 10002.

The Credit Handbook for Women. American Express Company, American Express Plaza, New York, N.Y. 10004.

FOOD

Shopping, cooking, eating—and thinking about food when we are hungry or dieting—interests many of us more than any other topic and occupies much of our time. Unless we live on a farm, complete with cows and chickens, or grow our own victory garden, we do our food shopping daily, weekly or in between.

As a share of the money we spend for goods and services, food accounts for about 18 percent in the United States. In many countries of the world, the percentages are much higher. If you live on a limited income, it may also be higher for you. Remember, however, that your so-called food dollar buys a lot more than food today. If you are the average American shopper, you spend $5.96 out of a $20 bill for nonfood items at the supermarket. Next time you shop, add up what you spent for food, and for nonfood— you'll probably be surprised. And don't count only paper goods, soaps, pharmaceuticals, gadgets and magazines as nonfoods; beer, soft drinks and candy aren't *food* either.

Because shopping in self-service stores is impersonal, and because you buy closed packages, trusting that they contain what the wrapper promises, there are laws that protect you. Government agencies supervise farmers and manufacturers who produce goods, and stores who sell them.

By law, labels must give you detailed information about weight and consistency of contents. Nowadays you will also find the nutritional value of food analyzed on the container. You may consider it well worth the time and effort to take advantage of this information.

If shoppers aides, family members or friends accompany you to the food store or do the shopping for you, be sure that YOU are familiar with your consumer rights so that you can advise your aides, in the market or at home. You get plenty of aid to educate yourself: from advertisers who want you to buy their wares, and from consumerists who tell you in books, pamphlets, newspapers, magazines and on the air how to buy wisely. On p. 132 you will find titles of publications that are yours for the asking. Requests on postcards will bring them to you, full of good information and practical suggestions.

Shopping by yourself or with an aide, by telephone or through an aide, you have two main choices: neighborhood stores and supermarkets.

Neighborhood Stores give you personal service, assemble your order, may deliver it to your home and extend credit. For all these reasons, they must charge higher prices than self-service markets.

When you order by telephone, ask about the day's "specials," and specify brand, size and weight you want. It's a natural tendency for the grocer to boost his sales by sending costlier brands or larger sizes when you do not order explicitly.

Supermarkets tempt you to buy, on impulse, more than you had planned. In 1977 alone, food makers spent about $4 billion on advertising.* Remembering those ads, consumers chose among 10,000 items what to buy in the stores. Mothers are pushed by their children, conditioned by TV commercials, to demand snack foods and sugared cereals.

Did you ever wonder why milk is placed way back in the store? Simple: on the way there, you may pick up a jar of pickles or olives, or a tea strainer,

---

* "The Way We Eat," *Wall Street Journal* (June 24, 1977).

high-profit items that had *not* been on your mind. While waiting to check out, how about chewing gum, cigarettes and the magazines with those flashy titles? Hard to resist? You are not alone. Unplanned purchases constituted 46.8 percent of what went into the nation's shopping carts in 1977.*

Your household shopping dollar will stretch further if you know some of the laws and common-sense shopping rules for the food market; apply them yourself, supervise the person who shops with you and instruct the aide who shops for you.

Here are some "Dos" and "Don'ts" that can be dollar stretchers.

AT THE FOOD MARKET

DO
prepare a shopping list.

DON'T
shop on an empty stomach;
be tempted to make impulse
purchases.

look for advertised specials. If they are not in stock, demand a rain check. The rain check is a courtesy, not enforceable by law.

let markets lure you into making trips for advertised specials that they never seem to have. Stores that advertise specials must have supplies on hand or they are in violation of the law.

look for the unit price, the price per pound, quart or count. This is the only price that lets you compare value between different brands and between various package sizes of the same brand. Unit price labels must be on the items or on the shelf below the display of the item.

be confused by all the numbers. The only figure to concern you is the unit price, per pound, quart or count; usually, house brands are cheaper.

expect unit price shelf labels in small stores. Only large markets may show them.

compare the cost of convenience foods. The more service is provided, such as seasonings, pre-cooking, freezing, the more you pay; it may have value to you.

automatically assume that the fresh form is always cheapest. A glass of home-squeezed orange juice costs almost three times as much as a glass made from frozen concentrate.

* Study by the Point of Purchase Advertising Institute and E. I. du Pont de Nemours.

DO

look for the date stamped on most dairy products and baked goods—either, say, "Apr 15" or "04 15." Breads are dated by days of the week, two days ahead of delivery.

read the labels on all packaged foods, including frozen, for net weight and ingredients, listed in descending order of quantity.

check the label on packaged meat, whole or chopped, for the original cut, like rib, chuck, sirloin. This must be stated.

watch the scale to be sure the indicator starts at zero and stops before weight and price are quoted.

make sure that you pay only for the *net* weight of what you buy. If it is weighed in a container, the total weight must show more than the exact weight of the contents you are charged for.

ask the manager to weigh or count the quantity you want, however small.

use the customer scale if your market has one. It should be near any store-packaged merchandise, like meat, fruit, vegetables; take the time—it could mean money.

make sure the cash register tape has a top and bottom print-out, indicating the register had been cleared before your purchases were rung up.

DON'T

buy the nearest date. If you shop on April 1, cream cheese dated Apr 15 will stay fresh longer in your refrigerator than one dated Apr 09. Look for the date furthest in the future.

forget your eyeglasses when you shop;

accidentally buy products that contain ingredients harmful to your personal health.

be fooled by fancy names on packaged meat. Only the USDA grades—prime, choice or good—indicate the quality.

let anything be weighed on a scale you can't see. On a blocked scale, your purchase could be short-weighed.

pay for a box at the price of its contents. By law, the container cannot be included in the total price you pay. A pound of candy, cookies or potato salad, is a pound without the container, not including the box!

buy more than you need, because you are too shy to ask.

be timid about weighing your purchases; it's your right to check weight. If you pay for more than you get, you've been cheated.

get charged for something you haven't bought.

DO

return to the store if you have a reasonable complaint about the
quality of merchandise you
bought. Return the unused portion and the sales slip and speak
to the manager.

DON'T

just get angry and throw freshly
bought, spoiled food away. In a
good store, the manager will
want to keep you as a satisfied
customer.

**If you have a complaint about a packaged product, by all means write
to the manufacturer whose name and address are on the package—by law.**

**Address your letter to "Consumer Affairs Department." You will hear
from them! Remember that producers spend millions of advertising dollars
to woo you; they surely will not ignore your letter. On the contrary, you
may receive samples of other, similar products of theirs if you were dissatisfied with the one you bought. (We know of a cat who received six
varieties of cat food when the owner told the producer that the cat hated
the kind he had been served. And it wasn't "Morris," the finicky TV cat.
Just an average pet!)**

**Of course, should you find insects, animal hair or other contamination
in packaged food—rarely!—rush and notify the Food and Drug Administration. They may have the product recalled and you will have done a
service to other consumers.**

Shoppers Aides

Next to your homemaker, social worker or other professional aide, you may
find shopping aides through your local Volunteer Service bureau, church or
nonsectarian groups who do volunteer work. Some senior citizens centers
may have members who will enjoy shopping for you.

In some areas Girl Scouts, thirteen to seventeen years old, have been
trained to become wise shoppers and assist disabled neighbors. If your local
troup is interested, the Girl Scout Council of Greater New York will be glad
to advise them: 355 E. 46th Street, New York, N.Y. 10017.

The Camp Fire Girls expressed interest in carrying out a similar project
on a national basis. Contact your local group or write to: Camp Fire Girls,
Inc., 1740 Broadway, New York, N.Y. 10019.

THINGS TO COME...OR ALREADY HERE

Kilograms, Liters, Meters and Degrees Celsius

Sooner or later you'll get used to the new measurements. The Metric Conversion Act of 1975 commits the United States to join most of the rest of the world in the metric system.

It's really quite easy: based on the decimal system, everything is multiplied or divided by ten. You already accept grams in your prescriptions, and millimeters in your cameras and films—and the U.S. dollar has one hundred cents!

In the food market you've got used to seeing preweighed meat and chickens marked in 2.5 lbs., meaning 2½ lbs. Soon you'll find the weight expressed in kilograms. Some manufacturers are beginning to mark their containers with both weights—to phase in the new, phase out the old. The weatherman on TV tells you degrees of Fahrenheit, the old, and Celsius, the new.

For free literature, write to:

American National Metric Council, 1625 Massachusetts Avenue, N.W., Washington, D.C. 20036.

National Bureau of Standards, Metric Information Program, Washington, D.C. 20234.

UPC—Universal Product Code

Universal Product Code is the meaning of those black stripes and small numbers on most packages and cans in the supermarket. They are codes, in preparation for check-out by laser beam; the checker will slide the product, code side down, over a scanning device. The scanner will *read* the code and send a message to the store's computer, which identifies the item and rings it up at the check-out counter.

Advantages and drawbacks to UPC include:

- Faster check-out—if stores don't use fewer check-out lanes
- Less human error—if the correct price is fed into the computer
- A detailed description of item and price on the cash-register tape so that the consumer can check purchases

When it was first introduced, markets who used the automatic check-out wanted to remove prices from individual cans and packages. Since the scanner only reads the striped code, the prices read by the consumer were to be posted on the shelves, next to the displayed merchandise.

Consumers protested. They want to compare prices with other items of the same type before checking out, and they want to remember how much they paid at the time they use the item, maybe a few weeks later—and they get angry about how much more they had to pay for the most recent purchase!

Consumer protest was effective. Today, voluntarily or by law, markets who use the electronic check-out also serve the human eye with prices in numbers on individual items.

☞ **If you want to learn more, write for free publications:**
"Computerizing Supermarket Checkout," DHEW Publication No. (FDA)
76-2043. U.S. Government Printing Office, Washington, D.C. 20402.
"Computerized Supermarket Checkout" (#547 F). How the Universal
Product Code check-out system works and how it affects the shopper.
Consumer Information Center, Pueblo, Colo. 81009.

HOW DOES YOUR LOCAL MARKET SERVE YOUR SPECIAL NEEDS?

People choose their favorite markets because they are close to their homes, clean, well stocked, charge reasonable prices, open at convenient hours and have pleasant salespeople. The following questions can help you grade your market on how well it serves you. If it fails in some points, ask for accommodations. The time has come to give Americans with disabilities equality with other shoppers. Environmental barriers and unconcerned personnel must become things of the past in America's marketplace.

Accessibility

- Is there a level or ramped entrance?
- Are doorways and aisles at least 32 inches wide?
- Is at least one check-out lane 32 inches wide so that a wheelchair can pass through?
      If not, why not? Ask to have one counter moved by a few inches if they wish to keep you as a customer. It's been done where people asked for it.

- Is there an exit post, installed to prevent the loss of shopping carts, but which can also prevent your wheelchair from exiting?

    It might be a violation of fire laws. Call the fire department for information.

- In the parking lot, are there some spaces near a level entrance reserved for disabled drivers?
- Is the International Symbol of Access featured in the store's advertisements?

Information

- Are vision-impaired shoppers informed about coupons or special offers advertised in newspapers and on store flyers?

    How about an in-house phone, connected to a taped message, that could give shoppers with poor or no vision the information without having to ask anybody? Suggest the idea to the management. They may thank you for it.

- When special sales are announced on the public address system, is the exact location of the merchandise described?
- When number indicators are used, for turn at service at crowded counters, such as bakery or deli, are flipped numbers also called out by voice?
- Do checkers verbalize and identify the values of dollar bills?

Communication

- If a hearing-impaired shopper needs some verbal information, do staff members know how to communicate?

Staff Assistance

- Do you get an aide assigned to you if you shop at non-peak hours?
- At all times, does store personnel assist in reaching items on high or low shelves?
- Can your order be delivered to your home, at not-too-busy hours?

Remember, your shopping dollar is your vote in the marketplace. Spend it where you are made welcome and appreciated as a customer!

HOME-DELIVERY FOOD SERVICES

You may receive, in the mail or by phone, offers for home delivery of groceries, with the help of catalogues, computers and the lure of supermarket prices. You may be invited to phone in your order a day ahead for delivery from a nearby warehouse on the following day.

Attractive as these offers may appear to you, go slow on committing yourself to long-term contracts. If you order from a new home-delivery service, try it first on an experimental basis. Don't let yourself be pressured by slick sales talk. Find out for yourself!

FOOD STAMPS CAN GIVE YOU EXTRA BUYING POWER

Food stamps can be used to buy extra food in a simple manner at most food stores. Persons receiving Social Security and recipients of SSI (Supplemental Security Income) may be eligible to participate in the Food Stamp Program which helps low-income people spend less money to buy more food for a healthier diet.

Food stamps are used like cash to buy foods and seeds at all stores that accept them. They cannot be used to buy tobacco, alcoholic beverages, pet food, or things you can't eat. The stamps help you stretch your dollars because they are always worth more than you pay for them. That's how food stamps give you extra buying power. The bonus value of food stamps depends on your income and the size of your family. A single individual can be a household, if he/she prepares and eats meals at home.

Standards of participation in the Food Stamp Program are the same for everyone without regard to sex, race, color, religious creed, national origin or political beliefs. Unfortunately, many people entitled to food stamps, among them disabled consumers, do not use them because they mistakenly think of them as charity. If you know such people, tell them that better nutrition is no alm but everybody's right.

___

To find out where and how to get food stamps in your neighborhood, contact your local state agency which administers the Federal Food Stamp Program. The toll-free Food Stamp hotline, 1-800-342-3710, will direct you to the office nearest to your home.

Home-delivery Meal Services

If you are elderly, you may use food stamps to purchase meals at communal dining facilities. If you are elderly and disabled, you may purchase meals from home-delivery services with your food stamps.

"Meals-on-Wheels" is a common name given to meals delivered to the home. All food-stamp recipients 60 or over who are physically handicapped, feeble or unable to prepare all of their meals may use food stamps for Meals-on-Wheels.

Find out from a local senior citizens center or Food Stamp office if you can be served.

Food Stamps for the Feeding of Guide Dogs?

Rumor had it that a governor was about to sign a state bill that would allow the use of food stamps for the purchase of food for guide dogs. Many of them are large and do eat a lot, but to owners, they are worth every ounce of their weight in gold.

Research did not confirm the rumor, and yet there is a kernel of truth: when filling out your application, you can include the money you spend on your guide dog, including veterinary bills, as medical expenses. This reduces your spendable income so that you will pay less for the food stamps you buy and thereby increase their bonus value to you. The money you save on purchasing your own food bill will help feed your trusted friend.

Tax-Deductible as Medical Expenses:

Special diets, if prescribed by your doctor, are deductible for the charge above what it would normally cost you to eat; special food or beverage, prescribed solely for treatment of an illness.

You will find these free publications full of useful information.

The Food Stamp Program (#551 F). Benefits of food stamps; who is eligible and how to apply; includes information on using food stamps for meals delivered to the home. Consumer Information Center, Pueblo, Colo. 81009.

The Food Stamp Program (Program Aid #1123) and *Shopping with Food Stamps* (Program Aid #1109). U.S. Department of Agriculture, Food and Nutrition Service, Washington, D.C. 20250. See also publications of your local state agency.

EATING OUT

Whether you are a gourmet diner, savoring five-course meals in elegant French restaurants, or the more popular type, grabbing hamburgers, pizzas or sandwiches in fast-food chains—before you can judge the quality of food offered, there's a primary problem to resolve: Can you get into the place at all? Once in, will you be seated comfortably and will the staff know how to serve you properly?

Let's evaluate some of your local eateries.

- Are they accessible through the front door, or do you have to enter through the back, past the garbage pails and through the kitchen, while the rest of your party gets the red-carpet treatment?
- Is there a parking attendant? Is there help available for those needing assistance in entering? If not, can help be arranged for in advance?
- Are rest rooms accessible?
- What is the distance from floor to edge of restaurant table?
- If there are booths, can a wheelchair be placed at the open end of the booth?
- Has staff been trained to serve guests with disabilities?—(See Chapter 9, "Barrier-Free Travel," p. 225.)
- Many restaurants and fast-food chains now offer menus in Braille. Does yours?
- Do the restaurant's advertisements, in papers and in the pages of the classified telephone directory, feature the International Symbol of Access?

A commendable idea is suggested in a national newsletter:

Report has intercepted a letter addressed to the "Dining Out" critic of a prominent metropolitan daily. Perhaps the suggestion contained therein can be whispered to similar columnists in other hometown newspapers:

Would it be possible for you to include, in your review of restaurants, a reference as to whether or not the restaurant is accessible to the handicapped? (Mainly wheelchairs—entrance, dining area, restrooms, etc.)

This would serve a double purpose. First, it would inform the handicapped person; and second, it would make the general public more aware of the handicapped and their needs. If you feel that a written explanation would take away from the general mood of your review, then, perhaps, a coded system could be used, with letters or symbols.*

* *Report*, Vol. 3, No. 2 (March/April 1977). Newsletter of the National Center for a Barrier-Free Environment, 8401 Connecticut Avenue, Washington, D.C. 20015.

For eager students, and for just about everybody who wants some advice about nutrition and wise food shopping:

- Choose in bookstores and public libraries from among books for every taste.
- Read consumer advice columns in newspapers and magazines.
- Study the free brochures food companies, banks and all kinds of businesses and government agencies distribute. Usually, they are up-to-date and full of timely ideas that will save you money and improve your nutrition.

Write for the publications listed below:

Series of Publications:

Family Food Budgeting for Good Meals and Good Nutrition; Safety for the Family; Food Quality—What You Can Do about USDA Grades; Food Guide for Older Folks; Storing Perishable Foods in the Home.
    —U.S. Department of Agriculture, Washington, D.C. 20250

Series of Publications:

Labels on Foods; Nutrition Labels on Foods; Cooking Utensils; Food Safety in the Kitchen; Protecting Your Family from Foodborne Illness; Some Questions and Answers about Canned Foods.
    —Food and Drug Administration, 5600 Fishers Lane, Rockville, Md. 20857

Fact Sheets:

Kitchen Ranges; Glass Bottles; Fondue Pots; Electric Blenders; Mixers, Choppers, Slicers & Grinders; Refrigerators; Pressure Cookers; Counter-Top Cooking Appliances (Portable).
    —Consumer Product Safety Commission, Washington, D.C. 20207

Consumer's Guide to Food Labels (#548 F). Discusses ingredient and nutrient listing, open dating, metric units, and symbols used on food labels.

Food Shopper Language (#550 F). Layperson's guide to product terms used in the grocery store and food ads.

Your Money's Worth in Foods (#552 F). Guides for budgeting, menu planning and shopping for best values.

Can Your Kitchen Pass the Food Storage Test? (#553 F). Checklist of food storage hazards and how to correct them.

Nutrition: Food at Work for You (#558 F). Functions and sources of major nutrients; how to estimate your daily food needs; tips on buying and storing food.

Read the Label, Set a Better Table (#560 F). How to use nutrition labels to save money and serve balanced meals.

Myths about Vitamins (#562 F). Discusses claims made about various vitamins.

—Consumer Information Center, Pueblo, Colo. 81009

Easy 'n Thrifty Recipes for 2. In large type and in Braille editions. The recipes were specially modified to remove visual directions like "Sauté until lightly browned." Researched with the assistance of the National Federation of the Blind and the American Printing House for the Blind. Rice Council, P.O. Box 22802, Houston, Tex. 77027.

Consumer's Guide to Food Additives (35 cents) Department of Consumer Affairs, 80 Lafayette Street, New York, N.Y. 10013

Books, tapes and films useful to individuals and groups interested in adaptations to daily living, in the home and in the community:

Mealtime Manual for the Aged and Handicapped. An authoritative guide, demonstrating in text and many illustrations how kitchen tasks can be streamlined to permit the aged and disabled to live active, self-sufficient lives. Institute of Rehabilitation Medicine, New York University Medical Center, 400 E. 34th Street, New York, N.Y. 10016. Contact the institute for cost of most recent edition of this book, and inquire about other available publications on Homemaking for Paraplegics.

The Wheelchair in the Kitchen. A 32-page booklet describing suggested kitchen layouts and procedures to adapt kitchens for wheelchair use. $2.50. Paralyzed Veterans of America, Inc., 7315 Wisconsin Avenue, Washington, D.C. 20014.

Adaptations and Techniques for the Disabled Homemaker, by Hodgeman & Warpeha. Simplifies housework and gives directions for accomplishing specific tasks. Special equipment and procedures are examined. $3.65. Sister Kenny Institute, Chicago Avenue at 27th Street, Minneapolis, Minn. 55407.

Housekeeping Skills Self-Study Kit for older adults with visual problems to learn many daily-living skills at home and at their own pace. Sixty tasks include eating skills, cleaning and hand sewing, food preparation, stove safety, electric appliances and special adapted equipment. Six cassettes of instruction with a large print transcript, packaged in a vinyl notebook. $18.

Personal Management; Basic Indoor Mobility; Sensory Development—$25 each.

The Community Handbook. A step-by-step guide for locating needed services such as recreational programs, housing, medical, rehabilitation courses, etc. In large print. $3. Center for Independent Living, 318 E. 15th Street, New York, N.Y. 10003.

What Do You Do When You See a Blind Person? 13½ minutes, 16 mm, color. A light touch personifies this film, which demonstrates the right and wrong way of dealing with blind people in various situations. The film shows Phil, a well-meaning but ill-informed character, who meets his first blind person on a busy New York Street corner. During the film, Phil faces what are monumental problems for him—problems like walking, talking and dining with a blind person. Rental: $20 per screening; purchase price: $110.

Also many other films on blindness and how to communicate with blind people. Write for listing, describing contents of films and prices. Public Education Division, American Foundation for the Blind, 15 W. 16th Street, New York, N.Y. 10011.

PRODUCTS FOR SPECIAL NEEDS

Products for special needs run the gamut from tongue depressors to iron lungs, from rubber-tipped canes to hydraulic van lifts. Though produced by manufacturers and distributed by merchants, they do not adhere to the laws of the marketplace. The reasons are manifold:

- Consumers have no free choice; frequently their lives depend on the use of the product.
- Mostly, consumers do not choose their suppliers, but are referred to them by physicians or therapists.
- Consumers may not pay for the product themselves, but third parties pick up the bill.
- Comparison shopping does not enter the process.

All this benefits suppliers who exploit their advantages. They like to maintain an aura of professional authority; fight against competitive price advertising; and frequently treat the consumer as a beneficiary of their services rather than a paying customer.

Yet, time marches on. Consumerism will reduce even those jealously guarded privileges. Legislation is beginning to break down barriers. What is needed is the cooperation of enlightened consumers who know their rights and demand them in action.

OTC . . . Rx . . . GENERIC . . . MAC—A LOOK AT THE MEDICINE MYSTERY

Medicines have progressed further in the last thirty years than in the previous thirty centuries. In fact, many of the medicines available today had not even been discovered in 1940.

Consumers now spend almost $9 billion each year on prescriptions, but this money doesn't always buy better health. People sometimes take medicines they do not need—to wake up, to relax from everyday tension, to stimulate or reduce their appetite, and to get to sleep at night. Health can actually be harmed as a result, and a lot of money is wasted.

This doesn't mean that you shouldn't use drugs when you need them, but you should know when and how to use them. You can protect your health and prevent accidents or illness by knowing the best ways to buy and use medicines.

There are two basic types of medicines: OTC, over-the-counter drugs, and Rx, prescription drugs. *Over-the-counter drugs* (also known as home remedies and patent medicines) include such common remedies as aspirin, laxatives and antacids. If used according to the directions on the label, they are relatively safe. You can buy medicines without a prescription in any drugstore and in many supermarkets and other stores. And you are conditioned to know them by constant and costly commercials on television.

Federal law requires that the following information be on all OTC drug labels:

- Name of the product and the name and address of the manufacturer, packer or distributor.
- The active ingredients. This information helps people with sensitivities or allergies avoid products which cause bad reactions.
- Directions for safe use.
- Cautions or warnings. These tell you what side effects may occur and who should not take the drug at all.

Prescription drugs (which bear the symbol Rx) can be ordered or prescribed only by a doctor and can be sold only by a registered pharmacist. Generally more powerful than OTC medicines, prescription drugs are also more likely to cause side effects.

The following information should be on the label:

- The pharmacy's name, address and phone number
- The prescription number
- The patient's name
- How often and when to take the drug
- How much to take each time
- Special instructions (refrigerate, shake well, etc.)
- The doctor's name
- The date the prescription was filled
- The name of the drug (if the doctor says it should be put on the label)

Would you like to decipher some of the mysterious-looking abbreviations the doctor scribbles on the prescription, like a secret-code message, to the pharmacist? Here's some help to break the code (the words in parentheses are in Latin):

ad lib. (*ad libitum*)—freely, as needed

A.C. (*ante cibos*)—before meals

b.i.d. (*bis in die*)—twice a day

gtt. (*gutta*)—drop

h.s. (*hora somni*)—at bedtime

p.o. (*per os*)—orally

p.r.n. (*pro re nata*)—as the occasion arises

q.4 h. (*quaque 4 hora*)—every 4 hours

q.i.d. (*quater in die*)—4 times a day

rep. (*repetatur*)—can be repeated (the number of times an Rx can be refilled)

Sig. (*signetur*)—let it be labeled (direction for the pharmacist)

t.i.d. (*ter in die*)—3 times a day

ut dict., or UD (*ut dictum*)—as directed

The dosage forms are frequently abbreviated as "cap" (capsule); "tab" (tablet); "el" (elixir); "syr" (syrup). The dosage strength is commonly given in metric measure (e.g., mg., for milligrams).*

Why "Generic" and What Does "Generic" Mean?

A generic drug is one which is identified by its official chemical name rather than an advertised brand name. Generic-drug manufacturers can sell at lower prices because the company does not have a sales force or expensive advertising campaign. (Pharmaceutical companies reputedly spend more than $5,000 per physician per year to have salesmen call, distribute free

* *Changing Times,* The Kiplinger Magazine (April 1977).

samples and fill the pages of medical journals with full-page ads to familiarize doctors with products and their brand names.)

Substitute and Save

In most instances, an equivalent generic drug can be substituted for a brand-name one at a lower cost to the consumer. This is made possible by the fact that the brand-name drug and its generic substitute have the same chemical make-up.

Generic-drug substitutes are safe and just as effective as the brand-name equivalent. All generic substitutions have been approved by the U.S. Food and Drug Administration.

Ask your doctor if he can prescribe a lower-cost generic drug for you.

When your doctor writes a prescription it is up to him or her to indicate on the prescription blank whether or not a lower-cost generic drug may be substituted for a brand-name drug. Sometimes a doctor has a good reason for prescribing a brand-name drug.

Not all medications have a generic equivalent.

When a pharmacist substitutes a less expensive generic equivalent, he will inform the consumer of that fact, as well as explain the difference in price between the two. The purchaser has the right to refuse generic substitution.

Packages without Safety Features

Manufacturers and packers must package certain dangerous substances and medicines in containers which meet safety standards for children. Elderly and handicapped persons may request noncomplying containers when the original container is too difficult to open. Physicians may also order that medicines be dispensed in noncomplying containers.

Prevent children from going through your medicine cabinet or purse; the Poison Prevention Packaging Act is a weapon to reduce poisonings among children.

Getting the Best Buy in Medicines

Comparison-shop!

Prescription medicines and over-the-counter drugs can vary in cost as much as 400 percent in different drugstores and pharmacies. When you have to get a medicine immediately, you'll want to go to the nearest pharmacy. But when you will be using the same prescription medicine for a long time, check various stores to find the lowest price.

Ask the pharmacist to quote you the price before he fills the prescription. If he won't tell you or you think the price is too high, try somewhere else. Some pharmacies will also quote prices over the phone.

Use the symbols codebreaker above to make sure you compare prescriptions identical in strength and quantities.

Prescription-drug-price advertising is now legal. In order for you to compare by reading advertisements, the FDA requires that the following facts be included in the ads:

- Brand name of the drug (if any)
- Generic name of the drug (if any)
- Dosage strength (e.g., 10 grains, 50 milligrams, 1 tablespoon, etc.)
- Form in which it is sold—tablet, capsule, liquid, powder, salve, etc.
- Price of specific quantity of the drug

When comparing prices, bear in mind that the lowest possible price comes with bare-bone service. Pharmacists who give more services charge higher prices. Look for the services you want—convenience, credit, delivery and a record of your personal drug history, which may help the pharmacist spot undesirable combinations of medicines that you and your doctor may not be aware of.

MAC

MAC is shorthand for "maximum allowable cost," the maximum price the government will pay for certain drugs dispensed to patients under the Medicare and Medicaid programs. The program is administered by the Social Security Administration. They establish the maximum price for which they will reimburse the pharmacist. Should he have filled the prescription with a similar but higher-priced medicine, he will still be reimbursed only for the lower, established maximum allowable cost.

If a generic drug is available that substitutes adequately for a prescribed brand-name drug, the cost of the generic drug will be maximum allowable cost. Be careful, if you belong to a health-care plan that reimburses you for medications. The pharmacist may have filled your prescription with a higher-priced brand, and when you present your claim to your insurance company, union or any other health plan, all they'll refund to you may be the MAC price, established for the lower-priced equivalent.

The Department of Health, Education and Welfare estimates that the MAC regulations will produce savings of $60 to $75 million a year for the federal and state governments by cutting the cost of prescription drugs under Medicaid and Medicare without reducing the quality or availability of the care provided under these tax-supported programs.

In addition to these savings it is expected that the setting of maximum costs for drugs under Medicare and Medicaid will reduce, or at least hold down, the cost of these same drugs for the general public as well.

Who Pays for Your Medicines?

Medicaid pays for medicines.

Medicare does not pay for medicines bought in pharmacies, but will reimburse you for medications charged in hospitals and nursing homes as a part of your total bill while you are a patient in the institution.

Some group and individual health insurance plans pay for all or part of the cost of prescription drugs. Generally, they do not cover OTC medicines.

Some senior citizens' groups offer policies which pay for prescription medicines not covered by Medicare.

Veterans Administration pays only for medications administered in their institutions.

Tax-Deductible Medical Expenses

Drugs must exceed 1 percent of your income before they become a deductible medical expense. After that, they are lumped together with other medical expenses, deductible to the extent that they exceed 3 percent of your adjusted gross income, on line 15c, Form 1040.

Some nonprescription drugs—aspirin, antihistaminics, cough syrups, antacids and many others qualify as deductible medicines, and so do vitamins, iron supplements, etc., prescribed or recommended by your doctor.

The Food and Drug Administration's Role in Drug Safety

The 1962 Drug Amendments to the Food, Drug and Cosmetic Act of 1938 require that every drug sold in the United States be demonstrated by well-controlled, scientific studies to be effective as well as safe. To fulfill this responsibility, the FDA:

- Approves all new drugs before they can be marketed;
- Decides whether a new drug should be sold OTC or only by prescription;
- Seeks to remove from sale any drug that is unsafe, ineffective, improperly labeled;
- Tests all batches of insulin, vaccines and antibiotics before they are shipped to pharmacies;
- Inspects manufacturing plants for sanitary conditions and proper manufacturing practices.

Frequently a target of criticism, the FDA is accused both of underregulation and overregulation. On one hand, they are accused of permitting manufacturers' new drugs on the market without adequate testing. Those holding the opposite view contend that FDA overregulation stifles drug development, for which the American public pays a heavy price: a slowing in the development of needed new drugs, denial to the American people of important new drugs already available in Europe, and damage to the American drug industry as foreign manufacturers surge ahead in new drug development because they do not face the burdens imposed by FDA.

The passions aroused by the Laetrile controversy in the 1970s and the shock about the thalidomide tragedy in Europe in the 1960s, avoided in the United States by an alert FDA researcher who kept the fetus-crippling substance off the American market, illustrate the interest the American public takes in such matters vital to everybody's health—and the problems in trying to do right by everybody.

Drug-related complaints should be addressed to the following agencies:

If you believe a just-acquired medicine has gone bad, is off-color, stale or harmful, don't just toss it out—report it to: FDA, 5600 Fishers Lane, Rockville, Md. 20582, or your nearest FDA field office

Suspected false advertising for OTC medicines: Federal Trade Commission, Washington, D.C. 20580

Suspected illegal sale of narcotics or dangerous drugs: Drug Enforcement Administration, U.S. Department of Justice, Washington, D.C. 20530

Unsolicited products by mail: the local U.S. Postmaster

Contaminated, mislabeled or suspect products made and sold exclusively within a state: local or state Health Department

Accidental poisonings: Poison Control Center or local hospital pharmacy

Dispensing practices of pharmacists and drug prices: state Board of Pharmacy

Prescribing practices of physicians: local medical societies

Write for these publications:

Mixing Medicines? Have a Care! (#587 F). Drug interaction in the body, stressing the hazards of combining drugs.

A Primer on Medicine (#588 F). How to buy, use safely, and store over-the-counter and prescription drugs.

Reading Prescriptions (#590 F). Understanding symbols used on doctor's prescriptions to permit comparison shopping for prescription drugs.

—Consumer Information Center, Pueblo, Colo. 81009

Series "We Want You to Know About": *Labels on Medicines; Medicines without Prescriptions; Prescription Drugs; Adverse Reactions to Medicines; Today's FDA.*

Reprints from FDA Consumer: Prescription Drugs and America's Patients (November 1972); *A Primer on Medicines* (January 1974); *Medicine, Handle with Care* (August 1975); *Holding Down Prescription Drug Costs* (January 1976); *Toward More Effective Drug Regulation* (January 1976); *Drug Instructions: The Importance of Being Earnest* (February 1976); *What Drug Price Ads Must Tell You* (March 1976).

—Food and Drug Administration, 5600 Fishers Lane, Rockville, Md. 20582

SPACE-AGE TECHNOLOGY PROMISES PROGRESS TOWARD AUTONOMY

"America's disabled citizens presently are unaware of the total scope of self-help aids, products and services available to help them reach their maximum personal fulfillment" states a report by the Panel on Research Programs to Aid the Handicapped, released by Congressman O. E. Teague of Texas, chairman of the Committee on Science and Technology, and quoted in the Summer 1977 issue of the NAPH Newsletter. The committee concluded that the lack of communication and contact between the researchers, product developers, manufacturers and consumers was the main reason for the information void and should be remedied quickly.

"Disabled people have never been able to perform comparative shopping for products and services under one roof, and rely solely on the doctor's or a second party's advice when determining which product or service will best serve the individual's disability," declared the president of the Paralyzed Veterans of America. Trade shows like the exhibits at the Washington Conference of the President's Committee on Employment of the Handicapped and the first International Disabled Expo in Illinois in August 1977 perform exactly this service: they show disabled consumers and professionals the technical marvels that will help them compensate for their disabilities and reduce their handicaps.

Talking calculators, Braille print-out computer terminals, breath-and-mouth-manipulated computers and home-environment control systems, mobility systems, wheelchairs that look like motor scooters and some that climb up stairs and curbs, hydraulic lifts that raise them into vans, and children's wheelchairs that adjust to the child's growth from tot to teen—all vie for attention and promise progress toward autonomy.

Don't expect any of these space-age technological marvels within reach of the average citizen by tomorrow. For the moment, take hope from knowing that they exist and will, in time, be ready for public distribution.

Meanwhile, if you want to find out what is within your immediate reach, consult these resources:

- **Your local rehabilitation center**
- **Periodicals relating to your type of disability**
- **National Buyers Directory of Products and Services for the Use and Rehabilitation of the Physically Disabled, contained in "Green Pages," Newsmagazine for the Disabled, Winter Park, Fla. 32789**
- **"Accent on Information," a computerized retrieval system containing information to help persons with disabilities to help themselves and live more effectively**

    AOI Search Request Form, contained in "Accent on Living" magazine and listing 33 categories with many subdivisions

    Basic research (includes up to 25 most recent references) costs $6; it will be returned if AOI has no information on the subject. Write to Accent on Information, P.O. Box 700, Bloomington, Ill., 61701 (Print or type your mailing address)

Premarket Clearance for Medical Devices

A new law, passed in 1976 in the form of amendments to the 1938 Food, Drug and Cosmetic Act, gives the Food and Drug Administration authority to require manufacturers of medical devices to prove that they are safe and effective, properly made and accurately labeled before they can be put on the market. It constitutes the most extensive enlargement of the FDA's authority since the 1962 drug-law changes enabled the agency to rule on the effectiveness of drugs.

Medical devices run the gamut from the very simple to the extremely complex, from bathroom scales and thermometers to kidney dialysis machines and artificial limbs. More than 12,000 different medical devices are estimated to be on the market, produced by more than 1,000 manufacturers. The total market value is put at more than $2.8 billion.

No one knows for sure how many deaths and injuries have been caused by unsafe medical devices. A search of the medical literature, made by the U.S. Department of Health, Education and Welfare in 1969, uncovered 10,000 verified injuries directly related to medical devices in a ten-year period, 751 of which had proved fatal. The Commission on Professional and Hospital Activities, an independent health group, estimated that 36,000 complications from medical devices occurred in one year.

Before the 1976 Medical Device Amendments, the FDA could act against such products only if a defect was discovered after a product was in use. Now all companies must meet new FDA reporting requirements which call on them to register all their new products with the FDA, keep up extensive records of complaints and comply with other FDA manufacturing regulations designed to ensure the quality of products.

Devices currently on sale will be given a grace period of more than thirty months to satisfy FDA testing requirements. But new and substantially different medical devices won't be permitted on the market until FDA endorses their safety and effectiveness.

For an interesting article, from which the information about complications caused by faulty medical devices was taken, write to the FDA:
"Medical Devices," Strengthening Consumer Protection. "FDA Consumer," Reprint from October 1976; HEW Publication No. (FDA) 77-4005, Food and Drug Administration, 5600 Fishers Lane, Rockville, Md. 20857.

The Acquisition of Medical Devices

In theory, the rules of wise consumer-buying—comparison shopping, full information on quality, warranties, repairs, return privileges, financing—should prevail in all consumer transactions, purchases or rentals, cash or credit.

In reality, the conditions under which purchases and rentals for special needs are carried out distort the economics of the marketplace.

Here are some of the reasons. If you are a member of long standing in the disabled minority, you may add some from your own experience. If you are a newcomer, they may help you understand some of the unusual conditions.

- Consumers of products for special needs are captive audiences. They must have the device that helps them cope with their disability, for mobility, information, communication, autonomy to participate in the mainstream of society, or simply for survival.

- Consumers are physically or psychologically restrained from comparison shopping.

- Consumers are frequently ignorant about the product, do not know what standards of quality and warranties for performance to demand.

- Consumers acquire their devices initially upon recommendations of a physician or rehabilitation service. When subsequent purchases or repairs are made by the user alone, the consumer is liable to all the risk and fraud possible in any consumer transaction.

- Suppliers, manufacturers and retailers constitute a monopolistic industry, dominated by relatively few and mostly old, established companies operating under the guise of quasi-professional extensions of the medical profession. This situation exercises little restraint on the profit motive of an industry whose profits have consistently been above average.

- Payments for purchase or rental of equipment are made or reimbursed, in the majority of cases, by third parties, such as Medicare, Medicaid, Veterans Administration, Vocational Rehabilitation, Workmen's Benefit or other types of insurance, which eliminates most cost-consciousness of employees who are spending other people's money.

ASSISTIVE DEVICES

"Unlike buying stereo equipment or a new car on which the advertised price may be lower than the *manufacturer's suggested retail price,* the wheelchair purchaser usually pays the price decided upon by the manufacturers," says the report by the Disability Rights Center, a nonprofit organization operated by disabled individuals working closely with consumer advocate Ralph Nader, and receiving some funds from him.

"The issue of price should concern the whole public," stated the center's director, Debby Kaplan, a lawyer, "because most of these devices are paid for by insurance companies or from public programs like Medicaid or by veterans' benefits."

"The 400,000 handicapped Americans who are bound to wheelchairs must rely on overpriced unsafe products, sold in a monopoly market," the report charges, and Ralph Nader adds the charge that "Government agencies like the Veterans Administration, which is the largest single consumer in the $30 million industry, have failed to exercise economic muscle for themselves or for disabled people."

At a cost of $3 million, 20,000 chairs were purchased by VA hospitals around the country in 1975. Everest & Jennings, the oldest and leading wheelchair manufacturer, fills a large portion of the VA's purchasing orders, claiming VA patients prefer E & J products.

E & J currently holds a 50 percent share of the wheelchair market and a 90 percent share of the more lucrative market of custom-made chairs for the severely disabled. In a civil antitrust suit, filed in May 1976, the U.S. Department of Justice charged the company with monopolizing the manufacture and sale of wheelchairs in the United States. The company claims that there is no basis for the suit. Reports that wheelchairs selling in the United States for about $400 were marketed in England for less than half the price were never officially disclaimed.

Here are, in their own words, some of the complaints from disabled consumers who responded to the author's nationwide survey:

The way items sold under the heading *Surgical Supplies,* wheelchairs, beds, prosthetics, etc., appear almost price rigged and are probably the most expensive class on the market. Rental equipment fees are outrageous.

D. M., New Jersey

Orthopedic appliance dispensers sometimes infer that *every repair* must be reviewed by a doctor before they will go ahead. Since these repairs are no more than a nuts-and-bolts procedure, I ignore the odd looks and smug remarks. The difficulties vanish when they find you are paying cash and on-the-spot, when satisfactory work is accomplished . . .

Better regulation of the pricing format for this industry would be in order. Often the charges are arrived at *off the top of the head* of the cashier.

W. D., New Jersey

When getting a new cane (Medicaid), I had to get what they gave me. I had no choice in the matter. I would have preferred a heavier one (I'm fat!). But because I wasn't paying for it, I felt ashamed to fight.

And the time I needed a stool or bench so I could get in and out of the bath tub. No one asked me what size I wanted. I had to take what the store sent. Again, Medicaid paid for it and I didn't argue. It doesn't seem all that fair that I have no word in the matter. Would love to see this corrected. Medicaid is so negligent in this.

A. D., Pennsylvania

In preparation for a law proposed to the City Council suggesting "licensing of persons engaged in the selling, fitting, repairing, servicing or making adjustments to products for the disabled," Sara Chew of the New York City Department of Consumer Affairs (DCA) conducted a survey of suppliers of wheelchairs, prosthetic and orthotic (straightening) devices in New York City, including *corsetières,* surgical-supply stores and department stores, selling postmastectomy breast prostheses. The DCA survey on wheelchairs largely confirms the statements reported here and adds two important observations:

1. Motorized wheelchairs start at about $1,000 and can run up to $2,200, depending on special controls and variations. According to the National Institute of Rehabilitation Engineering (NIRE), the E & J motorized chair is superior to other brands.

    A study conducted by the Center for Concerned Engineering (a Washington group sponsored by Ralph Nader) claims that wheelchair manufacturers have made little effort to compete on design or pricing. The study also points to design deficiencies in motorized wheelchairs, causing "explosion and fire hazards, thermal hazards, incomprehensible control box width problems, electrical, drive train and power waste problems."

    NIRE agrees about these potential hazards in motorized chairs—especially when controls are added, as they often are, by unqualified persons. They suggest that dealers be required to certify that all motorized wheelchairs and special attachments have been inspected, perhaps by an underwriter's inspector.

2. Several dealers stressed the advantage of renting over buying, particularly if the use was to be short-term, as it could be with a wheelchair or a hospital bed, or if the user had Medicaid or Medicare. Medicaid will cover the entire cost of rental, and Medicare will pay 80 percent of the cost. Dealers pointed out that with rentals there was no repair or servicing problem. They aso admitted that rental was financially even more rewarding to the dealer than profit on sales. An article in *American Druggist Merchandising* (June 1, 1973) quoted 40 percent as the yield on sales transactions, and goes on to suggest that if the dealer allocates the extra space needed for stocking rental equipment, his profit will escalate dramatically. "A wheelchair has a rental life of about 36 months . . . its complete cost to the retailer will be recovered in 6 months and over the period of its rental life it can easily return a profit of 400% or more."

With regard to prosthetic devices, the DCA report continues:

Physicians, prosthetists/orthotists and consumers alike will agree that medical involvement is essential in the fitting of a new device whenever the individual's physical condition is new or changing. Many physicians and practitioners further recommend that consumers avoid the risks of shopping on their own in all instances . . .

There are approximately 1600 certified prosthetists and orthotists in the United States. The maintenance of professional standards is entirely internal and voluntary, through the American Orthotic and Prosthetic Association. A survey by that Association and the National Academy of Sciences concluded that there is a 113% shortage of orthotics personnel and a 98% shortage of prosthetics personnel. By 1980 there will be enough to adequately meet the needs but numbers will still be way below optimal. (It must be admitted, however, that many old and experienced practitioners, sometimes second and third generations in the business, never bothered to take out certification and operate under what may be called a "Grandfather's clause.") . . .

Many consumers feel that prices are higher than they should be usually ascribing them to the lack of competition among few practitioners or to the fact that the buyer basically has no choice—he must have the device . . . This dependence also makes the consumer feel more vulnerable, so that City and State Consumer Affairs agencies have received, in the past, no appreciable number of formal complaints against prosthetists or orthotists. But such complaints exist, and the consumer should feel that there is a source of help.

Very few individuals need rely solely on their own resources, although many do not realize what other resources are available:

- After a hospital determines a child's prosthetic or orthotic needs, the *Bureau of Handicapped Children* of the Department of Health will review the family's ability to pay and often contribute whatever portion of the cost exceeds that ability.
- *For persons over 21* the state office of Vocational Rehabilitation can perform a similar function if the device contributes to the person's employability.
- *Medicare* will pay 80 percent of the cost for those who are eligible.
- *The Veterans Administration* pays for devices not only for the veteran but also for anyone in his family.

■ *Medicaid,* for those who are eligible, will pay a reasonable amount for devices, according to a rate formula, but only if the order comes through a rehabilitation-center physiatrist or a physician connected with such a unit. All costs are covered only if the person's income is low. Sometimes they pay only 80 percent. Also, Medicaid often picks up that portion of the costs that is not covered by Medicare or OVR.

■ *Major medical coverage,* written by private insurance companies, claims a policy of leaving the question of quality of devices up to the physician and not questioning prices.

■ *Sales-tax exemption* is applied in most states to wheelchairs, crutches, hearing aids and other medical equipment and prosthetic devices.

The DCAs Report on *Breast Prostheses* confirms largely the findings summarized in an excellent article in the November 1975 issue of *Consumer Reports,* the monthly magazine published by Consumers Union: "After Mastectomy: Find the Right Prosthesis."*

The article describes the various types of prostheses available, their cost, and the importance of finding competent and sensitive fitters at a time when the consumer's self-image and self-confidence are at an all-time low. "Shop around" is their advice. Now that even high-fashion stores and top designers have entered the market, the choices available to postmastectomy patients have increased considerably. "A commercial prosthesis should not be purchased until the doctor gives permission," advises Consumers Union, and maybe the best advice of all is this:

> Many women who undergo mastectomies have one valuable resource, *Reach to Recovery.* With the surgeon's permission, an RTR volunteer—a former mastectomy patient herself—visits a woman in the hospital to provide reassurance, and to describe appropriate exercises. In addition, she gives the patient a temporary, Dacron-filled prosthesis, describes the various breast forms available, and describes a list of suggested outlets for prosthetic devices.
>
> RTR also distributes lists of manufacturers and approximate retail prices. As an added aid, most local offices of the American Cancer Society (ACS) have on hand a variety of forms that a woman can examine in a noncommercial setting. Further, RTR volunteers will accompany women shopping for prostheses to give them guidance.
>
> *Reach to Recovery,* a booklet by Terese Lasser, national consultant and coordinator or RTR, is an excellent reference for the postmastectomy patient. It is available from most American Cancer Society offices.

* Reprint and Book Department, Consumers Union, Orangeburg, N.Y. 10962. 40 cents.

Most insurance policies with major medical provisions pay 80 percent of the cost of a prosthesis. Include a prescription from your doctor when you make your claim.

Medicare will pay 80 percent of the cost of what "they allow" for a breast prosthesis, which may be a far cry from what the store charges you. But cheer up . . .

The cost of breast forms (but not the bra) is a tax-deductible medical expense—as is the charge for "fitting" or "altering" a bra. To make certain of a deduction, ask the surgeon to write a prescription for the prosthesis, and be sure the store's bills and the checks written to pay them are marked "surgical."

Leasing

Leasing of automobiles and other personal property, such as furniture, power tools, television sets, hospital beds, wheelchairs and other items which will be needed only for a limited period of time or which are likely to be outdated quickly, has recently become a popular way of having the use of goods without having to make an expensive purchase. Like buying on credit, leasing involves regular payments over an extended period of time.

To enable consumers to make more informed decisions about leasing personal property (nonrealty) items, the federal government enacted the Consumer Leasing Act of 1976, amending the Truth in Lending Act, and Regulation Z, implementing it. Under this Truth in Leasing Act, cost and other disclosures about the rights and obligations of the customer (or lessee) and owner (or lessor) must be clearly made in writing before the lease is signed. The act applies to any leasing agreement for personal property which the customer will be using primarily for personal, family or household purposes, where the leasing period will be four months or longer and the total contractual obligation will be $25,000 or less.

The act requires meaningful disclosure of the terms of the lease, which will enable consumers to compare various lease terms available to them and to compare the costs of leasing with the costs of purchasing on credit. All leasing contracts must contain the following:

- A description of the leased property
- The amount of any payment required at the beginning of the lease
- The amount of the fees for registration; the amount for certificate of title, license or taxes that you must pay; the amount of other charges not included in the regular periodic payment

- A statement of the amount or the method for determining the amount of any charges that will be imposed at the end of the leasing period
- A statement indicating whether you have the option to purchase the property, and at what price and time
- A statement disclosing what warranties cover the property and who is responsible for paying the premiums on insurance
- The number, amounts and due dates of payments, and the total amount of the payments
- A statement of the conditions under which you or the business can end the lease before the contract is up (this section is to include the way in which any fees or late payments, failure to pay, or terminating the lease early are calculated)

The law also includes provisions to protect you from excessive charges when you return the item at the end of the leasing period, as well as providing that any penalty charges be reasonably related to the actual harm caused.

Servicing and Repairs

All of the dealers questioned in the DCA survey indicated that they did provide servicing and repairs, at the same time claiming that "buyers seldom had trouble with their chairs."

This assurance is in sharp contrast to the findings of the Disability Rights Center study, which reports that chairs frequently rust, bend and develop broken handles. "When a chair won't function properly," the report states, "it is difficult to get corrective servicing."

The same complaints were voiced by numerous disabled witnesses at the public hearing conducted by the Department of Consumer Affairs, also in preparation for the suggested licensing law quoted previously (p. 146). These witnesses told harrowing stories about being unable to go to work, or even, in some cases, to get out of bed for weeks, when spare parts took weeks or months to arrive from California. To prevent such problems, at least within their reach, the Center for Independent Living in Berkeley, California, maintains a twenty-four-hour emergency repair service, and stocks a vast array of replacement parts.

Most of the New York City dealers said that it would be possible to provide a replacement chair on a rental basis to a person whose chair required a lengthy repair job, but none of the dealers could say what a repair might cost. Wheelchair users insist that servicing is very expensive and a particular problem for people on Medicaid.

☞ **It was suggested that a person on Medicaid whose chair needs overhauling may be financially better off getting a new chair, as Medicaid will pay only a minimal amount toward an overhaul, but will most likely pay for a new chair.**

How about warranties (discussed in connection with other goods on p. 180). Don't they apply to wheelchairs? Yes, they do—and with the same qualifications. Moreover, an E & J representative at the company's exhibit at the May 1977 Conference of the President's Committee on Employment of the Handicapped in Washington, D.C., stated that because of the complicated regulations in the Moss-Magnuson Truth in Warranties Act of 1975, E & J now does not give any written warranty at all, but makes the consumer rely on the company's well-established reputation for reliability and service.

As the law reads, even without a manufacturer's written warranty the consumer still has the dealer's implied warranty; it is therefore all the more imperative for the consumer to buy his wheelchair from a reputable company and to assure himself before the purchase that the dealer carries spare parts for the chair. One manufacturer, Preston, supplies a kit of spare parts that it says are commonly needed: spokes, wheel-bearing components, rubber bumpers and small hardware parts.

The best advice seems to be that the consumer himself make provisions for breakdown and repair in order to minimize inconvenience and disruption of daily activities. If possible, store spare parts. For instance, storing spokes, or even spare wheels for wheelchairs, may save you much inconvenience. And if you recently hit a jackpot or have a rich Aunt Minnie, an entire spare wheelchair in your closet could keep you rolling, however long Chair Number One stays out of the running.

HEARING AIDS

An estimated 14.5 million people in the United States have hearing impairments. More than 5 million of them are 65 years old or older. About 3 million of them are school-age children. The hearing-aid industry describes impaired hearing as America's number-one handicapping disability. Industry sources place the total number of hearing-aid users at 2,388,000. Seventy percent of them have never seen a medical specialist, with the result that some people try to solve their hearing difficulties with a hearing aid when what they really need is an accurate diagnosis and medical care.

The 600,000 hearing aids sold at anywhere from $350 to $1,000 are produced by eight hearing-aid manufacturing companies; they control 70 percent of all sales in the United States. Such high market shares in any one industry indicate a shared monopoly of a kind which usually does not compete on price and product quality, but operates on promotion and product differentiation.

Distribution is handled by an estimated 7,900 hearing-aid dealers, attracted by markups of up to 300 percent. With this competitive situation it is very tempting for some dealers to make exaggerated claims. Many unscrupulous dealers have fitted walk-in customers with aids, whether or not they were indicated. High-pressure door-to-door salespeople sometimes give misleading statements about the benefits of the device and sell hearing aids that wind up unused in dresser drawers to people who can least afford financial losses.

One of this industry's greatest shortcomings is the lack of training on the part of their representatives. Of 15,000 hearing-aid dealers and salespeople, only 2,114 are certified, meaning that they have taken a twenty-week home study course offered by the National Hearing Aid Society.

"In a sense, the hearing-aids business is a profession where you can *do it yourself,*" advises the *American Druggist* magazine (February 15, 1974). "There are practically no roadblocks to becoming a hearing-aid dealer. Almost anyone can go into that business." Estimating the overall market for hearing aids, accessories and batteries between $75 million and $90 million, the magazine implies that pharmacists use their customers' confidence to sell them high-markup hearing aids.

Finally, acting under its newly acquired authority over the sale of medical devices, the FDA issued a regulation (effective August 15, 1977) designed to protect consumers from being sold hearing aids that won't help them and to make sure that people see a doctor to check if there is a medical reason for their hearing loss.

- The new regulation mandates that hearing aids can be sold only to people who have had a medical evaluation of their hearing loss within six months before the purchase of a hearing aid.
- Unless the examination is specifically waived by the purchaser, a statement from a physician that a hearing aid may help will be necessary for purchase.
- Waiver is not permissible for persons under 18 years of age.
- The regulation also requires manufacturers to provide—and let the prospective buyer read before the sale is completed—a detailed brochure which tells consumers what hearing aids can do, how they work and how to use them.

Although the regulation forbids a hearing-aid dispenser from encouraging prospective buyers to waive the medical examination, critics of the regulation consider this point a weakness because consumers may sign the waiver in order to avoid the effort and expense of examination by a physician.

Forty-five states now regulate hearing-aid sales/salespersons (all states except Alaska, the District of Columbia, Illinois, Kansas, Massachusetts and Utah). "Many but not all of these," comments the State Legislation Office of the American Speech and Hearing Association (ASHA), "are the type of hearing aid dealer licensure laws sponsored by the industry itself and found, in a Senate staff study, to offer more protection to the dealer than the consumer." Their statement continues:

> The newly issued FDA standards are very weak, as can be seen in the fact that both hearing aid dealers and manufacturers support the action of FDA, which is supposed to regulate them. The tragic irony here is such that its *weak regulations will supplant state laws*—even the tougher laws which protect consumers in many states. Already, the hearing aid industry has attempted to use the FDA standards to attach existing laws in New York, New Jersey and other states, which provide consumers with a reasonable assurance that they will not be sold unnecessary or inappropriate aids.
>
> The Federal Trade Commission proposes a trade regulation rule on sales practices in the field. The National Council of Senior Citizens and ASHA represented consumers in the hearings, generally supporting the FTC proposal. Groups representing hearing aid dealers and hearing aid manufacturers also took part, generally opposing the FTC proposal. Final action is not expected for several years.

If this makes your blood boil, as well it may, make your voice *heard*. See chapters 4, section called "The Voter's 'Right to Be Heard,' " p. 80, and 5, "How to Communicate with Federal Agencies," p. 85.

If you notice symptoms of hearing loss, see a physician. Some types of hearing loss can be corrected by medical or surgical treatment; others cannot. The physician may refer you to an otologist, otolaryngologist or an audiologist.

The *otologist* is a specialist in the diagnosis and treatment of the ear. He has a Doctor of Medicine (M.D.) or a Doctor of Osteopathy (D.O.) degree.

An *otolaryngologist* is an M.D. or D.O. who specializes in care of the nose and throat as well as the ear.

An *audiologist* is a specialist in the nonmedical evaluation and rehabilitation of persons with hearing disorders. He generally has an M.A. or Ph.D. degree.

Hearing aids may be worn in the ear or behind the ear, depending on the type and severity of the impairment. The device worn at the ear may be complete in itself, or it may require a separate unit—usually worn in the coat, shirt or dress—to house the microphone and amplifier. A complete hearing aid can also be built into the temple pieces of eyeglasses.

The essential components of a hearing aid include:

■ A microphone to pick up the sound
■ An amplifier to boost the loudness of the sound
■ A receiver (or earphone) to deliver the sound
■ A battery as a power source

A hearing aid is essentially a miniature sound amplifier. It cannot restore poor hearing to normal and often cannot help solve speech distortion or group conversation clarity. However, despite these limitations, the proper aid for the problem can benefit many persons.

How to Choose a Hearing-Aid Dealer

As with any other purchase, shop around for the best dealer. Compare the prices of at least three dealers before buying. Remember that when you walk into a hearing-aid-dealer's store, you are a customer, not a patient. Get all the facts about the device—including its complete cost and warranty—in writing before you buy.

What parts of the aid are *guaranteed,* and for what length of time? What are the terms of the servicing guarantee? How long is the instrument expected to serve? Is there the protection of an insurance plan? What are the benefits, and at what cost?

How available is *servicing?* Can the dealer make minor repairs or must the device go back to the factory? What is the cost of batteries and other upkeep? Is there immediate replacement in case of failure of the instrument or will the hearing aid be returned for repair, leaving you without it for weeks? Does the dealer or the manufacturer provide a loan replacement during repair?

If you are dubious about using an aid, find out if you can rent one temporarily. Don't let yourself be pressured or intimidated by the salesperson. Consider the purchase carefully for at least a day or two.

For informative literature, write to the Better Hearing Institute, 1430 K Street, N.W., Suite 600, Washington, D.C. 20005. This is a nonprofit, educational, charitable organization, which will give you information on medical and surgical and amplification help that is available for people with hearing problems.

Their toll-free "Hearing Aid Help Line" is 800-424-8576. They will not recommend to you a specific dealer or instrument. In case of complaints against a dealer or manufacturer, they may act as intermediaries.

Financial Help

- *Medicaid* programs in some states pay for hearing aids.
- *Medicare* pays for the hearing diagnosis and hearing-aid evaluation if done by a qualified audiologist or otologist, but does not pay for the hearing aid.
- *Most major health insurance companies* do the same, paying for diagnostic services but not for the instrument. Some insurers claim coverage of the cost of the aid.
- *State Office of Vocational Rehabilitation,* and
- *Federal Rehabilitation Services Administration* assist people whose hearing problems handicap employment. (This usually includes homemaking.) Information on this program is available from the Office of Deafness and Communications Disorders, Rehabilitation Services Administration, Office of Human Development, HEW, Washington, D.C. 20201.
- *Veterans Administration* provides hearing aids only to veterans whose hearing disability is the result of military service. Veterans should contact their nearest VA office or hospital.
- *Federal-income-tax-deductible* is the cost of hearing aids, as a medical expense. Medical and dental expenses are deductible only to the extent that they exceed 3 percent of your adjusted gross income, on line 15c, Form 1040.

You might want to write for some of the following helpful booklets:

"Is Hearing Your Problem?," *Consumer Close-Ups* (September 1976). Cooperative Extension, Cornell University, State University of New York, Ithaca, N.Y. 14850.

"Making Sure Hearing Aids Help," *FDA Consumer* (June 1976). Food and Drug Administration, 5600 Fishers Lane, Rockville, Md. 20852.

Hearing Aids Selected, Veterans Administration (1977). Supply Service Department of Medicine & Surgery, Veterans Administration, Washington, D.C. 20420.

Hearing Loss, Hope through Research. 45 cents. DHEW Publication No. 73-157, U.S. Government Printing Office, Washington, D.C. 20402.

"How to Buy a Hearing Aid," *Consumer Reports* (June 1976). 40 cents. Reprint & Book Department, Consumers Union, Orangeburg, N.Y. 10962. Quoted by ASHA as "the best thing written on the subject."

Ears to Ya', Consumer Survival Kit. $1. Maryland Center for Public Broadcasting, Owings Mills, Md. 21117.

Paying through the Ear, study conducted by Public Citizens Retired Professional Group. $3.50 for individuals, $8.50 for professionals and organizations. 3700 Chestnut Street, Philadelphia, Pa. 19104.

Telephone Pioneers

At a Press Conference and Exhibit (September 1977), Telephone Pioneers of America showed an ordinary transistor radio modified to amplify TV programs for the hard-of-hearing.

Telephone Pioneers of America is a volunteer-service organization of Bell Telephone employees with more than eighteen years of service, some still active, some retired. They render community services, and working on their own time, in home workshops, they use their electronic and inventive skills to create aids for disabled children and adults. While telephone companies maintain responsibility for providing modified telephone services for the handicapped, Pioneers have extended this commitment. "Working through eighty-eight chapters in forty-eight states and Canada, our volunteers draw on the same technological skills and manufacturing techniques they use in their daily jobs in the telephone industry," says a spokesman. "Pioneers adapt this know-how to create aids for the blind, deaf, retarded, motion- and speech-handicapped, after working hours."

Among the exhibits were "talking" dolls and animals that encourage responses from autistic children; beeping baseballs; a directional beeping "cricket," mounted on a lead bicycle for a blind cyclist to follow; voice-activated telephones; breath-activated dialers; and many more products of labors of love and ingenuity.

☞ Most of the Telephone Pioneers' inventions use inexpensive components, adapted for special purposes. People with problems that need technical solutions are invited to call the local Telephone Business Operator and ask to be put in touch with the local chapter of Pioneers. Upon presentation of the problem, the inquirer will be referred for assistance to a chapter in the United States that specializes in solutions to similar problems.

About the Audio Aid for Hard-of-Hearing Children and Adults, the news release states: "With less than $15, a standard nine-volt transistor radio and about an hour's work, persons with severely impaired hearing can enjoy radio, television, movie or theater performances which would otherwise be out of their hearing range."

"Converting a radio into an Audio Aid requires removing and adding a few electronic components and rewiring the radio," says one of the Pioneers who developed the sound amplification device. "Bell Laboratories Pioneers ave filled requests for circuit diagrams and conversion instructions from service organizations and nursing homes as far away as Hawaii."

☞ For technical information, write:
Telephone Pioneers of America, Frank B. Jewett Chapter, Bell Telephone Laboratories, Inc., 600 Mountain Avenue, Room 6H-412, Murray Hill, N.J. 07974.

Please note: This is neither an endorsement nor unsolicited medical advice! It's printed here for your information; the author saw the demonstration, heard the inventor, read the news release, and sends you on your way to your own research—after discussion with your physician!

EYEGLASSES, LENSES, ARTIFICIAL EYES

Eyeglasses

An imaginary advertisement in the New York *Times* (May 28, 1977) compares eyeglass prices:

Price paid for eyeglasses by the Defense Department, competitive bidding on mass basis:

simple lenses, black, plastic frames, carrying case,
assembled by the department $4.88

same type, purchased from private optometrist by
individual consumer $37.94

If you are one of the 112 million Americans who wear glasses, and if this fictitious ad makes you mad, try to hold down your blood pressure and keep on reading.

A Senate committee, the Federal Trade Commission and the Justice Department are investigating alleged monopolistic practices in the sale of eyeglasses that may cost American consumers as much as $400 *million a year in excessive prices.*

Senator Gaylord Nelson, the Wisconsin Democrat, chairman of the committee, stated: "We have found the same pair of glasses may be available for around $15 in one store and between $50 and $70 in another store nearby. In frames, we found a variety of types wholesaling for $2 and $3 that retail for as much as $32."

Such excesses take place more frequently in the forty-five states that either prohibit or limit the advertising of prices of glasses. Surveys have shown that in New York City, the prices of glasses in six neighborhoods varied by as much as 250 percent, that in Ohio such differences ran as high as 300 percent and that in New Jersey the variations were as high as 350 percent.

Consumer activists are urging the Federal Trade Commission to remove barriers to advertising by sellers of ophthalmic goods and to require optometrists to give written, signed prescriptions to consumers so that prices can be compared. "Laws that limit eyeglass advertising should be taken for what they are: a weapon against discounting," the New York *Times* said on June 11, 1977. No wonder the American Optometrist Association, representing 20,000 members, and other lobbyists try to hold on to them.

Consumer advocates also accuse licensing boards of various states of serving the professionals they license rather than the public, which is supposed to be protected by licensing.

◄═ **If eyeglass advertising is prohibited or restricted in your state, write to the Federal Trade Commission, Washington, D.C. 20580, and urge**

your legislators to support their efforts toward nationwide removal of those barriers.

Safety standards imposed by the FDA require that eyeglass lenses be impact resistant to prevent eye injuries from the accidental shattering while being worn. Manufacturers use many methods to make lenses impact-resistant, such as heat or chemical treatment, using impact-resistant material like transparent plastics, or using glass material thick enough to provide impact resistance. Details are described in: *We Want You to Know What We Know about Impact-Resistant Eyeglass Lenses.* DHEW Publication, U.S. Government Printing Office, Washington, D.C. 20402. 15 cents.

Lenses

Both contact lenses worn for cosmetic reasons and implanted intraocular lenses are considered medical devices, subject to FDA regulations.

Recently marketed soft contact lenses must be prescribed and fitted by a physician or optometrist. Because of the potential health hazard with soft contact lenses, FDA requires that physicians who prescribe them provide patients a "package insert," giving full information about the product and its use. An electric disinfectant unit must be used daily to boil the soft contact lenses in a solution of salt water. Read: "Soft Contact Lenses," *FDA Consumer* (reprinted from July/August 1976). HEW publication No. 76-4004, U.S. Government Printing Office, Washington, D.C. 20402.

Artificial Eyes

The sclerical lens is created to enhance an existent but nonfunctioning eye.

A complete artificial eye prevents the socket from shrinking and deteriorating.

Stock artificial eyes are mass-produced, less expensive, and in many areas, the only ones available.

Custom-made artificial eyes are created by an ocularist who is specially trained. A first artificial eye, and usually any replacement, will be ordered by a physician and checked for proper fit.

Prices vary greatly, with stock eyes usually costing under $100 and custom-made eyes up to $400, according to complexity of work required.

Financial Help

- *Medicaid* pays for ophthalmic goods, up to a scheduled maximum.
- *Medicare* reimburses up to 80 percent, according to the usual schedule. The balance is tax-deductible.
- *Health insurance plans* pay according to your contract with them. Check your clauses.
- *No sales tax* is charged on prescription eyeglasses, lenses and artificial eyes. Nonprescription sunglasses are taxable.
- *Tax-deductible as medical expenses* are all prescription ophthalmic items. Medical and dental expenses are deductible only to the extent that they exceed 3 percent of your adjusted gross income, on line 15c, Form 1040.

FASHIONS FOR THE FASHION-ABLES

An article in the New York *Times* (June 11, 1977) described in detail a Japanese fashion designer's newly opened boutique, in the accessible basement of an Osaka hotel, selling attractive, serviceable clothing and accessories for disabled customers. The report claims that the opening of this boutique also underlined the changing status of Japan's silent, but sizable, handicapped population.

We'll be glad to send you a reprint of the article. Write to me % the publisher.

Maybe it will arouse the entrepreneur in you to start such a business for yourself, aided by a low-interest loan from the Small Business Administration. Or perhaps you could talk your local department store into opening a boutique which would perform a service for disabled consumers, and at the same time, make them customers for the store's other departments. You could even offer your services as the manager of the boutique, if you are so inclined.

Progress is also made in this country. Courses in clothing designs for special needs are offered at the Universities of Nebraska and Kansas. A new book, published by the Sister Kenny Foundation, claims:

> Recognizing the need for attractive, well-fitted and functional clothing for the handicapped person, the staff of Sister Kenny has developed fashions for a variety of special needs.

Over 30 fashion designs are illustrated, with some adapted from well-known pattern companies like McCall's and Vogue. Problem areas and possible solutions are covered in concise outline form. Also included are hints on fittings and alterations, selecting the proper fabric and more. This book is an important guide for the person with limited hand functions or visual problems, spasticity, a colostomy, etc., who wants to improve his/her appearance.

Clothing for the Handicapped, by Miriam Bowar, R.N., O.T. Sister Kenny Institute, Chicago Avenue at 27th Street, Minneapolis, Minn. 55407. $2.40.

The following publications are listed in *General Information to Help the Recently Disabled* (No. 1), Insurance Company of North America and Human Resources Center, I.U. Willets Road, Albertson, L.I., N.Y. 11507:

Clothes for the Physically Handicapped Homemaker (Eco. Research Report No. 12). 30 cents. Institute of Home Economics, U.S. Department of Agriculture, Washington, D.C. 20250.

Flexible Fashions. Explains how to sew and adapt clothing. Arthritis Foundation, 221 Park Avenue South, New York, N.Y. 10003.

Fashion-able. Mail-order catalogue of clothing, adapted household devices. Rocky Hill, N.J. 08553.

Men's Fashions for the Wheelchair Set. Custom tailoring by mail order. Leinenweber, Inc., Brunswick Building, 69 W. Washington Street, Chicago, Ill. 60602.

Hearing Aid Vests

Hearing Aid Vests, hand-made from colorful materials, some gaily embroidered, were shown at the Telephone Pioneers of America exhibit (described on p. 156). "Hard-of-hearing youngsters from six months to six years of age can use a hearing aid without losing the freedom to move, crawl, explore their world," states the press release. "Pocketed vests eliminate cumbersome harnesses and straps; keep children comfortable so they don't pull off their hearing aids."

Photographs also showed elderly wearers of such vests, concealing the battery in a pocket and guiding the wire, safely and unnoticeably to the ear piece.

☎ For information and vest pattern, write to: Telephone Pioneers of America, Alexander Graham Bell Chapter, The Chesapeake and Potomac Telephone Company, 2000 L Street, N.W., Room 622, Washington, D.C. 20036.

Braille Color Clothing Tags

Small aluminum tags, called Braille color clothing tags, are embossed in Braille with names of colors and sewn into clothing. They allow blind people the independence to choose their own wardrobes and even color-coordinate household linens. Scarves or other identically shaped items can be stored in plastic bags, identified by such Braille color tags.

More than 100,000 tags are made and packaged yearly exclusively by Pioneers at Western Electric in Kearney, N.J., for the American Foundation for the Blind, which supplies them free of charge to blind persons nationwide.

☎ Write to: American Foundation for the Blind, 15 W. 16th Street, New York, N.Y. 10011.

IN THE DRIVER'S SEAT

Americans are accused of having a love affair with their automobiles. It was in 1968 that the first Secretary of Transportation called mobility the Fifth Freedom and discussed it in relation to the handicapped as well as the physically normal.

Mobility is a crucial freedom for the disabled. It enables them to engage in meaningful vocations, to participate in community affairs, to seek cultural and recreational outlets, to broaden the scope of their outlook and generally enrich their lives.

A car is the optimum means of transportation for the handicapped population. To meet the needs of this group more adequately, it is necessary to improve our driving technology, to improve delivery of service systems and to resolve such problems as funds for buying a car, parking, taxation and insurance.

Whether you are a member of long standing in the disabled community or a newcomer, you will be amazed at the variety of devices available to put you behind the wheel. Vans built for wheelchair accessibility, hydraulic lifts installed in existing vans, hand or foot control systems for arthritics, amputees, hemiplegics, paraplegics and quadriplegics and little people, and fish-eye bubble mirrors for deaf drivers. You may have seen advertisements for all these products in magazines like *Accent on Living, Paraplegia News* and others, and you will be inundated with descriptive, illustrated publicity material as soon as you make your interest known. Invariably, these brochures stress three features: quality of products, ease of handling, and contribution to the user's mobility and independence.

Manufacturers of hand controls, some disabled themselves, also stress the ease of installation so that controls can be put in place or removed instantly when a nondisabled driver has to use the same car.

A list of automobile hand-control manufacturers whose equipment has met Veterans Administration Prosthetic Center specifications is available free of charge from: Eastern Paralyzed Veterans Associations, 432 Park Avenue South, New York, N.Y. 10016.

Since you will be guided in the purchase of vans, cars and controls by your VA, OVR or rehabilitation center, we list here only some central sources you may wish to contact for your own reasearch:

"Vans, Lifts and Hand Controls." Special Feature, by Joe Laurie, editor, *Rehabilitation Gazette*, 4502 Maryland Avenue, St. Louis, Mo. 63108.

Personalized Licensed Vehicles for the Disabled. Rehabilitation Engineering Center, Moss Rehabilitation Hospital, 12th Street and Tabor Road, Philadelphia, Pa. 19141.

Vehicle Controls for Disabled Persons. American Automobile Association, 1712 G Street, N.W., Washington, D.C. 20006.

Driver Education for the Physically Disabled

Jiri Sipajlo, instructor and research associate, Driver Education, the Center for Safety, New York University, a man with unlimited skill and infinite patience, ascribes the above-average safety record of disabled drivers to three factors: formal driver education; defensive driving; knowing the importance of their driver's licenses to getting around.

For accident victims, the experts recommend driving lessons as soon as possible so that aptitude in substituting for the use of immobilized or lost limbs will conquer their fear and lift their spirits.

To receive their driver's license, students are given the standard written test and a road test administered by inspectors. The license will indicate what adjustments the driver must have on his car. In case of temporary disability, the restriction can be removed from the license if the individual passes a new road test after recovery.

Deaf drivers rely on visual signals for changes in traffic patterns—for instance, when ambulance or fire-engine sirens alert hearing drivers. They have to depend on maintenance lights, vibrations, smells for warning signals about their car's working order. "People sometimes think I am paranoid about my car," admits Professor Martin Sternberg of the New York University Deafness Research and Training Center. "Not at all. I'm just asking my hearing passengers if their ears can pick up some messages that the car is trying to send me."

If you do not live near a rehabilitation center to receive driver's education, you may wish to consider the advice an owner of a private driving school suggested in a letter to the author:

> The handicapped are wide open to exploitation simply because of the fact that they will make any sacrifice to regain their mobility. More often than not a handicapped student is charged for the considerable time it takes to help him out of the house and into the car and vice versa.
>
> An unscrupulous driving instructor can stretch a driving course ad infinitum especially with a handicapped person. Some offer *special care* to the nervous, the aged and the handicapped, knowing quite well that practically all student drivers are nervous.
>
> Since bills for state-assisted student drivers are sent directly to the paying agencies, rendered services are frequently overstated. Students should keep a record of the lessons they received and insist to see a copy of the invoice submitted to the agency, to compare what was charged with what was actually delivered. If these figures differ, students should request an investigation. Otherwise, there is a total lack of control.
>
> Students without such public assistance probably spend somewhat less, as it is so much easier to rip off anonymous taxpayers through their government agencies!
>
> I am turning into a maverick of the driving school industry. Speaking out of school, so to say.

Auto Insurance

Many companies refuse to insure disabled drivers, giving various excuses. This discrimination does not seem justified in view of handicapped drivers' safety records: "Driving records of physically handicapped drivers appeared to be equal to, or better than, the normal driver," concluded a study of the California Department of Motor Vehicles. "Both male and female handicapped drivers had a similar involvement in total accidents and a lesser number of convictions than the normal driver. From these results it does not appear that differential licensing standards or insurance rates can be justified on the basis of the handicap alone."

A person may not be denied insurance on the basis of his or her handicap. Drivers rejected by private insurance companies should be able to obtain insurance from state automobile insurance plans, under an "assigned risk" category. Because these plans are designed for persons considered high risks, premiums are above average. "This is intolerable discrimination based on disability, not justified by driving records," says Julius Shaw, a New York City Administrator and disabled consumer activist.

For postaccident or illness-handicapped drivers, their previous driving record is considered, with tickets or accidents counting against them.

Automobile insurance may only be canceled for certain reasons specified by law. Insurance companies may not cancel a motor vehicle policy simply because the policy-holding individual is handicapped.

For more information:

"Managing Your Auto Insurance," Series of three reports; "Consumer Reports" (June, July, August 1977). Your local library.

"No-Fault" Automobile Insurance, "Transportation Consumer Fact Sheet" (January 1976) U.S. Government Printing Office: 1976-678-996/403 Region No. 8, Washington, D.C. 20402

Special Plates

A total of approximately 31,000 special handicapped license plates or permits are issued annually in all states except Missouri and Wyoming. The general definitions of "disabled driver" involve a person who uses a wheelchair or crutches because of mobility problems, and one who obtains a doctor's signature on the application for special plates, indicating eligibility. Such plates or permits allow parking (but not double-parking) in otherwise prohibited places except for bus stops, taxi stands, within fifteen feet from a fire hydrant, a fire zone, a driveway, a cross-walk, a no-stopping zone or a no-standing zone.

Departments of Traffic who issue these plates or permits usually also demand proof that the driver needs the permit to get to work or studies. The cost of special plates or permits vary from the same as that for standard plates to $10 more or $10 less in different states. Many states issue free plates to eligible veterans.

Parking privileges are not uniformly accorded to out-of-state handicapped permit holders, especially in places with severe parking problems like New York City. The reason given is not inhospitality, but the lack of the criterion of need for work or study.

Reserved Parking Spaces

In addition to the privilege of parking on street spaces prohibited to the general public, reserved spaces in private parking lots, churches, museums, and shopping centers are intended to serve disabled drivers.

In letters to the author, disabled consumers write:

> The town has reserved 6 or 8 parking spaces in mall-parking lots for handicapped persons. I have only used them 3 or 4 times in the last year, because they are always occupied. Either there are more handicapped (and perhaps elderly) persons than I had thought or there are many inconsiderate people using those spaces.
>
> Parking is a big problem in all shopping areas. All public places should have special areas marked for handicapped parking and should find some way to enforce it. What good is it to have an accessible entrance, if they continue to block it with automobiles.

As a self-help defense measure, "Advocates for the Handicapped," 77 W. Washington Street, Chicago, Ill. 60602, offers parking "tickets" which any law-enforcement official, museum or shopping-center guards, security personnel, disabled persons and their families and friends, and agencies and organizations serving handicapped individuals can distribute. They are placed on the windshield of cars parked illegally in handicapped-parking spaces or across ramps used by persons in wheelchairs. The tickets have no legal significance, but ask physically able people to use other locations next time. Books of ten tickets each cost 20 cents; distributed to parking guards, organizations and friends, they could help improve the handicapped-parking system.

Rental Cars with Hand Controls

Rental cars with hand controls are available at airport locations in major cities. There is no extra charge for installation of special equipment; a $25 cash deposit for hand controls will be credited against rental charges when the vehicle is returned to the rental location. Avis (toll-free reservation number: 800-331-1212), Hertz (800-654-3131) and National (800-328-4567) service Atlanta, Boston, Chicago, Dallas, Detroit, Houston, Los Angeles, Miami, Minneapolis, Phoenix, San Francisco and Washington. Advance reservations are requested from forty-eight hours to ten days, to "reasonable lead times" in other cities.

Licenses for Nondrivers

Special licenses are being advocated by spokesmen for the blind, among others, who claim that nondriving people should enjoy the same convenience of identification that the driver's license provides in check cashing or charging for purchases and services. No concrete action has been taken as yet, except in Ohio: the state plans to sell photo-identification cards to people over 65 and those over 18 who are handicapped, to enable them to cash checks and make other transactions, even though they can't produce a driver's license.

Financial Help with Purchase of Car, Adaptations and Driving Instructions

Under Public Law 91-966, veterans who receive VA assistance toward purchase of a new car may be eligible for additional assistance on a new car as well as the purchase of handicap driving controls. See your VA prosthetics officer or write to: Prosthetic and Sensory Aids Service, Veterans Administration, Washington, D.C. 20420.

Consult your local rehabilitation center about financial aid from the Rehabilitation Services Administration, state offices of Vocational Rehabilitation, and Workmen's Compensation and Major Medical Insurance Plans.

Tax-Deductible Medical Expenses

- Hand controls, cost of installation and equipment
- Mechanism to lift you into the car
- Specially designed car to accommodate you and your wheelchair
  Note: The cost of power steering is not deductible.

Note also that if and when an environment-protective gas-guzzler tax is imposed, your van or car will surely fall into that category because of the special gas-consuming features your car needs, such as power steering, automatic gearshift, electric windows, hydraulic lifts, let alone its size, large enough to accommodate your wheelchair, which surely would not fit into a fuel-economic compact.

Disabled consumer advocates will cross that bridge when they come to it, but it won't do any harm to alert your legislators now that you will need tax exemptions when the occasion arises.

For more information, write for free publications and rental film:
"Driver Education for the Physically Disabled," Evaluation, Selection and Training Methods, by Jack M. Hofkosh, M.A., RPT; Jiri Sipajlo, M.A.; Leon Brody, Ph.D. Institute for Rehabilitation Medicine, New York University Medical Center, 400 E. 34th Street, New York, N.Y. 10016.
"Tips on Car Care and Safety for Deaf Drivers." U.S. Department of Transportation, National Highway Traffic Safety Administration, Washington, D.C. 20590.
"Driving," Quadruplegic Functional Skills. Film, showing various methods of unaided transfer into van or car; chair storage; use of hand controls. Film No. M-3062-X. Department of HEW, National Medical Audiovisual Center, Atlanta, Ga. 30333.

VALUE RECEIVED FOR SERVICES RENDERED

Services, from "your friendly banker" to "man's best friend," are not always performed by friendly service people—at least not overly friendly to your pocketbook. Automobile mechanics, TV-repair people, home-improvement contractors are not above taking advantage of consumers' ignorance of what goes on under the hood, behind the glass or inside the walls.

How can consumers protect themselves? We can't all become mechanics, but we can learn about and apply laws created to protect all consumers and working for those who know and apply them.

YOUR FRIENDLY BANKER

Nobody can accuse banks of not courting consumers for their money. Inducements include promises of free checking accounts, highest interests on savings accounts, free toasters and other gifts, an array of banking-related services—and branch offices all over town.

As a wise consumer, you know of course that you should apply the rules of careful shopping to your choice of a bank as well. Comparison-shop, critically evaluate advertising claims, read the fine print.

- What do you have to do to receive the *gifts?*
- Are checking accounts really *free,* or do you have to keep a sizable amount of money in a savings account?
- Are there hidden costs, like charges for checks or a per-check fee?
- Are you penalized for stop-payment orders or bounced checks?
- Do various methods of computing interests on savings accounts produce different yields from those advertised as *highest in town?*
- What other services does the bank offer?
- Can you cash a check at another, not your regular branch of the same bank?
- If you bank by mail, will the bank pay postage?
- What consideration will you be given if you wish to request a loan?

These are some of the questions you should ask—in theory! In fact, if you act like most people, you will choose a bank by location, nearest your home or your place of work. That's why there are more bank branches than supermarkets and gas stations. In a choice between neighborhood banks, you may consider their banking hours so that you can get there when it best suits you.

As we did with food markets and stores, let's put your local bank branch to the *Accessibility Test:*

- Are entrances in front, and from parking lot, level or ramped?
- Is there a hinged door, 32 inches wide, next to a revolving door?
- Are parking spaces reserved for disabled drivers?
- Is at least one teller's counter low enough for transactions from a wheelchair?
- If not, does teller come around the counter or must a third person assist?
- Do tellers help vision-impaired clients in identifying bills?
- Do they display sensitivity in communicating with hearing impaired clients?
- What services do they provide that make it possible for clients with impairments to maintain independence and privacy in their bank transactions?

In a 1976 access survey, conducted by the author on behalf of the New York City Department of Consumer Affairs, the smallest percentage of responses was received from banks. (The best responders were the airlines!) Outside of assurances about courteous service and check-cashing privileges in other branches if an account was maintained at the bank, only one bank reported on a special service.

When opening an account at Chemical Bank, a legally blind person receives a Braille account kit, consisting of a checkwriter, instructions in Braille and a supply of checks. The checkwriter is a set of hinged aluminum plates into which the check is inserted. Cutouts correspond to blank lines on a check. In addition, the checkwriter has Braille cells that enable the user to imprint the information he will need to identify the check after it is paid and returned to him. To complete the vision-impaired depositor's independence and privacy, the monthly statement is rendered in Braille.

Since it can be done, why not suggest the procedure to your bank as a good idea for a needed service? Or perhaps your local newspaper could report about the service and challenge your local bank to follow suit? It's worth a try!

EFTS—WHAT IS IT? IS IT FOR YOU?

Even if you don't know what the letters EFTS stand for, you may already use the service if you have made arrangements for the U.S. Treasury to deposit your Social Security check directly in your checking account, without any paper changing hands.

That is the meaning of paperless banking—Electronic Funds Transfer System. It is a computerized system that transfers funds from the payer's to the payee's account without the use of checks.

- Shoppers may pay for goods at retail stores by using a card inserted in an electronic terminal. Their accounts are charged electronically; they carry less cash.
- Bank customers may deposit or withdraw cash at any time of day or night by using their cards in unattended machines.
- Employees or recipients of any income, such as Social Security, rents or dividends, can have their payments deposited directly into their checking or savings accounts without ever receiving a check.
- Bills may be paid by telephone, authorizing the bank to debit the account

and transfer funds to the various payees. The voice at the other end may be a human being's or a computer's; the call will be charged as only one telephone unit, regardless of length of conversation.

If you choose this way of paying your bills, now or in the future, you will save the work of writing checks, affixing postage stamps and taking envelopes to the mailbox. And if you have any difficulties with eyesight or handwriting, this may be just the thing for you.

Today there are 5,800 electronic tellers or cash dispensers operating, and 225,000 terminals in stores that could be tied into an EFT system. Do consumers make a beeline for these electronic marvels? Not quite—yet.

Many consumers are reluctant to give a bank that much control over their funds, and they do not like the elimination of canceled checks as proof of payment. Also, people are afraid of potential harm that could be caused by a computer error—and you know how frustrating it is to argue with a computer.

Moreover, there is a potential of invasion of privacy if all financial transactions of the month are laid out in one consolidated statement. To that argument, advocates of the system respond that there will be no more privacy problem than already exists now. The decision is yours—for now. Sooner or later, the electronics will take over.

At the moment, however, it's a good idea to make arrangements for your Social Security checks to be deposited directly into your bank account. The bank will be glad to assist you in notifying the U.S. Treasury. This method avoids the risk of having a check stolen from the mail box or cashing the check and keeping too much cash in your pocket or at home.

For more information:

"A Guide to Banking Services." 4-part series. Picking the Best Checking Account; How to Pick the Best Savings Account; How to Shop for Credit; Shaking up the Banks. *Consumer Reports* (January, February, March, May 1975). Consumers Union, Reprints, Orangeburg, N.Y. 10962. $1.25.

Break the Banks! A shopper's guide to banking services. $3.50.

It's in Your Interest. A consumer's guide to savings accounts. $4.

Both above: Consumer Action, 26 Seventh Street, San Francisco, Calif. 94103.

Shopping for a Loan: A Truth in Lending Survey. 50 cents. California Citizens Action Group, 909 12th Street, Sacramento, Calif., 95814.

Truth in Savings Publication List. Includes over 40 publications concerning savings. Free with stamped self-addressed envelope.

13-question questionnaire—what to ask to compute savings-account earnings. 5 cents with stamped self-addressed envelope.

Both above: Kansas State University, Department of Family Economics, Manhattan, Kan. 66506.

EFT and the Public Interest. A report of the National Commission on Electronic Fund Transfers (February 1977). 1000 Connecticut Avenue, N.W., Washington, D.C. 20036. U.S. Government Printing Office, Washington, D.C. 20402. $2.60.

INSURANCE—LIFE, HEALTH, PROPERTY, WORKMEN'S COMPENSATION

Insurance is one of the services most consumers buy with little knowledge, and less information or ability to comparison-shop than any other item they purchase. Insurance policies are forbidding-looking documents with more exemptions hidden in their fine print than ten of the proverbial Philadelphia lawyers might discover, let alone the unwary layman.

"Here you are. Read it for yourself."

Drawing reprinted with permission

Life Insurance

"Who needs a life insurance policy only a lawyer can understand?" reads the caption of a full-page advertisement in the *New York Times Magazine* (June 5, 1977), in which the life insurance companies in America offer readers a free booklet, "What's in Your Life Insurance Policy?" "Several companies are already issuing new policies written in language easier for people to understand," claims the ad.

⟨✍⟩ **Write for the booklet to: American Council of Life Insurance, 277 Park Avenue, New York, N.Y. 10017.**

Such change of heart may not have happened entirely unprodded, by companies which for years were accused of selling insurance policies that fattened the coffers of the companies and the commissions of their agents rather than benefiting consumers.

The late Senator Philip Hart opened a subcommittee hearing in 1973 with this statement: "More than 300,000 times a day, all year long, American consumers pay a bill without having more than a vague idea of what they are buying. These 14 million consumers, at an outlay of about 23 billion dollars a year, are buying life insurance policies."*

Ralph Nader, probably the most articulate consumer advocate of all time, went on record with these unflattering remarks: "The life insurance industry is, perhaps, the last giant industry to come under the legislative microscope . . . For almost 70 years the life insurance industry has been a smug sacred cow feeding the public a steady line of sacred bull."

Herbert Denenberg, the Pennsylvania Commissioner of Insurance, testified as one of the best informed men in the industry. His abrasive manner was possibly intentional: "The life insurance industry—however pure its motives and morals—is inflicting confusion on the public, with policies that the public cannot understand, with a pricing system that prevents intelligent shopping, with agents that are often incompetent, and with many companies that are unsound financially. . . . We have competition, but it is competition by confusion. So life insurance, which is supposed to provide protection, has become another of the leading consumer frauds."

However confused, most heads of families want to provide some security for their families in case a tragedy should befall them. The best advice is to comparison-shop carefully, making every effort to fully understand the protection one buys in relation to the cost.

Term insurance is a type of life insurance which provides pure protection only. It is the type of insurance that gives the family the greatest amount of protection for a limited period for the least cost.

Term insurance sales have soared dramatically in recent years, amounting to 31 percent of life insurance sold in 1975, and the trend since has been

* Reported in *How to Save Money on Your Life Insurance.* Insurance Research Service, P.O. Box 468, 571 East Main Street, Brevard, N.C. 28712.

perpendicularly up. "Millions of life insurance policy holders are finding term preferable to the more expensive whole life, believing they can invest their funds in superior ways than in whole life or endowment insurance," contends Sylvia Porter in the New York *Post* (August 1, 1977).

In the state of New York, savings banks first received authority to go into the life insurance business—up to $30,000—in 1939, and lately they began to use that right by opening *insurance stores* in popular department stores and shopping centers in middle- and low-income areas. Some savings-bank officers believe their insurance meets the needs of a segment of the population neglected by traditional insurance sources. Priced to compete with insurance companies, their premiums can be less than half those of other institutions, according to the Savings Bank Life Insurance Fund. Your state may have similar laws or consider their introduction.

Request information from your State Insurance Commission, located in your state capital.

You will find good advice in the U.S. Government pamphlet, "Insurance for Your Health, Car, Life," by Charlotte George, State Family Economics and Management Specialist at the University of Missouri, Columbia (U.S. Government Printing Office, 1976-680-141/5 Region 8, Washington, D.C. 20402). Here's some of that advice:

> Life insurance is not a savings plan or an investment plan. Neither is it the answer for building an educational fund for children. Life insurance is often sold for such purposes, but there are better ways for obtaining these objectives than through life insurance . . . When you and your family are establishing a life insurance program, consider these very important factors:

- Buy the policies which will give the most protection at the least cost.
- Insure the right family members.
- Consider the family's financial needs.
- Buy the insurance from companies that are financially sound and are represented by honest, well-trained agents.

Life Insurance and Disabling Accidents

Among the clauses in life insurance contracts there may be some relating to temporary or permanent disabilities occurring to the insured during the coverage of his policy.

Waiver of Premium

If you should become disabled, and you are covered by life insurance, in many cases you will not have to continue to pay the premiums. Under a waiver of premium benefit, payments will not have to be made as long as you are totally disabled from performing the duties of your occupation or profession for a given length of time, in accordance with the terms of contract. For instance, your life insurance contract could specify that if you are totally disabled for nine months, then your life insurance coverage would continue without further payment of premiums until you are able to return to work.

Mortgage and Credit Insurance

This insurance covers your mortgage payments, in accordance with the terms of the contract, during the time you are disabled.

Accidental Death and Dismemberment Insurance

These policies provide set amounts, either in a lump sum or in monthly payments, for the loss of life, sight or limb, as a result of an accident, on or off the job. Payment is in accordance with the terms of your contract and is in addition to any other benefits.

The American Council of Life Insurance, 277 Park Avenue, New York, N.Y. 10017 will be glad to send you these informative booklets:
"Life Insurance—for Your Family Security"
"Life Insurance Fact Book, 1975." 123 pp.

Life Insurance and Disabled Applicants

Is discrimination practiced against disabled applicants? The answer is "YES"! Though this fact is denied sanctimoniously by all companies, closer investigation reveals facts denying the denials.

"Insurance companies are out to make money—appeals to civil rights roll off their backs," a longtime insurance agent confided.

An insider reports that a group at Gallaudet College complained that agents made no efforts to sell insurance to deaf clients. Possibly communication difficulties deterred salesmen—or could it be that deaf applicants would not be welcomed by the salesmen's companies?

In some states the law prohibits declining solely for blindness or physical handicap. "Mostly, underwriters give insurance to handicapped persons who are functioning," another expert claims. As in all insurance policies, the premium depends on age. But medical or occupational risks may get substandard premiums, which are higher in cost. Clients are informed that their premiums are above average for their age group. They are also told that if an occupational hazard ceased to exist, the premiums could be reduced.

"You can shop around and perhaps find a better deal," another interviewee suggests. "New and younger companies may be more flexible; the older ones can be stodgy."

Applicants are "rated," revealed further investigation, the extent of their disability determining whether or not they will be granted a policy, and the cost of the premium. The origin of the disability—whether congenital, through accident or illness—is weighed, as well as the person's mobility and adjustment to the condition. The required use of a wheelchair definitely is reflected in the rating. Different actuarial tables are used, resulting in higher premiums. Accidental-death benefits and disability premium waiver most likely will not be granted.

You won't find any of these conditions spelled out in any of the companies' publicity materials or in their policies, not even in the fine print. But neither will you find an insurance company executive who'll swear on the Bible that they don't exist.

Health Insurance

Health insurance can be in individual or group policies, through the employer or a fraternal organization. Health insurance contracts are detailed and not the easiest to understand. It is often very hard to sort out the facts and obtain the kind of health insurance you are seeking.

If you are nearing 65, it is particularly important to review what you have, because many policies reduce benefits when you qualify for Medicare.

Health Insurance for the Disabled

If you are disabled, health insurance may be more difficult to obtain. In some cases, major medical coverage may be accepted, while disability insurance will be declined. A clause referring to "pre-existing condition" will exclude anything relating to the disability. Costs incurred, for instance, in relation to a bladder infection in a wheelchair-bound individual, or a blind person falling off a step ladder, may not be compensated for, yet the same individuals will be covered for expenses connected with appendectomies. However, some laws require health insurance policies, once they have been issued, to continue, covering individuals for certain handicapping conditions.

Many mentally retarded persons have health insurance coverage to help pay their medical costs, reports the Health Insurance Institute. An estimated 87 percent of all mildly retarded adult males have jobs, as do 33 percent of females. All of these persons who are employed where health insurance is provided are insured along with other workers.

For more information: "What You Should Know about Health Insurance." Health Insurance Institute, 277 Park Avenue, New York, N.Y. 10017.

Look carefully into offers of additional health insurance to supplement Medicare payments. Don't be fooled by high-pressure salesmen or official-sounding names, like "Voluntary Medicare." They have no connection with the government.

"Health Insurance for Older People: Filling the Gaps in Medicare," *Consumer Reports* (January 1976). 50 cents. Reprint and Book Department, Consumers Union, Orangeburg, N.Y. 10962

Property Insurance

Property insurance may not discriminate against disabled applicants, except for the glaring automobile insurance injustice, discussed on p. 164.

Write for: "Insurance Coverage for the Renter and the Home-owner." U.S. Government Printing Office: 1976-680-139/1 Region 8, Washington, D.C. 20402.

Workmen's Compensation

Workmen's compensation refers to weekly cash benefits and the provision of all necessary medical care to a worker who is disabled because of accidental *injury arising out of and in the course of employment* or because of an *occupational disease,* and in case of death resulting from such injury or disease, weekly cash benefits payable to his dependents.

Disability Benefits

Disability benefits are temporary cash benefits payable to an eligible wage earner when he is disabled by an *off-the-job injury or illness.* Supplementing the workmen's compensation law, the disability benefits law ensures protection for wage earners by providing for weekly cash benefits to replace, in part, wages lost because of injuries or illnesses that do not arise out of and in the course of employment.

Disability benefits are also provided to an unemployed claimant to replace unemployment insurance benefits lost because of illness or injury. Each state has a worker's compensation law, usually under the direction of the Executive Department, the Governor's Office. Benefits are variable from state to state. An analysis of workmen's compensation law is available from the U.S. Chamber of Commerce, comparing the laws throughout the country.

Write to the Workmen's Compensation Board in your Governor's Office for:
"On the Job Injury," What Every Worker Should Know about Workmen's Compensation.
"Off-the-Job Disability," What Every Worker Should Know about Disability Benefits.

The Second-Injury Law

The second-injury law is a part of the workmen's compensation law which limits the workmen's compensation liability of employers who hire handicapped workers, or retain handicapped workers in employment.

The purpose of the second-injury law is to protect employers who hire physically handicapped workers against a disproportionate liability in the event of subsequent employment injury.

Many surveys show that handicapped workers are safer on the job than their nondisabled co-workers. But even with this good record, handicapped people still have a hard time finding a job. Sometimes, during an interview, the employer will say: "We are sorry. We can't hire you. Our insurance rates would go up."

The employer may use this as an excuse because he is not familiar with handicapped people and does not know what to expect or how to handle the situation, or he may not understand the insurance laws in his state. There is no change in worker's compensation insurance rates when a company hires handicapped employees. The rates do not depend on the physical conditions or ages of workers, but on the hazards involved in a company's work and on its accident experience.

Sometimes handicapped workers have accidents on the job. This injury is considered a "second injury." This second injury, combined with the pre-existing disability, may result in a greater percent of disability. The second-injury fund says that the employer is liable only for the percent of disability that results from the second injury. The second-injury fund pays the worker the difference between what the employer covers (single accident loss) and the total disability award.

Each state has its own worker's compensation law and second-injury fund. In some states deaf people are included among those who are protected by second-injury funds. In some states they are not.

☎ **For additional information and assistance, contact one or more of the groups below. These organizations can explain the worker's-compensation and second-injury laws in your state:**

The President's Committee on Employment of the Handicapped, Washington, D.C. 20210

Your state office of Vocational Rehabilitation
Your state Division of Employment Security
Your state Human Rights office

You can find their addresses and telephone numbers in the telephone directory.

Finally, one more example of discrimination, even in workmen's compensation insurance. One of the author's survey-responders writes from Long Beach, California:

> We recently formed an Independent Living Center in this area, necessitating the acquisition of Workmen's Compensation Insurance coverage for our employees—who are all handicapped.
>
> All private carriers refused coverage. In making application to the State Compensation Board we anticipated a *clerical* rate of 42¢ per $100. We were charged $1.06 per $100 and rated as a *training* situation.

Insurance by Mail

Mail-order insurance could be a trap, warns the Federal Trade Commission. "Even though a mail offer looks good, shop around for the best policy. Don't be fooled by come-ons like *Veteran Policies,* or *Medicare Policies.* If you don't understand the policy, ask your neighborhood legal service, an insurance agent, or a businessman you know, to explain it."

The Federal Trade Commission is concerned about misleading insurance offers that you may receive in the mail, and it needs your help in stopping illegal practices.

Report any mail-order insurance problems you have to your FTC regional offices and field stations and also contact your State Insurance Commission, located in your state capital.

For more information: "Mail Order Insurance" (Buyer's Guide #1), Federal Trade Commission, Washington, D.C. 20580.

REPAIRS

If your watch stops running, your toaster stops toasting, the TV is on the blink, and worst of all, your automobile gives you trouble, the warranty *may* help, but don't bank on it.

In theory, in a full warranty the warrantor must remedy the product within a reasonable time and without charge in the case of defect or malfunction. If the product is still defective after a reasonable number of attempts to fix it—in other words, if it's a lemon—the consumer must be offered a refund or replacement.

In fact, you may have quite a time to see these things happen. There may be conditions in the fine print you have not read; the limited warranty—"guaranteed" for 30, 60 or 90 days—frequently tends to be more a protection to the seller than to the buyer.

In complaints about automobile repairs, the second most frequent category of consumer complaints (mail-order-related complaints rank first), dealers' repair shops are frequently accused of making "Band-Aid" repairs during the warranty period of 90 days, causing the hapless motorist to bring the new car in, time and again. Then, when the warranty period has expired, the more extensive repair is done, for a hefty charge.

If you have purchased your malfunctioning product from a reputable retailer or a reliable manufacturer, you will get satisfaction. Your first steps are:

- Return the product to the retailer, or manufacturer, according to instructions, for repair or replacement.
- Be sure to hold on to all documents relating to your purchase, to establish your claim by date of purchase. You may have sent in a card supplied in the wrapping, but that usually serves more for the seller's statistical purposes.

Informative and easy-to-read publications tell you what you should know about warranties to take full advantage of the protection the law provides:

Warranties, There Ought to Be a Law . . . There Is. Federal Trade Commission, Room 130, Washington, D.C. 20580.

Warranties (#533 F.) Types of warranties required by law; how to use them for comparison-shopping; what to do if you have a problem with a product under warranty. Consumer Information Center, Pueblo, Colo. 81009.

Amendments to the law are in the hearing stages. Questions such as "Who should pay the shipping costs for a heavy article that has to be returned to the manufacturer for a warrantied repair?" are hotly disputed between manufacturers and consumer advocates. Don't expect quick resolutions of such conflicts, but DO read and listen to news items. When consumer protective legislation is passed, it is always publicized in consumer columns and media presentations. It's to your advantage to know laws that protect you and to apply them when needed in personal situations.

If your item in need of repair is of older vintage, you are on your own. Try to find reputable repair shops, recommended by neighbors or based on your own satisfactory previous experiences. Comparison-shop for repairs. This is especially important on *blind* repairs, radios, TV sets, automobiles, where you may be in the company of most consumers who don't know what is behind the lens or under the hood.

Usually, repair shops charge a fee for the estimate and apply the amount toward the cost of the repair. If the estimate seems exceedingly high to you, it may save you money to pay for the detailed written estimate, and then, armed with it, get another estimate. The second repair shop, not knowing what his competitor had quoted, may go lower—or higher. He may claim different parts in need of replacement, making you wonder who is a phony. If both agree on repairs and cost, at least you won't have any nagging doubts on having been had.

The New York City Department of Consumer Affairs, a strong regulatory agency, has some good regulations. You may apply their recommendations, even if they are not the law in your locality. And you may suggest them to your legislators:

- Get a written cost estimate of the repair.
- Do not let the repairman start to work before you have accepted his cost estimate and authorized him with your signature to proceed.
- Instruct him to notify you before going ahead should he find during the course of the repair that the final cost will have to exceed the estimate.
- Ask him to return to you the old parts he claims to have replaced (he may find that difficult if he has charged you for something he didn't do).
- Insist that a repair or delivery man keep his appointment with you on the

day promised. Your time is as valuable as his; the least he can do is notify you the preceding day if he cannot keep his appointment.

🐟 **Write for: Regulation 26, "Repairs," and Regulation 43, "No-Shows," of the New York City Consumer Protection Law against Unconscionable Trade Practices. Department of Consumer Affairs, City of New York, 80 Lafayette Street, New York, N.Y. 10013.**

HOME IMPROVEMENT

Home improvement is probably the most costly repair you'll ever commission. It's also the one where more people come to expensive grief than in any other consumer transaction. Homeowners' gullibility leave the field wide open for con artists.

There's that fake *inspector* who notices that a furnace or water heater not only is in violation of local ordinances but will blow up the house if not speedily replaced. Fortunately, the con artist's buddy will give the scared homeowner a good price; he'll also *not* report the existing violation to the authorities. Incredible? Not at all; happens every day.

Then there's the man with a truck who just happens to have enough material left over from a neighbor's job to tar your roof or blacktop your driveway. For immediate cash only, so that the boss shouldn't find out what a steal he gave you. He did—literally. And he won't be around when the next rain washes off the bargain-price black *paint*.

Even with legitimate contractors, there is always the run-of-the-mill shoddy workmanship, and the "certificate of completion" you may have signed unwittingly, enabling the contractor to get his money from the bank which is financing your job, before it is satisfactorily completed.

Perhaps you are planning to refit an old house or apartment to your needs or remodel your current lodgings to new needs, created by accident, illness, old age or a disabled child in your family. Here is some important advice:

- Find a reputable contractor, recommended to you by friends or neighbors who are satisfied with the jobs he had done for them. If your locality requires licensing of home-improvement contractors, be sure you deal only with a licensed contractor.
- Get at least three competing estimates.
- Have all specifications *written* in the contract, down to the last detail.
- Don't rush into signing. Take your time. Think it over carefully.

■ And remember, even after you signed the contract, you have a 72-hour cooling-off period to change your mind. No excuse needed. During these 72 hours, the contractor is not permitted to start the work or store materials or tools on your premises, trying to coerce you into sticking to the agreement.

If you plan to have any home improvement done, you may avoid a lot of trouble later if you use the following questionnaire as a guideline now:

Before you sign the contract   Yes No

Does the contract heading clearly state the contractor's name,
   address, telephone and license number?   — —

Is the date of the contract filled in?   — —

Does the contract clearly state when the job will begin and how
   much time is estimated for completion?   — —

Are all advertised or verbal representations, guarantees and warranties spelled out and made a part of the contract?   — —

Is every item on the repair or renovation clearly printed or typed
   in?   — —

   Quantity __ Quality __ Brand name __ Model number __

Are both labor and material guaranteed against defects or poor
   workmanship?   — —

   For how long? _____

Does the contract contain a clause to the effect that shortcomings and defects in both material and labor will be
   corrected without charge?   — —

On brand-name items, will the contractor provide manufacturer's
   warranty cards for you to complete and mail in?   — —

   Don't rely on the contractor to send these in.

   All products manufactured after July 4, 1975, must state
   whether warranty is *full* or *limited*. Which type is on the
   product the contractor intends to use? _____

Will there be any hidden charges used as a device to disguise
   the actual cost of the job?   — —

Will the contractor procure all permits required by law?   — —

Is there any charge for procuring these permits?   — —

Does the contractor have a performance bond?   — —

Are his workmen's compensation, public liability and property
   damage insurance in force?   — —

   Don't let work begin until the contractor provides you with
   certificates of insurance.

Does the contractor or salesman try to rush you into signing?   — —

After you signed the contract   Yes   No

Did the salesman sign the contract and list his own license
    number?   —   —
Did he tell you that you may cancel this contract within 3 days
    for any reason and without penalty? (Sundays are not
    counted, but Saturdays are.)   —   —
Is the cancellation notice attached to the contract?   —   —
    Do not permit the contractor to *spike* the job during the
    3-day period of cancellation. By law, he may not deliver
    material, start demolition or construction until the 72-hour
    grace period has elapsed.
Did you obtain a clearly legible copy of the entire contract?   —   —
    It's an important document. Keep it in a safe place.

Payment

Keep deposit payments small, regardless of the total amount of
    the contract.
Make no substantial payment until work actually begins.
    Match subsequent payments to the progress of the job.
Under no circumstances be pressured to sign, or inadvertently
    sign, a completion certificate until the job is finished.

Financing

Did you comparison-shop for the cost of credit as carefully as
    for the service?   —   —
    Contractor? ___ Bank? ___ Credit union? ___
Did you scrutinize all conditions of any loan agreement?   —   —
    Annual rate of interest in % ___ Finance charges in $
    and ¢ ___ Amount of each installment ___ Number of
    payments ___ Penalties for late payment or default ___
Did you multiply the amount of each installment with the number
    of payments to find out the real, total cost of the repair,
    renovation or improvement?   —   —
Could you afford larger individual installment payments, paying
    off the loan faster and reducing the total cost, compared to
    smaller installments, strung out over a longer period of time? —   —

If you are not satisfied

Don't fret—complain!
    First, to the contractor. No satisfaction?
Complain to your local Consumer Affairs Office. This is the
    information they will need:

a) Your name, address, zip, phone number (from 9 A.M. to
   5 P.M.)
b) Contractor's name, address, zip, phone number, license
   number
c) Your complaint—complete, brief
d) *Copies* of all pertinent documents—contract, warranties.
   Do not part with any original documents. Mail copies only.

LET THERE BE LIGHT . . . AND HEAT!

There's little you, as a consumer, can do about spiraling rates of gas and electricity—unless you are the activist type and protest loudly at the public hearings of your State Utility Commission, when your local power company applies for yet another rate increase. State utility commissions regulate the rates, service and practices of utility companies—electric, gas, telephone, water and steam.

There is, however, quite a lot you can do to conserve the use of power, by carefully investigating the energy consumption of appliances, as well as their price, before you make your purchase, and checking your utility bills to make sure you pay only for the power you have consumed, not more, due to billing errors.

Conservation

With only one seventeenth of the world's population, our country uses one third of the world's energy. While in years past your utility company urged you to use a lot of their product, electricity, now they will be equally eager to help you save it.

Ask the Consumer Service Department of your utility company for their free consumer education publications. They'll be happy to mail them to you.

Here are some pieces of common-sense advice:

DO	DON'T

Upstairs, Downstairs, in My Lady's Chamber

DO	DON'T
■ turn off all lighting, heating, cooling, not being used.	■ light, heat, cool, entertain empty rooms.

DO	DON'T
■ get proper-size air conditioner, heater—undersize rather than oversize. ■ close quickly doors of heated or cooled rooms.	■ let accumulated dirt reduce output of vacuum cleaner. ■ overcool or heat; each degree up or down adds 4% to 5% of energy. ■ let in too much cold or warm air.

Bathroom

■ shower rather than bathe—uses less water.	■ let leaky faucets waste hot water.

Kitchen

■ use small amounts of water in cooking. ■ cover boiling pots; use lowest setting that will do the job. Turn off heat a few minutes before food is cooked; let retained heat complete cooking. ■ open refrigerator, freezer doors as few times as possible. ■ before opening door, know what you want. ■ for peak efficiency, fill to capacity. ■ defrost as soon as frost is ¼″ thick. ■ keep all items sealed properly. ■ clean coils, check gaskets. ■ use small appliances to save energy. ■ accumulate dishes from several meals. ■ turn off dishwasher when wash cycle is complete; open door slightly. ■ use only cold water for disposer.	■ preheat oven for broiling or roasting. ■ preheat oven for foods cooking longer than one hour. ■ waste oven space; cook casserole meals together with roasts or cakes. ■ let in more warm air than unavoidable. ■ let your refrigerator work overtime. ■ stand there with the door wide open. ■ overfill refrigerator or freezer. ■ let accumulated frost act as insulator. ■ store foods in heavy wrapping paper. ■ tolerate dirty coils, leaky gaskets. ■ waste range or oven for toast or popcorn. ■ use dishwasher unless fully loaded. ■ use dry cycle if dishes not needed immediately. ■ waste hot water on anything.

DO   DON'T

Laundry

- plan your washday schedule.
- wait until you have a full load.
- match wash time load and soil levels.
- use cold water whenever possible.
- sort clothes to thickness before drying.
- remove permanent-press garments promptly.

- use washer more than you have to.
- overload your machine.
- omit soaking heavily soiled garments.
- use hot water unless unavoidable.
- run additional cycle for a few items.
- dry wrinkles into permanent-press items.

Energy-Labeling of Household Appliances

Approximately 20 percent of all energy consumed in the United States is used in apartments and single-family dwellings. Much of this energy is needed to operate the vast number of appliances found in American homes. These include some 31 million room air conditioners, 70 million refrigerators, 23 million freezers and 55 million water heaters.

Just as there are variations in design and purchase prices among competing appliances, so there are variations in the amount of energy different appliances require to perform essentially the same task or service. For example, some room air conditioners are more efficient than other competing models—that is, they use less energy than others having the same cooling capacity.

To encourage manufacturers to provide point-of-sale information on appliance energy use, and to encourage consumers to buy the most efficient products that will meet their needs, the U.S. Department of Commerce, working with the Council on Environmental Quality and the Environmental Protection Agency, has developed a voluntary energy-conservation-labeling program.

 ■ **When shopping for a new appliance, use the manufacturer's information on the label.**
- **Look for the EYOC (Estimated Yearly Operating Costs) figure.**
- **Consider this figure, and the type of warranty offered, in comparing prices of competing appliances. A low purchase price alone**

may not be a bargain if yearly operating costs and not warrantied repairs will more than exceed initial savings.

Write for: "Energy Labeling of Household Appliances," U.S. Department of Commerce, National Bureau of Standards, Washington, D.C. 20234.

Understanding Your Utility Bill

If your household budget and utility costs conflict, you need to know how to read your electric and gas meters and bills. With this skill, you can figure out how much energy costs by the unit and whether your attempts to conserve energy are effective. You can also check the accuracy of your bills, and find out how much energy is used to heat and cool your home.

- Write for *"Understanding Your Utility Bill,"* a publication of the Federal Energy Administration, Washington, D.C. 20461, or for a similar one published by your utility company.
- Study these booklets and apply your skills to checking if your meter registered more than your actual consumption or whatever other mistakes you suspect in your utility bills.

If you think there is an *error in your utility bill,* you have the following rights:

- First, complain to the company, by telephone, letter or in person. You do not need any special form, and the company must answer within a reasonable time.
- If you are not satisfied with the company's response, complain to your State Utility Commission. It's a good idea to send your letter by certified mail, return receipt requested. Keep a copy of your letter and the receipt in a safe place.
- The commission will investigate your complaint and report to you.
- Your service cannot be shut off while the company or the State Utility Commission is investigating your complaint, but you may be required to pay bills or parts of bills about which there is no reasonable dispute.

If you get a *disconnect notice,* you have a certain number of days to pay your bill or contact the utility company in the fashion described above, informing them that you think they made an error in your account.

- You can also make arrangements to have another person, a friend, relative, neighbor, notified if you ever receive a disconnect notice. This *Third Party* does not have any obligation to pay a consumer's bill, but would call or contact the consumer to be sure everything is OK and to be sure the consumer understands what the disconnect notice means.

Request from your utility company an official Third Party form to designate the person you wish to be notified at the same time as a disconnect notice goes to you.

For recipients of Social Security, disability payments, pensions or other limited, fixed incomes who let their utility company know that they have fallen behind in their payments because the utility's billing dates do not coincide with the receipt of their income, the utility will work out a payment plan to clear up the arrears over a period of several months. Once the arrears have been paid and a customer's payment pattern adjusted, the utility expects that future bills will be paid on time.

Life-Sustaining Equipment

Some utility customers have life-sustaining equipment which runs on electricity. Iron lungs, respirators, kidney machines, ultrasonic nebulizers, suction pumps, rocking beds—these are the kinds of machines on which human lives depend. The number of these machines is growing, and so is the number of people who rely on them.

If you, a member of your family or someone in your household depends on life-sustaining equipment, let your utility company know so that you may receive preferential service in case of power failures or other emergencies.

Consumer Action

Ellen Logue, a spunky consumer who shares her Brooklyn apartment with husband Andy and their two guide dogs, has some very definite ideas about how blind people should have the right to read for themselves information about the utilities. Here's what she accomplished with Con Edison, the New York utility company:

1. Con Edison asked the New York Association for the Blind, and "In Touch," a radio network for the blind, to inform their clients and listeners about Third Party notification and Life-Sustaining Equipment procedures.

2. "Con Edison, through the Public Service Commission," Ellen writes, "is going to have my electric bill written for me in Braille by the Lighthouse. Everything that pertains to the bill will be written in Braille. The back bill will also be written and the present amount. I will also know about the kilowatts that I use for clocks, refrigerators, radios, TVs, washing machines and driers. I think this is a very good idea. As it is now, I know nothing about anything."

If you agree with Ellen that her idea is a good one—and accomplished what she wanted—maybe you'll want to become such a pacesetter in your community!

As a New Yorker, paying Con Ed's rates (the highest in the country), the author is no defender of the company. However, accommodations for disabled subscribers are commendable. They are due mainly to the efforts of Con Ed's Director of Consumer Affairs, Grace Richardson.

Recently she instituted a service for blind customers, who may request that a sighted person of their choice will receive a duplicate of their bill to help them check for accuracy.

Upon the author's urging, Grace is now suggesting to management the installation of a TTY phone, so that deaf subscribers may have the same access to information and registration of complaints as do their fellow hearing New Yorkers. The TTY may be in action by the time this book is in print. If not yet . . . write and ask for it! Request the same service from YOUR local utility company.

BAKER'S AID

A special service for their blind customers is performed by one of New York's utility companies. The Brooklyn Union Gas Company Brailles consumers' oven control dial of the gas range to make it easier to select the temperature. Nailheads set in the dial correspond to the temperature settings, up to the "Broil" position. Consumers bring in the dial and when the work is completed, the dial is mailed back to its owner.

Why not suggest this service to *your* gas and electric companies?

Appliances which are particularly useful to those persons with visual limitations are simple to operate and clean, and have raised letters and/or numbers on the control dial. If the appliance you wish to purchase does not have the raised or Braille dial, write the company's consumer affairs department, enclosing the model and serial number of the appliance. Some companies will exchange the dials free of charge. A free service in Brailling of oven dials is available from the Robert Shaw Control Co., Youngswood, Pa. 15697.

The above information is part of a long and informative article, "Household Appliances for the Visually Impaired," in *On Your Own* (December 1977), A Special Program of Continuing Education in Home Economics, P.O. Box 2967, University, Ala. 35486.

AS CLOSE AS YOUR NEAREST TELEPHONE

In a public relations sales promotion campaign on television, the telephone company shows emotional scenes: new grandpa telling new grandma "It's a boy!" Small boy telling Grandpa "I love you." In magazine ads, young mother and child tell absent Daddy "We miss you." "Your loved ones are as close as the nearest telephone" is the message the company wants to convey. For many people, hard-of-hearing or physically handicapped, the telephone instrument may be close-by, but its effective use is out of their reach. Yet for many of these people, the telephone could be an even more vital life line to communication with the outside world. Fortunately, modern technology has developed ultrasophisticated coping devices. Telephones responding to breath control or head movement, and phone communications for the deaf and deaf-blind boggle the mind.

Ask your Telephone Business Office for the booklet "Services for Special Needs," published by the Bell Telephone System. It describes devices developed to help persons with physical impairments to communicate.

Your local area telephone company may also list their special services in a booklet of their own. Read about "Telephone Pioneers of America," p. 156. These volunteers may be able to help you with much less costly coping devices. Your local Business Telephone Operator will refer you to the nearest chapter.

Financial Help

Financing such special equipment may present a problem. Telephone companies insist that the cost for special equipment must be borne by the user, or it would have to be distributed over charges to all subscribers in the form of increased rates.

Medicaid does not consider telephone a medical necessity, therefore instruments are not covered by Medicaid.

Vocational Rehabilitation may pick up some of the cost if the telephone contributes to employability of the user.

In *service charges to handicapped subscribers,* concessions are being made by some telephone companies that can serve as models for consumer activitists to request similar money-saving rates from their local companies:

Charges for information calls are waived for disabled users; they are also exempt from charges being placed on local or long-distance operator-assisted calls; a credit-card account allows blind subscribers to be billed at the direct-dialing rate, even though they had assistance from the operator in making "collect" calls from pay phones because they have trouble identifying coins and coin slots.

If your local telephone company grants these concessions, contact the company for information on qualifying for the exemptions.

A *special budget rate* may be most economical for people who need the telephone mainly for incoming calls. The basic charge covers incoming calls only; each outgoing call is charged in message units. There is no message-unit allowance.

If you need the telephone mostly for security and reassurance, this economy service could be for you; if you like to call friends and chat—stay away from it; the message units can pile up to a costly end-of-the-month surprise.

Not all telephone systems carry a budget rate, and even those who do keep rather quiet about it. If the operator claims never to have heard of it, ask for the supervisor to make sure you get competent and complete information. If they really don't feature the budget rate for incoming calls, there's another accommodation to lobby for.

The Bell System's Telephone Adapter

If you find new types of telephone receivers in coin phones preventing you from using your hearing aid as you did in the past, you are a victim of progress. The new receivers are supposed to give better service—but to you, they interfere with service.

☞ **Call the Business Office for information and booklet about the Adapter ($8.25), which enables wearers of hearing aids to use the new types of receivers in coin phones.**

Upon the urging of consumer groups, the Bell System has embarked on a program to make all coin telephones compatible with hearing aids that have the inductive telephone pickup switch. Meanwhile, it is the system's objective that in all public places, such as airports, railroad stations and bus terminals, at least one compatible phone be placed in each bank of public telephones.

☞ **Look for a booth that has a phone with a blue cap where the cord joins the receiver.**

When installing a new telephone or having a current phone serviced, be sure to request an old-style receiver that permits direct use of your hearing aid.

Special Booths

Wheelchair accommodations are now frequently found in at least one of a line of pay phone booths; removing the door leaves a 30-inch entrance; coin-slot height is 54 inches. This makes phoning a lot easier for people confined to a wheelchair. It's also convenient for children and some adults.

☞ **Impress on the sales representatives of the Classified Telephone Directory that they should suggest to advertisers in the Yellow Pages the inclusion of the accessibility symbol in their ads. Tell them that your fingers could "do the walking" on paper, but you'd also like to know where you can have access in person. An "ear" might symbolize captioned movie films.**

Telephone Complaints

Complaints against the telephone company and billing disputes can be directed to the Public Service Commission or an equivalent regulatory agency in your state.

If you are the argumentative type and want help in fighting the system, you'll get it from a book produced by one of the Ralph Nader–inspired groups:

A *Consumer's Guide to Telephone Service.* Complete information on how to challenge inaccurate phone bills; long distance telephone rates; connecting your own extension phones; new modular plugs, jacks and adapters, and more! New York Public Interest Research Group, Inc., 5 Beekman Street, Room 410, New York, N.Y. 10038. $1.95, check payable to NYPIRG.

GA MEANS "GO AHEAD"

TTYs, teletypewriters for deaf people, is a system which permits deaf individuals to communicate with others over the regular telephone system by typing. In the TTY (developed in 1964 by a deaf engineer), an electronic device connects two teleprinters by means of acoustic/inductive coupling to the standard telephone.

Deaf persons with TTYs generally have some form of visual signaling equipment to alert them when the telephone rings. They answer the phone by placing the telephone handset in a cradle on the acoustic coupler, turning on their TTY and typing out their identification, e.g., "Mary Jones here. GA."

TTYs give to deaf users freedom from dependence on children, relatives and neighbors in making telephone contacts. They also give them peace of mind in knowing that they can secure help in emergencies.

The present national network of teletypewriters consists of over 10,000 such stations, including over 400 schools and other organizations serving deaf people. Of the 410,000 pre-vocationally deaf people, however, less than 2 percent have teleprinters. *Teletypewriters for the Deaf* lists on only 120 pages subscribers in all fifty states, Canada, England, Israel and the Philippines.
Teletypewriters for the Deaf, P.O. Box 28332, Washington, D.C. 20005.

Several government agencies that list general information numbers for use by the public now also list TTY numbers.

The Federal Communications Commission installed a TV-phone system to make FCC information as accessible to the deaf as to anyone else in the community. For example, if the deaf person has a compatible teletypewriter in his/her home and wants to know something about connecting privately owned equipment to company-owned telephones, he/she should dial FCC's special number (202/632-6999) to receive a print-out. The system can also be used to complain to the FCC about telephones, television, radio or other communication systems regulated by the FCC.

Other government agencies are: the Internal Revenue Service (IRS), see p. 90; Amtrak (National Railway Passenger Corporation), see p. 229; The President's Committee on Employment of the Handicapped; the Office of Deafness and Communicative Disorders at HEW; and the National Visitors Center. The National Bureau of Standards and the General Accounting Office have installed TTY equipment for the use and benefit of their deaf employees.

Implementing Section 504 regulations that make *access* mandatory for all programs receiving federal funds, all agencies accessible to direct contact with the public may soon have TTYs as a matter of law.

Private business too will soon have to recognize that deaf people are potential customers. TTY phone number listings in the classified directories AND in the alphabetical listings will guide the purchasing power of deaf consumers to businesses that care enough for them to make the relatively small investment of a TTY phone.

If YOU are a deaf consumer, write to the presidents of stores, hotel chains, bus companies, air lines you would patronize if they made it possible for you to communicate with them. And tell your friends, relatives, colleagues to write, until business gets the message. (For where to find names of company executives, see p. 205.)

On April 19, 1977, then-Congressman Edward I. Koch (Dem.-N.Y.) introduced a bill "to provide for the use of telecommunication devices by the Senate and the House of Representatives to enable deaf persons and persons with speech impairments to engage in *toll-free* telephone communications with Members of the Congress."

In response to inquiries about the status of the bill a few months later, Congressman Koch wrote on August 11: "You will be pleased to learn that Senator Dole, who introduced my bill in the Senate, recently obtained such a device for the use of the Senate. Plans to install the device for a trial period are currently being developed. It is my hope that the House of Representatives will soon follow suit, and also retain this equipment."

(Congressman Koch was elected mayor of the city of New York on November 8, 1977. It can be hoped that as a mayor, he will be as sensitive to the needs of disabled citizens as he had been in his Congress days.)

Going one step further, Congresswoman Gladys Noon Spellman (Dem.-Md.) introduced on April 27, 1977, a bill "to provide for the installation of telecommunications devices for the deaf in agencies of Federal, State, and local governments, in offices of Members of Congress, and in other locations; this Act to be cited as the Deaf Services Act."

While Representative Spellman's bill is more comprehensive than the Koch-Dole bill, it is also more costly and does not include the word *toll-free*, which is important to TTY users, whose typed conversations consume more time than spoken ones. She is, however, quite right in demanding communication for deaf citizens with all government agencies.

Both bills have been referred jointly to the committees on Government Operations and House Administration. And there they sit. If they still do by the time you read this, write to your representatives and make clear that you want them to act on those bills, because it is services you need, not sleeping bills!

You may also write to the Honorable Frank Thompson, Chairman of the House Administrations Committee, H 326, The Capitol, Washington, D.C. 20515, requesting his support for the Spellman and Koch-Dole bills. Send copies of your letters to the sponsors of the bills, Congresswoman Gladys Noon Spellman, Longworth Office Building, Washington, D.C. 20515, and the Honorable Edward I. Koch, Mayor of the City of New York, City Hall, New York, N.Y. 10007. If you want to inquire about the current status of these—or any bills that interest you—call or write Legis, Washington, D.C. For address and phone number, see p. 83.

Some city and county police headquarters have TTY installations and forward emergency calls to fire departments and hospitals.

New York City has also introduced Fire/Police emergency call boxes on city streets, which persons who do not have speech or hearing capabilities can use by means of coded "tap" signals not known to the general public, to prevent misuse.

☛ If you wish to suggest such a system to your municipality, write for information to :
Community Relations Bureau of the N.Y.C. Fire Department, 110 Church Street, New York, N.Y. 10007.

Costs

Teletypewriter costs range from $50 (used machines) to $800 or more new. Complete installation for a TTY is from $250 and up. Costs after installation includes monthly telephone service charge, replacement of paper and ribbon, plus minimal maintenance.

There is, however, a problem if TTY users are charged the same monthly service charge as regular users. It is estimated that even between fast typists, conversations between TTY users take about ten times as long as the same spoken communication, resulting in much higher bills.

Directed by the Public Service Commission, in November 1977 the New York Telephone Company agreed to reduced charges for teletypewriters used by deaf persons. It is sad to report that this decision has not yet been implemented. It's being batted back and forth between the PSC, the telephone company and the courts. The argument of costs having to be distributed among all subscribers is again raised. Meanwhile, deaf subscribers pay exceedingly high telephone bills.

☛ You can help to hasten indecision and bureaucratic wrangling into action in your favor. Write to the Bell Telephone Company, your local telephone company, your local State Service Commission and enlist consumer action groups and your elected representatives in the good fight!

Braille phone TTYs, teletypewriters for deaf and blind persons, produce a Braille print-out and notify the user that he is being called by means of a small fan activated by the incoming signal, or by an impulse on a wrist-worn instrument. These installations are quite costly and not in wide use.

TV phone is a recently developed new concept in telephone communication. A small portable unit, clipped to the antenna of any TV set and plugged into an electric outlet, translates incoming electronic impulses, produced by the sender's keyboard, into letters and words visible on sender's and recipient's TV screens simultaneously.

"SK" means "Signing off"!

INTERPRETERS—FACILITATORS OF COMMUNICATION

In October 1975 a deaf man in Baltimore was sentenced to prison for a homicide he had allegedly committed. Later it was found out that, having an unqualified interpreter, the accused had never fully understood the court's proceedings. He was set free.

Today, sign-language interpreters are qualified professionals with established standards of skills and ethics. Several colleges have programs leading to a bachelor's degree in interpretation.

The Registry of Interpreters for the Deaf, Inc. (RID) is a national organization with over 52 chapters and a membership of 3,000. A program of national evaluation determines the skills of members. Certificates, awarded by the National Certificate Board, are valid for five years and must be renewed. The RID certifies interpreters in the following areas: expressive interpreting (EIC), expressive translating (ETC) and reverse skills (RSC). Interpreters who attain certification in all these areas may, if their scores are high enough, be awarded the Comprehensive Skills Certificates (CSC). Interpreters holding the CSC may apply additionally for specialist certificates. Currently, the only specialist certificate being offered is in the area of legal interpretation (LSC), but specialist certifications in other areas, e.g., educational, mental health, medical, artistic, religious, etc., are being planned.*

"What use is a doctor if you can't communicate with her or him?" asks Ruth Brown, communications teacher at the New York Society for the Deaf. "Skilled interpreters are needed to tell deaf patients what their doctors say, what medication they need, and to help them ask questions. The number of psychiatrists and therapists trained to work with deaf patients is also much smaller than the demand for such services," she adds, "but Medicaid will not pay for interpreting services."

"The Legal Interpreter is sworn in as an Officer of the Court," explains Professor Sternberg. "He is a facilitator of communications, not a friend to whom the client may reveal a confidence as in the lawyer-client relationship."

* "Teaching Deaf Students How to Purchase and Use Interpretation Services," by Robert M. Ingram, *Deaf American* (May 1977).

Legislation mandates the provision of interpretation services in judicial proceedings in at least half of the states, including several states with special commissions on the deaf. A bill before Congress, the Bilingual Courts Act, would provide for interpreters in all federal courts and perhaps in lesser courts as well.

In increasing numbers, interpreters are becoming more specialized, better educated, more aware of their roles as professionals and more visible on TV screens and at public events. In any program involving federal funds, their presence is mandated under the "access" provisions of Section 504 of the Rehabilitation Act of 1973.

Consumers of interpretation services must understand clearly that interpretation services are not free, but must be contracted in the same way as legal or other professional services. When a deaf consumer enters into a contract with an interpreter, he is purchasing a communication service. He is not purchasing a mother, a teacher, a helper or a chauffeur. The role of the interpreter is not to do things for the deaf consumer, but to allow the deaf consumer the opportunity of doing things for himself. The interpreter is the channel through which communication between deaf and hearing partners of the conversation flows. The deaf person speaks directly to the hearing person and insists that the hearing person speak directly to him. Neither communicator begins his sentences "Tell him . . ." or "Ask her . . ."

In cases where the interpreter will be compensated by a third party, the deaf person should confirm the arrangement. He must not expect the interpreter to seek reimbursement, but must seek as a consumer whatever funds are available through third parties, such as Vocational Rehabilitation, Medicaid, community service centers, relatives or other sources. Even then, the deaf consumer should make some contribution, however small, to the interpreter's fee. His payment not only takes responsbility for the purchase of the services, it also gives him the right to register a complaint when these services are not satisfactory.

The first option open to the consumer is to approach the interpreter with his complaint and try to work out an agreement satisfactory to all parties, or he may secure the services of another interpreter.

Complaints can also be made to the agency who provided the interpreter or to the National Review Board of the RID, which has the authority to recommend disciplinary action against members, when necessary.

For more details, read the quoted article by Robert M. Ingram in the May 1977 issue of the *Deaf American.*

RID publishes a directory which lists members by states, certified members, chapter officers and suggested reimbursement for professional services.

For further information concerning learning the language of signs, developing interpreting skills, establishing an interpreter training program, securing interpreting services at the local or national level, contact: Registry of Interpreters for the Deaf, Inc., P.O. Box 1339, Washington, D.C. 20013.

MAN'S BEST FRIEND

In the days before television newscasts, newsreels in movie theaters were preceded by a crowing rooster and the words "The Eyes and Ears of the World." Today, 25,000 blind and about 100 deaf people rely on the eyes and ears of well-educated, loyal animals to substitute for their own missing sight and hearing. To the blind, guide dogs give mobility and a more independent life. Deaf owners are alerted to the ringing of door bells or TTY phones; alarm clocks; fire, smoke or burglar alarms; and the crying of babies.

"Temperament qualities which we require in a guide dog," says Jeff Lock, director of Guiding Eyes for the Blind, a training school in New York State, "are soundness, tractability, overall willingness to please and acceptance of responsibility, together with a basically soft, sweet disposition, suitable for control by a blind person." Guiding Eyes runs its own breeding program, mostly Labrador and golden retrievers, and occasionally German shepherds. Young puppies are placed in foster homes for "socializing," before starting their intensive training for their work.

When the dog has learned absolute obedience and the proper sense of leadership, dog and blind person are brought together. Eleven times a year, blind people arrive for training classes from all parts of the United States and from abroad. During 26 days of training, the dog lives with the student, sleeps in his room and remains quietly under the dining-room table during meals. Together, student and dog face the realities of crossing streets, boarding buses, riding in elevators, shopping in stores, even attending church services—just about everything a sighted person does in the course of the day.

The cost of breeding and training the dog, transportation for the student, a month of instruction and living at the school run to about $4,000; the charge to the student, however, is only $150 and waived for students who cannot afford it. The program is maintained entirely by private donations.

The school stays in touch with their graduate-teams. When one shepherd dog became ill with colitis and had to be taken out three times a night, the owner was asked if he'd want to return the dog and train with a new one. "What's a friend for?" was the blind man's answer.

Write for full information to: Guiding Eyes for the Blind, Yorktown Heights, N.Y. 10598, or The Seeing Eye, Inc., Morristown, N.J. 07960, or ask a local agency for the blind about a training school nearer to your home.

Acceptance or Rejection of Master-Dog Team in Society?

A guide dog may be "man's best friend" and more, but not every human is the team's friend. Discrimination is still practiced by some people. Employers may not like dogs on their premises, restaurants won't allow dogs, landlords will not rent apartments and blind students can't live in dormitories with their guide dogs. Where access is denied to blind people because of their guide dogs, the law will have to remove such obstacles.

In 1976 New York State enacted a strong law to that effect. Specifying activities and places, the law summarizes:

"It shall be an unlawful discriminatory practice for any person to discriminate against a blind person on the basis of his use of a guide dog."

If you wish to submit a copy of this law to your legislature as an example, write to: New York State Senate, Albany, N.Y. 12224. Ask for Article 4-B, Sections 47-47-c of the Civil Rights Law, adopted June 29, 1976.

(See also "Guide Dogs on Common Carriers," p. 62, and "Canine Air Travelers," p. 233.)

Consumer Action

Andy Logue, perpetual advocate for rights of the blind, and his dog, Heath, were refused admission in a popular Times Square restaurant. Andy sued in Small Claims Court for violation of the Civil Rights Law. The restaurant was fined $500 and the owner invited Andy, his wife Ellen (the Social Security Administration and Con Edison fighter), plus Heath and Star, their guide dogs, to celebrate the victory in the restaurant's private dining room.

Andy also brought Heath with him when he checked into a New York City Hospital for surgery. A dog in a hospital? Wasn't there a rule against that? No, there wasn't, because the case was a first. Had the Department of Health been consulted? It had. No negative ruling either, because the request was unprecedented.

"Heath saves the nurses' time," Andy said, grinning. "Want to see how he walks me in the corridor?"

"And who walks Heath?"

"The nurses do," Andy admitted. "But the dog would be unhappy without me at home, and here he gives me emotional solace. Isn't that the best medicine for a patient?"

Right, Andy—right on!

Hearing Dogs

Hearing dogs are newcomers to the man-animal relationship. So far, the only place they are being trained is in Denver, under the auspices of the American Humane Association. Because the standard for hearing-dog service does not require particular breeds or sizes, many dogs in the program come from animal shelters. Instead of being destroyed for want of a home, they will be loved and needed by their deaf masters.

When Rin-Tin-Tin or Lassie performed in front of movie cameras, they obeyed hand signals by their trainers, who were out of the camera's view. Hearing dogs also are trained for hand signals, for deaf people who have speech difficulties. A large doll and babies' taped crying are used to teach the dog to alert deaf parents. The ringing of an alarm clock makes him jump on the bed and wake his sleeping master with a loving lick.

Before being delivered to his assigned family, the dog gets a few days of additional training. Bumper heard taped crying of his future family's baby, and Banjo had to be conditioned to living with cats, his new family's pets. Happy, on his way to a newly married deaf and blind couple, was trained to lead one person to the other on the command "Find!"

Agnes McGrath, chief trainer, delivers the dogs to their new masters and stays nearby for a few days until the relationship has been established. Identified by a bright-orange collar and an identity photograph, hearing dogs may travel with their deaf masters in the passenger sections of airplanes. (See "Canine Air Travelers," p. 233.)

Training and delivery of dog run to about $1,800, but no charges are made to recipients. The demand for hearing dogs far exceeds the supply. The American Humane Association hopes that foundations will keep the program going.

☞ **If you wish to be placed on a waiting list, write to: Robert J. White, Administrator of Special Programs, American Humane Association, P.O. Box 1266, Denver, Colo. 80201.**

HOW TO COMPLAIN-SUCCESSFULLY!

"An ounce of prevention is better than a pound of cure" may soon read "A dekagram of prevention is better than a kilogram of cure." (100 dekagram = 1 kilogram)

Either way, *preventive* consumerism will save you money, time and aggravation. You know the principles of wise buymanship—comparison-shop, gather all available information, deal with responsible suppliers. However, if you've done all this and yet are dissatisfied with a product or service purchased, by all means, exercise your RIGHT TO BE HEARD!

You are entitled to redress of a legitimate grievance. Reputable retailers and manufacturers prefer intelligently registered complaints brought *to* them to disgruntled gossip *about* them. Sound business depends on repeat customers; only trick artists want to make a one-time fast buck and disappear into thin air.

No buyer expects to run into trouble with his purchase, but just in case . . .

☞ **Always save all documents pertaining to a transaction: sales receipt, contract, warranty. Keep them in a safe place.**

In case of disputes, emotional outbursts won't help. Documented, calm, factual presentation of your case will get most reasonable complaints adjusted by responsible business people. So eager are suppliers to retain their customers that they often staff an entire complaint department, frequently called Consumer Affairs Division. Management watches this department carefully. They want to know what consumers complain about and how fast problems are resolved.

For added self-policing by peer groups, many an industry has formed a Consumer Action Panel, which acts like an arbitrator if customer and company can't agree. Where no such industry panel exists, trade associations or a Better Business Bureau may act on your behalf. Remember that though these organizations are supported by their membership, they will try to achieve redress from individual companies for the sake of overall consumer good will for their industry or business in general.

Government agencies should only be approached after business sources haven't provided satisfaction. State or local consumer affairs departments may work on many complaints with limited staff; it may take a while until they get to yours. Spectacularly resolved cases presented on your TV consumer program may be few among many they received.

Resort to government and/or state and local consumer affairs agencies only after you have tried the retailer–manufacturer–trade association route.

Complaints about products and services for special needs will follow the same steps. Here, in addition to peer pressure exercised by trade associations, backup of your complaint by agencies, rehabilitation centers, physicians and therapists may be useful. Later steps, such as recourse to consumer groups, government agencies and political support should be as effective as in all complaints about any other consumer goods and services.

Files of government consumer agencies contain fewer complaints from disabled consumers than statistical averages would warrant. On the other hand, complaints voiced at public hearings reveal the catastrophic impact that malfunctioning and slow or unsatisfactory repairs of assistive devices can have on mobility and lives of disabled consumers. Could it be that disabled consumers are more inhibited in registering their complaints than other people? If you have been one of those silent sufferers—speak up!

Follow the steps outlined below for your complaints about any consumer goods and services, for your special needs or for your nondisabled self:

1. Make sure you have read and followed all instructions: check the warranties to see what is and what isn't covered.
2. Return to the salesperson; it helps to know his or her name.
3. Speak to the manager; if neither the salesperson nor the manager will listen, the president of the company may; ask for name and mailing address. Many companies have consumer affairs representatives. Write to them.
4. If you don't get a reply within a reasonable time (tops: one month), write to the president of the company, certified mail, return receipt requested. Send copies to local, state or federal consumer agencies, TV consumer personalities or consumer columnists. Indicate this on your letter by adding in the lower left-hand corner:

> cc: Department of Consumer Affairs
> District Attorney
> Congressperson
> Ralph Nader

These are just examples; use your own imagination. You'll be surprised how fast you'll hear from the company.

5. Write to the trade association, Better Business Bureau or national Industry Consumer Action Panel.

6. Inform a local consumer action group, government consumer affairs department, district attorney.

7. Write to your representative in city or state government or in Congress. Don't bait with your vote; just ask for intervention. The politician will get the message; so will the company.

8. If no one else can help you, take your case to a Small Claims Court. You do not need a lawyer; plead your own case. You do not have to lose a day from work; courts sit at night. You do not have to pay a large fee; cost per case is a few dollars. Upper limit of cases handled is usually $1,000. If you use a sign-language interpreter, be sure he or she is certified (see p. 198).

Where to Find the Names and Addresses to Write To

In your local library: *Moody's Industrial Manual; Poor's Register of Corporations; Standard Directory of Advertisers; Million Dollar Directory; Dun and Bradstreet Middle Market Directory. Directory, State, County and City Government Consumer Offices,* Office of Consumer Affairs, HEW, Washington, D.C. 20201.

Or save wear and tear and invest $1.25 in *Complaint Directory for Consumers,* issued annually by the Credit Union National Association, Inc.

"Everybody's Money," Box 431 B, Madison, Wis. 53701. The booklet lists names, addresses, phone numbers of industries, government agencies, consumer organizations, U.S. senators and representatives—just about everyone you'll need if you want to complain successfully.

For names of consumer affairs officers in companies, who will attend to your complaints and suggestions, write to SOCAP (Society of Consumer Affairs Professionals in Business), 1430 K Street, N.W., Washington, D.C. 20005.

What Your Complaint Must Contain:

- Your name, address, zip code, telephone number. (Where you can be reached between 9 A.M. and 5 P.M.)
- Name, address, zip code, telephone number of vendor.
- Description of complaint. Brief, factual. No emotional commentary, please!

- Enclose *copies* (never originals!) of pertinent documents: sales receipt, contract, canceled check.
- What you want to receive: refund; exchange; repair.

Write on standard-size paper; small, personal notes can get lost in a pile of mail. Type, if at all possible, or have someone type the letter for you. Handwritten letters take time to decipher and can wind up at the bottom of that pile of mail. Send your letter by certified mail, return receipt requested. Keep a copy of your letter and receipt in a safe place; you may need it to prove later to a government agency that you've tried previous steps with the company.

On the other hand, if you are satisfied with product, service or complaint resolution—write that too. Business people will appreciate hearing from you when you are pleased, not only when you're angry.

THE FINE ART OF FRAUD

All kinds of schemes have been thought up by con men who want to make a fast buck, and new frauds are being perpetrated every day against unsuspecting victims. On preceding pages you've been warned against several types of frauds related to the topics discussed, door-to-door sales, mail orders, home improvement and perhaps mail-order insurance.

The United States Postal Service reported that consumers lost $514 million in 1976 due to mail fraud. Figures proved that Americans were as gullible as ever. The losses were $110 million greater than in the previous year. The number-one complaint involved failure to deliver mail-order merchandise. Victims ranged from persons looking for quick money investments in land or stock, to others shopping for a variety of "vanity" items, such as blemish removers, diet pills and breast enlargers.

Here are just a few examples of the many schemes in circulation:

Charity rackets: Donate only to causes or organizations registered at local authorities. Don't get taken in by the sympathy approach, in person or by mail.

Correspondence schools: Before you enroll in a course that promises jobs to graduates, find out if you will really be able to find employment in the field.

Extra income claims: Never rush into a get-rich-quick scheme, especially if you have to "invest" in an inventory.

Fake contests: When you "win" a prize, it should not cost you money to collect.

Health claims: Don't buy false hopes; check with your doctor or a clinic about "miracle cures."

Phony inheritance schemes: You may be asked to send money for information which could help you claim an estate of considerable value left by someone with your last name. Chances are, many others with the same surname have received the same offer. If you really are a lucky heir, the estate's lawyers will find you without Mr. In-Between.

Referral selling: Be wary when you are told you will receive a discount by providing the seller with names of friends who may buy the product. The salesperson has probably made this offer to everyone in the area, and you are stuck with a contract for an overpriced gadget that you didn't need in the first place.

Withdrawing money from your bank account: Never, never withdraw money from your account for anyone who says he's investigating a problem or examining accounts, or claims he's a government agent, without first notifying your bank. Your bank is aware of such schemes and will tell you what to do.

Moving

Should you plan to move into another state, watch out. "Weight bumping"—the illegal adding of weight to the moving of household goods—takes at least $20 million annually from the pockets of U.S. consumers who move across state lines. The Interstate Commerce Commission (ICC) said 10 percent of the one million household moves each year result in families being "victimized by a dishonest minority of movers that may add bricks, iron bars or even people to moving vans when they are weighed."

Before contracting with a company, check with the ICC, the Better Business Bureau or your Consumer Affairs Office if it has on file any complaints against the company you consider choosing. None of these agencies will recommend a company to you, but they will warn you if you are about to deal with one that has a bad record of complaints against it.

Interstate Commerce Commission, Washington, D.C. 20423, Household Goods Branch: 202/275-7852.

Complaints about household movers, toll-free: 800-432-4537, Florida only; 800-424-9312, all other states.

Looking for Some Ways to Supplement Your Income?

There's a delightful book that may give you suggestions for occupations you never even thought of: *On Your Own: 99 Alternatives to a 9-to-5 Job,* by Kathy Matthews (New York: Vintage Books). $3.45.

But beware of the "work-at-home ripoffs." Here, quoted with the author's permission, are some pointers on how to avoid them.

How an advertiser will tip you off to a fraud:

- He will require money for instructions or merchandise before telling you how the plan operates.
- He will promise you huge, incredible, astonishing amounts of money.
- He will never offer you regular salaried employment.
- He will insist that experience or special skills are completely unnecessary.
- He will assure you that there is a large guaranteed market for your works.

If you suspect an ad is fraudulent, or even if you have no suspicions but want to be cautious before responding to a work-at-home ad, do the following before you send any money: check with postal inspectors, the local Better Business Bureau, the state labor department and any consumer protection agencies you can think of. All of these agencies serve as watchdogs against consumer fraud and will have on file any complaints lodged against specific advertisers. They will be able to advise you on the particular ad you want to answer.

Are you intrigued by the topic of consumer frauds? You'll find any number of books about it in your local library. It seems that quite a few writers earn honest money by warning innocent consumers against dishonest cheats. Better read about it than be a victim of consumer frauds!

IV. RECREATION

8. ARTS, LIBRARIES, SPORTS

THE ARTS–ACCESSIBLE TO EVERYONE

Leisure-time activities have become the nation's number one industry, as measured by people's spending. Latest figures show that Americans spent more than $160 billion on leisure and recreation in 1977. Sports activities draw more than 700 million participants a year. Attendance at sporting events has increased by 25 million during the past three years. Seventy-eight million Americans visited museums in 1976, and 62 million attended at least one performance of live theater. More than a billion tickets were sold to films. For millions, recreation is largely sedentary, watching programs on television.

In the fact of such a national boom, it is difficult to believe that any group of people could be denied access to the arts. Nevertheless, architectural, attitudinal and admission barriers deny millions of handicapped citizens their right to enjoy and participate in our country's rich cultural resources. Aware of this inequity, Congress, state legislatures, the courts, and now Section 504, have decreed that no public service or facility may discriminate against the handicapped person no matter what or how severe his handicap. This means that, for instance, if a museum's lectures, art education programs, displays or performances are open to the public, then these programs must also be made accessible by means of special material or equipment to the blind and deaf if there is a demand.

Today virtually hundreds of organizations of and for the handicapped are challenging institutions and businesses that do not provide equal opportunity for handicapped citizens. Museums are particularly vulnerable to legal action and government sanctions because they are public institutions supported by public taxes and contributions.

Most of the current challenges against cultural institutions involve simple accessibility. Obviously, museums can no longer ignore the accessibility issue. A lack of funds is not an excuse for inaccessible programs and facilities. The courts have ruled repeatedly that equal access for the handicapped must be accomplished even at the expense of regular program funding.

The most successful programs have always incorporated handicapped people in the earliest planning stages. Many museums have advisory councils that include the handicapped and a broad cross section of the local community. Careful planning requires time, thought, ingenuity and a great deal of information about user needs, alternative solutions, technical assistance and funding sources.*

A national center has been designed to help artists, architects, administrators and teachers develop new approaches to arts accessibility. The National Endowment for the Arts and Educational Facilities Laboratories are cooperatively sponsoring a "consumer demand" information service providing information that can be used to make arts programs and facilities more accessible to handicapped persons. Enrollment in the service is open to everyone interested in arts and the handicapped, and there is no fee.

☛ **You are invited to make suggestions for topics that you would like the service to research. Address your request, and write for publications, to: Arts, Box 2040, Grand Central Station, New York, N.Y. 10017.**

We're pleased that you are interested in making the arts accessible to everyone . . .
    Arts programs and facilities that have been designed to overcome barriers to children, the elderly, and the handicapped.
Materials from the National Arts and the Handicapped Information Service: Architectural Accessibility; Arts for the Blind and Visually Impaired; Technical Assistance; 1977/78 Conferences.
Arts and the Handicapped: An Issue of Access. Over 150 examples of how arts programs and facilities have been made accessible to the handicapped,

---

* Excerpted from "The Case for Accessibility," by Larry Molloy, director of the National Arts and the Handicapped Information Service. Reprinted from *Museum News* (1977), American Association of Museums, 1055 Thomas Jefferson Street, N.W., Washington, D.C. 20007.

from tactile museums to halls for performing arts, and for all types of handicaps. $4.

Art on the Road

A traveling exhibit, produced jointly by the National Arts and the Handicapped Information Service, was exhibited at the White House Conference for Handicapped Individuals in May 1977. In beautiful photographs and text in letters 5/8 inches high, the exhibit presents five evolving levels of awareness: (1) architectural accessibility, (2) program and communications accessibility, (3) access to all the arts for handicapped people, (4) benefits of accessible arts to the nonhandicapped public, and (5) careers in the arts—a focus on artists whose work bring new perspectives to the arts.

The fifteen 8' by 3' panels comprising the exhibit are available to museums, schools and art centers.

For information, write to: **Charles Wyrick, Director, Delaware Art Museum, 2301 Kentmere Parkway, Wilmington, Del. 19806.**

ACCESS TO THEATERS AND CONCERT HALLS

Accessibility will not present a problem in new structures, where it is incorporated in the design and a number of aisle seats are removable, to make space for patrons in wheelchairs. Older theaters, however, frequently cite fire laws as an excuse to refuse or complicate admission. They claim that such fire laws prohibit placement of wheelchairs in aisles.

Placed in undesirable locations at rear or side of theater, patrons in wheelchairs are nevertheless required to pay full admission price for orchestra seats they do not occupy. Surely, making some aisle seats removable so that wheelchairs could be placed there is no major alteration. Lacking that, patrons in wheelchairs should at least not be charged more for admission than standees, who do not occupy seats either. What fire laws would such accommodations violate?

Verify the claims with your local fire department.
Write letters to the editors of your local newspapers, complaining about the discrimination.

Alert a reporter or feature writer to do a piece on the problem in the Sunday theater section of a metropolitan or local newspaper.

Perhaps the theater critic of your local TV station could discuss the issue on an evening when he doesn't have to review an opening.

Radio essayists may appreciate your suggestion for a topic that has appeal for handicapped and nondisabled theatergoers.

Send copies of your letters to theater owners, just in case they missed the broadcasts!

Russian, Chinese or Amplified Sound?

Visitors to the United Nations Building in New York City are treated to a fascinating experience. When a meeting is in progress, one can put on earphones attached to delegates' seats and dial for simultaneous translation of the speakers' words into any of the official UN languages. Many people are familiar with another version of the same technology at work: in airplanes, your choice on the earphones is between classic or light music, news or the in-flight-movie sound.

What "major" technical installation would be required to equip several theater seats with earphones to amplify sound for hearing-impaired patrons? A very minor technical problem indeed, but it would make live theater accessible to art lovers whose hearing needs more technical support than their own hearing aids.

Include this topic in your lobbying campaign for accessibility. It'll make for a more complete story and have a better chance of getting written or spoken about.

Canine Audiences

Guide dogs may not be excluded from museums and theaters in states where laws prohibit discrimination against users of guide dogs. Generally, canine appreciation of the proceedings is confined to a quiet snooze under the master's seat. Not so during a recent show on Broadway. "A Howling Night on Broadway," *New York* magazine (August 1977), describes a hilarious incident:

> It's a doggy tale, all right. At a recent performance of the Broadway Comedy "Same Time, Next Year," two blind men were seated in the front row, along with their Seeing-Eye dogs, which were lying under the

seats. The dogs were well behaved throughout the play until one of the final scene changes.

To indicate the passage of time, music or radio excerpts of each period are played—including Richard Nixon's Checkers speech. When Nixon's voice came over the loudspeakers, the dogs began howling and barking. The audience and actors were convulsed with laughter. After Nixon's voice stopped, the dogs stopped too, and were quiet for the rest of the show.

Films for the Hearing-Impaired

Captioned Hollywood films are available on loan, at no cost from the Bureau of Education for the Handicapped. Any group of six or more deaf adults need just fill out an application form to receive one of these captioned films for their enjoyment. The reels hold 16-mm. film, suitable for home-movie projectors.

Contact: **Captioned Films for the Deaf Distribution Center, 5034 Wisconsin Avenue, N.W., Washington D.C. 20016.**

LIBRARIES ARE NOT MADE; THEY GROW

Libraries are more than collections of books and magazines. The library is also a natural information place for its community. Libraries always have furnished information to the public by searching among the books, magazines and other printed materials on their shelves for answers to citizens' in-person and phone queries. They also have been keeping pace with the nonprint media explosion by adding films, film strips, audio-cassettes, mini-computers and microfiche to their collections.

For readers with disabilities, libraries perform yet another service: they create access to the world of thought for people whose physical limitations may otherwise exile them to an intellectual wasteland.

LIBRARIES—FOR MORE THAN BOOKS

Under the Library Services and Construction Act (LSCA), Library Information and Referral Service Centers are springing up around the country to answer citizens' questions on almost anything from "abandoned houses" all the way down the alphabet through "youth counseling to zoning." The service is a catalyst between those in need of information and those who can supply it.

Modern life is complex, and information can be difficult to obtain. Information needs are felt at all levels of society regardless of a person's social condition or level of intellectual achievement. The public library, its branches within walking or driving distance, or as near as the phone, can answer the greatest number of questions for the average person. Queries such as "Where do I look for a job?" "How can I start a dude ranch?" or "What should I do for my sick pet lizard?" can all be answered at the library.

Most current Information and Referral (I & R) programs serve disadvantaged neighborhoods because it is there that the information gap is widest. But eventually the service should be made available to every neighborhood, reaching into community grass roots, with backup resources at the central library or county or state centers to assist with the more complex queries.*

Check out your own public library to see if an I & R service exists or is being planned.

Does your library have reserved parking spaces for wheelchair users? Experience has taught some libraries that these spaces are more respected by members of the public when they are designated by the International Symbol of Access. Suggest the idea to your local library!

LIBRARIES FOR SPECIAL-BOOK READERS

Limited eyesight need not take away the joy of reading. A free national library service is available to all Americans with disabilities that prevent them from holding or reading a book. Whether a person cannot see, or hold a book, or turn its pages, whether the disability is permanent or temporary— for whatever the reason—the Library of Congress has a free program, administered by the Division for the Blind and Physically Handicapped, to help that individual read books. The division provides books on records, open-reel tape and cassettes—called "Talking Books"—as well as books in Braille. Phonographs with special adaptations and, on a limited priority basis, cassette

* "Your Library: Neighborhood Ombudsman," by Eleanor Touhey Smith and Paula Winnick. *American Education*, U.S. Department of HEW, Office of Education (November 1976). Reprint: U.S. Government Printing Office, Washington, D.C. 20402. (35 cents; minimum charge of $1 for each mail order).

players are provided on free loan. Accessories supplied on request include earphones, pillowphones, and remote- and speed-control units. Appropriation by House and Senate for fiscal year 1978 is $28,720,700.

This national program is administered through a network of cooperating libraries that serve readers in specific geographic locations. Fifty-four regional and nearly a hundred subregional (local) libraries circulate the material to eligible borrowers. Approximately 478,000 readers, both children and adults, are served through the program. Of this number, 20,000 readers borrow Braille, 428,000 borrow materials in recorded formats, and an additional 30,000 borrow large-type materials. Over 12 million items per year are circulated to readers in the United States and its territories, as well as to American citizens temporarily living abroad.

Available to individuals or institutions, these free services can be obtained by submitting a certified eligibility form, either to the division or to one of its cooperating regional libraries. Eligibility forms are available upon request.

Upon certification, eligible readers will receive from their regional library a catalogue of books and magazines currently available, and detailed information as to ordering and returning reading material by *free* mail. Talking-book readers will receive phonographs and free copies of *Talking Book Topics*, a bimonthly publication, announcing the latest available selections. *Talking Book Topics* also includes a flexible phonograph disc on which the content of the magazine is recorded.

Readers who prefer Braille materials may request the bimonthly *Braille Book Review*, which is published in both print and Braille.

Specialists at the division select materials to be made into Talking Books or Braille books. The selections include thousands of titles, both fiction and nonfiction. Seventy magazines are available, including *Harper's*, *National Geographic*, *Good Housekeeping*, *Sports Illustrated* and *Jack and Jill*. Current best sellers, classic novels, mysteries, poetry, essays, the Bible, history, biography, travel and Westerns are among the choices available to readers. How-to-do-it books are in demand; print/Braille and other special-format books are popular with very young children and with visually handicapped parents of young children. A summary of the bills affecting handicapped persons that were submitted to the 94th Congress has also been produced in cassette form. A similar compilation of bills submitted to the current Congress is being planned. Talking Books are also produced in foreign languages. Current emphasis is on Spanish, the language which is much in demand by users of the division's services.

The music collection consists of a large selection of Braille music, music scores in large type, recorded music books and texts, elementary instruction on cassette for piano, organ and guitar, and demonstrations and discussions of music subjects on discs and cassettes. Braille and recorded music periodicals are also available.

Request: "Library Resources for the Blind & Physically Handicapped," 1977. A Directory of DBPH Network Libraries and Machine Lending Agencies Division for the Blind and Physically Handicapped, Washington, D.C. 20542.

Questions on various aspects of blindness and physical handicaps may be sent to the division or to any network library. This service is available without charge to individuals, organizations and libraries.

"Reference Circulars" are available from the Library of Congress, Division for the Blind and Physically Handicapped, Washington, D.C. 20542, on selected topics, including:

Aids for Handicapped Readers (1972)
Bibles in Special Media (1973)
Blind People in the Teaching Profession (1973)
Braille Instruction and Writing Equipment (1974)
Closed Circuit Television Reading Devices for the Visually Handicapped (1977)
Closed Circuit Television Systems for the Visually Handicapped (1974)
Commercial Sources of Spoken Word Cassettes (1973)
Directory of Local Radio Services for the Blind and Physically Handicapped (1976)
Library Services to the Blind and Physically Handicapped (1975)
Magazines in Special Media (1976)
National Organizations Concerned with the Visually and Physically Handicapped (1974)
Reading Materials in Large Type (1975)
Sources of Children's Book/Record, Book/Cassette, and Print/Braille Combinations (1974)

The division trains and certifies volunteers in Braille transcription and in Braille proofreading. In one year, nearly five hundred volunteers became Braillists, tape narrators or Braille proofreaders. Thousands of volunteers are actively engaged in producing books for libraries or individual readers. Approximately 3,000 Telephone Pioneers (senior or retired telephone-industry workers) volunteer their time and skills to the maintenance and repair of playback equipment.

☞ **If you have a pleasant voice and good diction, and your mobility impairment leaves you some spare time that other people may spend in physical exercise, why not exercise your vocal chords as tape narrator?**

Additional sources of materials for low or no-vision reading:

Magazines of special interest (e.g., religion) National Braille Press, Inc., 88 St. Stephen Street, Boston, Mass. 02115.

Choice Magazine Listening, 14 Maple Street, Port Washington, N.Y. 11050. A bimonthly audio anthology, available at subscription, free of charge. The best articles, fiction and poetry, chosen from over fifty current periodicals, including the *Wall Street Journal,* the New York *Times,* the *New Republic,* are read by professional voices onto 8 rpm phonograph records, which is the speed of the Library of Congress, free on permanent-loan record players.

College textbooks in Braille for blind students, in the fields of the sciences, mathematics and foreign languages, are produced at the NBA Braille Book Bank, operated entirely by volunteers, completely nonprofit.

☞ **For information, contact:**
National Braille Association, Inc., 85 Godwin Avenue, Midland Park, N.J. 07432.

SPORTS FOR DISABLED ATHLETES

"Stoke Mandeville, England, the sports resort capital of the world, hosted a very successful 25th International Wheelchair Games from July 24–30 1977," reports *Sports 'n Spokes* in its September/October 1977 issue. "Thirty-four countries from around the globe vied for the prestigious Gold, Silver, and Bronze medals.

"The U.S. team nailed down 37 gold, 21 silver and 11 bronze medals while excelling in all events of the international meet."

Such a report may surprise nonhandicapped readers, who think disabled athletes are confined to the traditional aquatic sports, popularized by a great disabled man, President Franklin D. Roosevelt.

Disabled readers know better! Newly disabled people, however, may yet have to hear about the many athletic opportunities open to them.

Write for: "Recreation is for Handicapped People" and "News-letter," the Committee on Recreation and Leisure, the President's Committee on Employment of the Handicapped, Washington, D.C. 20210.

WHEELCHAIR SPORTS

Wheelchair sports began in the United States in 1946, when disabled World War II veterans started forming wheelchair basketball teams, adapting the rules of regulation basketball to fit their own needs. War-injured paraplegics were soon joined by those with many other kinds of disabilities, and the wheelchair sports movement was under way.

In the years that followed, adaptations of sporting events for wheelchair competition have added archery, bowls, table tennis, shotput and swimming, dartchery, discus, wheelchair slalom, precision javelin, weight lifting, the Individual Medley and the Pentathlon.

In 1958 the National Wheelchair Association was founded to organize and govern wheelchair sports in the United States. Membership in this association is open to all men and women wheelchair athletes, and to officials and coaches, either involved or interested in wheelchair sports, as well as affiliate members of general interest. Members range in age from 13 to 65.

For more information, contact:

National Wheelchair Athletic Association, 40–24 62nd Street, Woodside, New York, N.Y. 11377.

National Wheelchair Basketball Association, 110 Seaton Building, University of Kentucky, Lexington, Ky. 40506.

American Wheelchair Bowling Association, 2635 N.E. 19th Street, Pompano Beach, Fla. 33062.

"Sports 'n Spokes," The Magazine for Wheelchair Sports and Recreation, 6043 North Ninth Avenue, Phoenix, Ariz. 85013. Bimonthly; $4 annually.

BLIND BOWLERS AND "BEEPING" SPORTS

Two thousand members of the American Blind Bowlers Association meet annually for their National Tournament. Competing are teams from as far as Hawaii and Canada, male and female, from ages 18 to 70. Some bowlers are partly sighted, but for the competition, each team must have at least one totally blind member.

☞ **Contact: American Blind Bowler's Association, 150 North Bellaire Avenue, Louisville, Ky. 40206.**

Vision-impaired bowlers are oriented for their starting position by guide rails; another bowling aid which uses lights and raised prongs on a panel lets them know which pins remain standing. "Touch and Tel-a-Pin" was recently invented by one of the Telephone Pioneers, who are also responsible for some of the "beeping" sports for blind children and adults.

Initiated by a "beeping" softball with an electronic beeper and amplifier buried inside, aids were developed which enable blind children to share the experience of team sports. Beeping cone-shaped bases, a fan-shaped field open up the world of leagues, playoffs and mini–World Series. Audio basketball laced with bells and played against a backboard wired for sound; "sona disc" audible hockey puck; a beeping horseshoe game; a beeping putting device for blind golfers; an audio ring-toss game for blind and brain-damaged children are some of the devices that open athletic group experiences to blind participants.

A versatile spinoff from the audio sports program is the "Cricket," a battery-powered, highly directional beeping unit which serves as an audio beacon for cycling, boating, hiking or cross-country skiing.

☞ **See p. 157 for "Telephone Pioneers" and how to get in touch with them through your local Business Telephone Operator.**

HAPPY LANDINGS!

On May 19, 1976, at the First National Fly-In of Wheelchair Aviators in Denver, Colo., the Federal Aviation Administration presented a Certificate of Commendation to William H. Blackwood, who led the Fly-In. Mr. Blackwood, a paraplegic pilot, a licensed flight instructor and FAA Accident Prevention Counselor, lost the use of his legs in 1962 when he was ejected from a crashing Air Force plane. He received the commendation for designing portable hand controls which paraplegic pilots can install on general aviation aircraft, avoiding the costly construction of specially built adaptations.

According to the Federal Aviation Administration, there are 780,408 licensed pilots in the United States. Dr. Charles Booze, of the Airmen's Certification Branch of the FAA's Aeronautical Center in Oklahoma City, supplied these (January 1, 1977) statistics about licensed pilots with disabilities: 4,855 are either legally blind in one eye or are actually missing an eye; 334 had polio at some time in the past; 531 had leg amputations, 175 miss an arm, 60 had a foot amputated; 23 airmen are deaf; almost 2,000 have a waiver because of impaired hearing.

Airline pilots? No. Flying sports enthusiasts? You bet!

For information, contact: Federal Aviation Administration, Department of Transportation, Washington, D.C. 20591; tel.:202/426-1960.

SPECIAL OLYMPICS

The Special Olympics is the world's largest sports and recreation program for the mentally retarded. More than 600,000 young athletes participate. At least 20,000 communities in the United States support Special Olympics activities. There are active programs in over 85 percent of the counties in the United States.

Many other countries are joining Special Olympics, such as Australia, Belgium, the Bahamas, Brazil, Canada, El Salvador, France, Germany, Hong Kong, Mexico, Okinawa and the Philippines.

Special Olympics is open to all mentally retarded, age 8 or older, and aims at improving physical fitness, emotional well-being and social adjustment. Ten official sports are offered—track and field, swimming, diving, gymnastics, floor hockey, basketball, ice skating, bowling, volleyball and wheelchair events. Participation is encouraged in many other worthwhile sports. International Games are held every four years.

"Families Play to Grow" supplements Special Olympics. It is a way for special children of any age to enjoy a regular program of play and sports with their families. Special Olympics was created and is sponsored by the Joseph P. Kennedy, Jr., Foundation.

🖎 **Printed materials and films can be obtained by writing to: Eunice Kennedy Shriver, President, Special Olympics, Inc., 1701 K Street, N.W., Washington, D.C. 20006.**

Special Olympics Instruction Manual. 138 pp. Published jointly by the American Alliance for Health, Physical Education and Recreation and the Joseph P. Kennedy, Jr., Foundation, 1201 16th Street, N.W., Washington, D.C. 20036. $2.25.

SCOUTING PROGRAMS

Scouting is for all youth. Charters are issued to community organizations to operate scout packs, scout troops, and explorer units that provide a program for handicapped youth both within and outside of institutions.

🖎 **For information and guidance, write to: Education Relationships Service, Boy Scouts of America, North Brunswick, N.J. 08902.**

Available manuals for leaders:

Scouting for the Physically Handicapped, No. 3039
Scouting for the Mentally Retarded, No. 3058
Scouting for the Deaf, No. 3060
Scouting for the Visually Handicapped, No. 3063
All above: Supply Division, Boy Scouts of America, North Brunswick, N.J. 08902

Braille, Talking Books, cassettes and large-print editions of scouting literature:

On cassette: *Scout Handbook;* Selected merit-badge pamphlets
In Braille: *Scout Handbook* (4 volumes); *Boys' Life* magazine; Merit-badge pamphlets (all subjects); Cub Scout books—Wolf, Bear, Webelos
On records: Merit-badge pamphlets (all subjects)
In large print: *Scout Handbook* (3 volumes)

For *Scout Handbook,* and Cub Scout books in Braille and large print (for sale), write to: American Printing House for the Blind, 1839 Frankfort Avenue, Louisville, Ky. 40206.

For *Boys' Life* magazine in Braille, write to: Clovernook Printing House for the Blind, 7000 Hamilton Avenue, Cincinnati, Ohio 45231.

For merit-badge pamphlets on records (on loan), write to: Recording for the Blind, Inc., 215 E. 58th Street, New York, N.Y. 10022.

9. BARRIER-FREE TRAVEL

BARRIER-FREE TRAVEL INFORMATION

The world has opened up for disabled travelers. Airlines, railroads, interstate buses, highways, accommodations, places of interest are becoming accessible and willing to serve this newly emerging sector of the traveling public. Whether you travel independently or in a group, preparation is the key to a successful trip. It pays to investigate carefully every detail of your intended journey: the carrier, tour operator, travel agent, accessibility en route and at your destination. You may be able to get a refund for an ill-fitting garment, but you can't return a spoiled vacation. Besides, anticipation and planning are half the fun. Reserve your resilience for the unexpected which no amount of planning can eliminate. Plenty of help is available to guide you in your research.

The United States Travel Service (USTS), the tourism branch of the Department of Commerce, reports that the federal and state governments, the travel industry, and parks and museums across the country have made a concerted effort to make transportation and tourist sites accessible to disabled individuals.

You will find information on areas of your interest in the publications listed below.

National Park Guide for the Handicapped #2405-0286. Superintendent of Documents, U.S. Government Printing Office, Washington, D.C. 20402. Accessibility of area by motor vehicles, attractions with paved walks and roadways, sites where signs are available in Braille. 40 cents.

Highway Rest Areas for Handicapped Travelers. The President's Committee on Employment of the Handicapped, Washington, D.C. 20210. Lists nearly 400 accessible rest stops in 49 states.

A List of Guidebooks for Handicapped Travelers. The President's Committee on Employment of the Handicapped, Washington, D.C. 20210. A listing of 86 cities in USA, Canada and some European countries to whom to write for the local guidebooks.

The Wheelchair Traveler, by Douglass R. Annand (author is paraplegic). Ball Hill Road, Milford, N.H. 03055. Contains over 3,500 listings from 50 states, Canada, Mexico, Puerto Rico, more; lists hotels, motels, restaurants and sightseeing attractions that are particularly usable by the handicapped traveler, whether ambulatory with a bad heart, amputee, arthritic or in a wheelchair. $4.95; add postage: 65 cents third class; $1 first class.

Easy Wheelin' in Minnesota, by Robert R. Peters, One Timberglade Road, Bloomington, Minn. 55437. A Wheelchair Accessibility Guidebook, made available as a public service by Education Services Department, the Minneapolis *Star* and the Minneapolis *Tribune,* 425 Portland Avenue, Minneapolis, Minn. 55488.

Vacationlands New York State. Supplement for Handicapped and Senior Citizens. The Easter Seal Society, 2 Park Avenue, New York, N.Y. 10016. Ten sections, covering all of New York State. Accessibility of historic landmarks, tourist attractions, park areas, building entrances, interiors, restrooms and parking facilities. A joint project of the New York Easter Seal Society and the New York State Department of Commerce Travel Bureau.

Access New York. NYU Medical Center, Institute of Rehabilitation Medicine, 400 E. 34th Street, New York, N.Y. 10016. An Accessibility Guide of Selected Facilities in East Midtown Manhattan. 50 cents.

Access Washington. Information Center for Handicapped Individuals, Inc., 1413 K Street, N.W., Washington, D.C. 20005. A Guide to Metropolitan Washington for the Physically Disabled.

Information also at the Handicapped Visitor Services Booth, Union Station, 50 Massachusetts Avenue, N.E., Washington, D.C. 20002. Open 7 days a week, 8 A.M. to 10 P.M. Tel: 202-523-5033.

A free information service to help disabled people throughout the United States plan trips here and abroad is available from: the Travel Information Center, Moss Rehabilitation Hospital, 12th Street and Tabor Road, Philadelphia, Pa. 19141.

This is not a travel booking service. Rather, the hospital provides the necessary data so that a disabled person can plan his own excursion. The center asks that requests for information include an outline of the cities or countries the traveler wants to visit and what his special interests are. Moss then sends him all available information on these sites, and their suitability and accessibility for the handicapped. The center also supplies names of people or agencies who might be able to provide more detailed information.

The hospital has assembled an extensive library of facts for disabled travelers, such as:

- Which hotels and motels have wheelchair ramps
- Which cruise ships and airlines make an extra effort to accommodate the disabled
- Which historical sites, national monuments, public facilities and tourist attractions are accessible
- Which cities and countries have special arrangements for disabled visitors*

BARRIER-FREE HOTELS AND MOTELS

In preparation for the White House Conference on Handicapped Individuals, the Sheraton Park Hotel in Washington, D.C., made extensive renovations and modifications to create a barrier-free environment for handicapped guests. Exterior and parking-lot ramps were built and ramps were installed in the public areas and meeting rooms. Doors were removed and grab bars installed in 396 sleeping rooms, and 25 percent of the public bathroom facilities were modified for wheelchair users. Telephones were lowered, and amplified hand sets installed. Raised letters and/or Braille signs were placed outside meeting rooms and elevators, and on most elevator control panels. In the restaurants and food-service outlets, Braille menus had always been available. Five hundred employees underwent sensitivity training, such as teaching restaurant workers to help blind persons find the coffee and the salad by using the clock positions to describe locations.

When asked why, with all this preparation, no flashing-light telephones or bed vibrators had been installed for the convenience and security of deaf guests, the manager replied frankly: "Because nobody has asked us." This

* NAPH Newsletter (Summer 1977).

simple statement may be the key to frequent omissions of services for disabled consumers. If you ask, you may get what you need.

Several of the national hotel chains are beginning to react to the public demand. Sheraton (toll-free reservation numbers: 800-325-3535) and Hyatt (800-228-9000) incorporate full-access architecture and specially equipped rooms in their new structures. Holiday Inn (800-238-5510), TraveLodge (800-255-3050), Howard Johnson's (800-654-2000), Best Western (800-528-1234) and budget motels and independent hotels around the nation are following the trend to accessibility. Several fast-food chains and independent restaurants are offering menus in Braille. The Century Plaza, Western International's hotel in Los Angeles, has printed all its restaurants' menus in Braille; the floor numbers on each elevator and all room numbers are raised; and in each room there is a relief map indicating the layout of the room.

As yet, no accommodations for deaf guests have come to the author's attention. "I often wonder," says Professor Sternberg, "when I check into a hotel room, what would happen in case of a fire. I wouldn't hear the alarm bell; firemen knocking at my door wouldn't get a reply and would think the room was empty. While other guests would escape to safety, I'd roast."

Why don't hotels provide portable TTY phones with flashing lights and bed vibrators to be installed temporarily, while a deaf guest occupies the room? Surely it would present neither technical obstacles to connect such instruments to the alarm system, nor would costs be prohibitive. Deaf guests would not only be safe in emergencies, they'd even enjoy the luxury of getting messages and using the telephone—like any other paying hotel guest.

☞ Write for: "Motels with Wheelchair Units," National Easter Seal Society, 2023 W. Ogden Avenue, Chicago, Ill. 60612.

HOW TO GET WHERE YOU WANT TO GO: PUBLIC TRANSPORTATION

What does consumerism mean in travel? Simply stated, it is the customer receiving what he pays for—no more, no less. It is the holder of a transportation ticket expecting and receiving certain minimum standards of service en route to his destination, and an uneventful reunion with his baggage once he arrives there.

For travelers with disabilities, it means also access to the conveyor and its services at points of departure, arrival and en route, and consideration by a staff that has received orientation training in communication with disabled passengers.

RAIL TRAVEL

"Access Amtrak: A Guide to Amtrak Services for Elderly and Handicapped Travelers" (August 1977) National Railroad Passenger Corporation, 955 L'Enfant Plaza, S.W., Washington, D.C. 20024.

This booklet describes in detail Amtrak services, gives door and aisle measurements and shows blueprints of Amclub, Amcafé, Amdinette, Turbo-club, Superliner Coach and Superliner Sleeping Car designs.

To find out what services Amtrak can provide to meet your special travel needs on any particular trip, call Amtrak's toll-free reservations and information number listed in your telephone directory.

The nationwide toll-free numbers to the teletypewriter (TTY) in Bensalem, Pa., are 800-523-6590 or 91; in Pennsylvania only, call 800-562-6960.

Blind passengers who travel on Amtrak with an attendant are entitled to a 25 percent discount for themselves and the attendant. They must have coupons from the American Foundation for the Blind, 15 W. 16th Street, New York, N.Y. 10011 (see p. 230). Guide dogs are permitted to ride in passenger cars at no extra charge.

Those deaf or blind passengers who need assistance should identify themselves to the conductor when he stops to collect tickets. He will make sure you are advised of station stops and will help you get off the train safely.

Whether you are riding short or long distance, reserved or unreserved, it is best to call a reasonable time before your trip to ensure that any special services or accommodations you require can be arranged.

Comments, both positive and critical, should be addressed to Adequacy of Service Bureau, Amtrak, 955 L'Enfant Plaza, S.W., Washington, D.C. 20024.

BUS TRAVEL

Both Continental Trailways and Greyhound allow a companion to ride free on interstate trips with a disabled traveler who needs assistance in boarding, exiting and traveling on a bus. A letter from a physician is required. New terminals and those scheduled for remodeling include barrier-free design features, such as ramps, handrails, low-level phones and water fountains and accessible rest rooms.

🖝 **Call your local Greyhound or Trailways office to help you work out your trip, determining where to make rest stops based on the accessibility of terminals. Write for "Helping Hand Service for the Handicapped," Greyhound Lines, Greyhound Tower, Phoenix, Ariz. 85077.**

TRAVEL CONCESSIONS FOR BLIND PERSONS

A blind person and his sighted companion may travel for one fare on most railroads and bus lines in the United States. In some parts of the country, one full first-class fare is charged, while elsewhere concessions are available on coach rates.

A blind person accompanied by a guide dog and a sighted companion is not eligible for this privilege, nor are two blind persons traveling together. Airlines do not give fare reductions; some steamship companies do.

Eligible is anyone who is totally blind or whose vision is so defective that he requires a companion in unfamiliar surroundings, and for whom it would be a hardship to pay two full fares.

You must have an identification card, and a coupon book for bus and rail travel, issued by the American Foundation for the Blind. The coupon books are issued annually for a nominal fee of $2, which is necessary to partially defray the cost of the program. No matter how many coupon books you use in a year, you pay just $2 during that year.

🖝 **An application card is contained in the booklet "Travel Concessions for Blind Persons," American Foundation for the Blind, 15 W. 16th Street, New York, N.Y. 10011.**

TRAVEL BY AIR

Air travel for disabled passengers has come a long way from the days when some determined individuals took airlines to court for refusing them passage. In March 1977 the "Rules for Transporting Handicapped Persons by Air" was issued by the Department of Transportation's Federal Aviation Administration. It is a set of regulations designed to "ensure that as many physically handicapped persons as possible can enjoy the benefits of commercial air travel with safety and comfort." Rather than issuing across-the-board regulations, the FAA allows each carrier to develop procedures appropriate to its own operations and aircraft. However, all certified air carriers must include in their tariffs all rules and practices used by the carriers in the transporting of handicapped passengers who may need help evacuating an aircraft in an emergency.

I suggest you write for: "Air Transportation of Handicapped Persons," Advisory Circular No. 120-32, Federal Aviation Administration Department of Transportation, Distribution Unit, Washington, D.C. 20590.

Though this is a government publication addressed to the airline industry, with the stated purpose "to identify the problems handicapped air travelers face and to provide guidelines to airline personnel to help alleviate these problems," you'll find the brochure good reading. After all, you should know for yourself what the airlines and their staff are supposed to do for you and what you can claim as your rights if their performance does not live up to your expectations and the government's demands.

In the guidelines, "a handicapped passenger" is defined as a person "who may need the assistance of another person to expeditiously move to an exit in the event of an emergency."
Handicapped passengers are categorized as:

a. *Ambulatory.* A passenger who is able to board and deplane from the aircraft unassisted and who is able to move about the aircraft unassisted. This includes the blind, deaf, mentally retarded, etc.
b. *Nonambulatory.* A passenger who is not able to board and deplane from an aircraft unassisted or who is not able to move about the aircraft unassisted.

Conditions which still permit airlines to refuse passage to a disabled individual are:

1. Passenger fails to comply with an airline's requirement for an advance notice.
2. Passenger cannot be accepted in accordance with the airline's procedures

concerning acceptance of passengers who may need help in being evacuated in an emergency.

3. The pilot exercises the prerogative of refusing passage to ANY passenger.

If you feel that the second point, allowing airlines to establish their own refusal procedures, offers too big a loophole in the FAA regulations, you may agree with Eunice Fiorito, former director of New York City's Mayor's Office for the Handicapped, who considered "a violation of her constitutional rights" the fact that airlines could "take away the right of an individual to make his own decision and make the decision for him."

However, let's look at the progress that has been made. During the summer of 1976 I sent questionnaires about accessibility and customer service to airlines, banks, department stores and food markets. By far the most responsive group was the airlines. All expressed their eagerness to serve disabled passengers and described procedures and staff training to make these passengers' flights smooth and enjoyable.

Delta Airlines has added stretcher patient facilities that permit stretcher patient service to approximately 95 percent of the cities served.

TWA publishes a booklet that they will be glad to send you. Write for *Consumer Information about Air Travel for the Handicapped,* TWA, 605 Third Avenue, New York, N.Y. 10016.

This booklet, first issued in 1976, was a pioneering effort of TWA's Director of Consumer Affairs, Janet Garlough. At present, the airline is considering more innovations: TTY installations in their 8 reservations offices. They also are experimenting with filling a need expressed by many deaf travelers: TTY phones at airports, to inform deaf passengers about changes in departures or arrivals and any unusual activity, and to give such passengers the opportunity to communicate by phone with their relatives, a privilege taken for granted by hearing travelers in case of schedule changes due to unforeseen conditions.

Pilot installations in selected airports will be watched for frequency of use, before the system will be installed in more or all airports served.

Hearing-impaired travelers, take note: Use the systems where they exist and ask other airlines for similar accommodations!

The new FAA guidelines devote many pages to "Attitudes of Airline Personnel" and ways of "Assisting Disabled Persons," describing types of disabilities the crew will encounter and should know how to be most helpful.

Advance notification of the passenger's special needs, including diets, is required, and the convenience of pre-boarding will be arranged, if desired.

Among the recommendations, one seems to be noteworthy for the fact that it had to be made at all: "When a passenger is pushed in a wheelchair to the ticket counter, the agent should speak to the person in the chair, not to the person pushing it."!!!

Have you, disabled reader, ever had the experience of a waiter addressing your table companion to find out what you want to order? More people than airline personnel must be told that "a handicapped person is usually not different from the nonhandicapped, especially with respect to pride and competitiveness."

The guidelines recommend seating arrangements which provide for the comfort of handicapped persons, as well as for the safety of all passengers in the event of an emergency evacuation. Each airline must establish procedures for carrying people who cannot move quickly to an exit during an emergency. And before takeoff, each such passenger and his/her attendant must be briefed on procedures to be followed in an evacuation.

Crutches and canes would slow emergency evacuation procedures, and are stored in an approved stowage compartment. Wheelchairs are transported in the baggage compartment. Shipping of batteries of motorized wheelchairs should be checked with the airline. Spillproof caps, sealed or jell batteries (instead of acid) may be recommended.

CANINE AIR TRAVELERS

Guide dogs give their owners the independence they wish to exercise in getting around, on the ground and in the air. Not surprisingly, the FAA Advisory Circular devotes an entire page to "Dog Guides," extensively quoting from *Seeing Eye Dogs as Air Travelers,* Information for Air Lines Personnel, The Seeing Eye, Inc., Morristown, N.J. 07960.

"Seeing Eye" is a trademark, designating dogs trained by the Seeing Eye, Inc., of Morristown, N.J. Generically, such dogs are called guide dogs. They are selected for intelligence, responsibility and gentleness, and have been thoroughly trained for their job. The blind person, too, has received intensive instruction in the care and control of the dog. (See "Man's Best Friend," p. 200.)

Guide dogs for the blind have been airline travelers since the 1930s, when United Airlines made a landmark decision in permitting blind passengers to keep their dogs with them in the passenger cabins of their aircraft. Since then, antidiscrimination laws have secured dog guides' rights to accompany their blind owners wherever they wish to go.

The dog should remain with its owner throughout the flight. A seat in the first row is recommended, where there is more room for the dog. A window seat will avoid other passengers having to step over the dog to reach the aisle. Guide dogs are gentle and friendly and are taught to accept strangers calmly. However, they should not be touched or petted, and flight attendants should discourage children from yielding to their natural desire to pat the dog.

In case of emergency evacuation, the owner should go down the chute with the dog in his lap. The dog should wear its harness, to activate his sense of responsibility and to help the man-dog team to leave the evacuation area quickly once they are on the ground.

Hearing guide dogs are newcomers to public transportation. Most public carriers are in the process of amending regulations to permit carriage of hearing dogs. Amtrak and the two major bus lines favor the service and are studying the program. They see no problem in applying the same policy that admits guide dogs for the blind. (See identifying collar and card, "Man's Best Friend," p. 202.)

United Airlines was the first to receive a request to carry a hearing dog. After filing with the Civil Aeronautics Board (CAB) for a regulation change, United began carrying hearing dogs at no charge in April 1977. By June, nineteen airlines—including nearly all major U.S. carriers—had filed with the CAB to allow transportation of hearing dogs.

Drawing reprinted with permission

ACCESSIBILITY OF AIRPORTS

The accessibility of most major airports will increase in the future. Public Law 94-352, Airport and Airway Development Act Amendments, was enacted in July 1976. Airport terminals constructed or maintained under provisions of this new law will have to meet accessibility requirements. Since federal funds assist in airport constructions or renovations, Section 504 of the Rehabilitation Act of 1973 will further assure the accessibility of airports.

Where local airports are deficient, airlines offer staff assistance for boarding, deplaning and making connections. American and Pan Am offer hydraulic lifts when there is no jetway boarding, and TWA announced a new "Handicapped Lift," an enclosed elevator type lift which will also be used to drive between gates and aircraft to aid handicapped passengers making connections.

Access Travel: Airports, a new and expanded edition of the federal Architectural and Transportation Barriers Compliance Board's airport access guide for handicapped travelers, has been published by the Federal Aviation Administration of the U.S. Department of Transportation.

The 20-page guide lists 69 accessibility features to 220 airport terminals around the world, beginning with Aberdeen, Scotland, and ending with Zurich, Switzerland. The booklet also includes information on how travelers with special needs can make advance arrangements to ensure a pleasant and comfortable trip.

Distributed free by the U.S. General Services Administration, Washington, D.C. 20405.

Rental cars with hand controls are available at airport locations in major cities. (See Chapter 7, section titled "In the Driver's Seat," p. 162.)

HOW TO HANDLE AIR TRAVEL PROBLEMS

If you have a problem with an airline—whether fares, baggage, poor service, delayed flights, or any kind of treatment which you feel was unfair or discourteous—your first action should be to report the difficulty to the airline company. The field of air travel is a competitive business, and airlines are anxious to provide service that is satisfactory to the customers. Some have even established consumer offices to handle problem situations.

If the airline does not respond or fails to settle your claim within a reasonable period of time, write to the CAB Office of Consumer Affairs for assistance: Office of Consumer Affairs, Civil Aeronautics Board, Washington, D.C. 20428; tel.: 202/382-7735.

Even without problems, or to prevent them from happening, ask CAB for their handy booklet, "Air Travelers' Fly-Rights," that should be read by all air travelers, regular or occasional. Airline personnel may not volunteer information about your rights. It's up to you to know what they are and to use them.

If your luggage is lost or damaged, file a complaint immediately, and keep copies of your claim, stubs and emergency expenses that you incur as a result of the difficulty. The maximum limit of airline responsibility for lost or damaged luggage is $750, but you'll have to prove that the contents were worth $750 or more.

Should you be "bumped" from a flight, in spite of confirmed reservation, due to the airlines' policy of overbooking to compensate for no-shows, the airline must arrange to get you to your destination within two hours of your scheduled time of arrival, or pay you a compensation from $25 to $200, depending on the price of your ticket. Thanks to a new ruling by the Civil Aeronautics Board, you'll now find notices about overbooking policies and the airlines' responsibilities to "bumped" passengers posted at all counters and included with your ticket.

Of course, you won't be the one to be bumped if you avail yourself of your pre-boarding privileges!

You may also write to the airline about good or bad experiences during your flight. The airlines' customer relations departments are extraordinarily courteous and will respond to you. Jack Gannon, Director of Public Relations at Gallaudet College in Washington, D.C., sent a letter to Piedmont Airlines describing, not critically but constructively, his experiences as a deaf passenger on one of their flights. He also sent them some marvelous "Tips on Dealing with Deaf Passengers." Here's an excerpt from the reply he received:

> Admittedly, we, as most businesses that deal with the public, have not done the job we should have in training our people to deal with handicapped persons. I honestly believe, however, that many of us are beginning to make some progress in this direction—primarily as a result of people such as yourself, *bringing to our attention* the correct ways of dealing with the handicapped. We recently received some very good material from a blind persons' organization.
>
> I am taking the liberty of making your letter and its attachment available to the manager of each city (49) we serve, and to the flight attendant supervisors for their further use in training our flight attendants.

☎ **If you wish to read "Tips on Dealing with Deaf Passengers," write to: Jack Gannon, Director of Public Relations, Gallaudet College, Washington, D.C. 20002. He'll be glad to send you a copy.**

GROUP TRAVEL

Even if you are an indomitably independent spirit, you may find great advantage in group travel. You'll be with congenial travel companions, all arrangements will be made for you, foreseeable problems will be eliminated. On trips abroad, immigration and customs procedures are simplified, and most important, you are not alone and stranded far from home in case of accident, illness or any other emergency.

You will find many group tours advertised in periodicals addressed to people of your type of disability. Your most important piece of research is to check and double-check the reliability of the tour operator or travel agent. The agent's experience and knowledge of the places you plan to visit can be very valuable to you, and his services don't cost you anything. He earns his fee from the discounts he receives from the carriers and hotels where he books you as a passenger and guest. If possible, speak to somebody for whom the travel agent arranged a trip or who traveled with a group tour conducted by the tour operator you plan to sign up with.

Before booking any tour, group or individual, find out if the travel agent or tour promoter are members of ASTA, the American Society of Travel Agents. In order to obtain and retain membership, travel agents must comply with the Society's Principles of Professional Conduct and Ethics, guidelines that have been established to protect consumers against unethical business practices.

What is a Travel Agent?
15 Travel Reminders from ASTA
American Society of Travel Agents, 711 Fifth Avenue, New York, N.Y. 10022. Be sure your travel agent or tour operator gives you satisfactory answers to many of the questions ASTA suggests in these publications. Cancellation privileges are just one of the conditions you should get in writing.

Handicapped persons, physically and financially able to travel, are so much being recognized as a responsive, virtually untapped reservoir for travel agents seeking new clients—and profits—that a new organization has been founded, the Society for the Advancement of Travel for the Handicapped. SATH defines itself as "a nonprofit marketing forum created for the exchange of knowledge and the gaining of new skills in how to facilitate travel for the handicapped."

Write to Murray Vidockler, Executive Director, SATH, 26 Court Street, Brooklyn, N.Y. 11242, for a list of agencies serving handicapped travelers.

Also ask for "Bibliography of Material concerning Travel for the Handicapped" and "Bibliography of Articles," of which reprints can be obtained on payment of $1.

Handy-Cap Horizons, Inc., is a nonprofit organization, chartered in Indiana, with tax-exempt status, which strives to bring the world to the door of the handicapped and elderly, either by actual travel throughout the United States and other parts of the world, or by articles in its quarterly magazine of the same name.

All who become members are eligible for Discount Tours, planned to fit the disabled and the older person who wishes a slower pace. "Our tours," they claim, "are planned to receive the most for the least sum possible. Much cheaper than commercial tours, for we are completely volunteer. We're people-to-people too. Being international, we have members in so many places to help with the planning, not only in all of USA and North America, but most of Europe, the Middle East, Africa, the Far East, to Singapore and Australia."

Handy-Cap Horizons do not plan independent travel. They are not a travel agent, rather a travel club. Tours are limited strictly to members. Membership dues are Active, single $6 per year ($6.50 outside USA); Active, family $7 per year.

To learn more of the organization, write for: "Once Upon a Time," History of Handy-Cap Horizons, written by a paraplegic minister and a quadriplegic teacher. Handy-Cap Horizons, Inc., 3250 E. Loretta Drive, Indianapolis, Ind. 46227. 50 cents for postage.

Flying Wheels Tours, a Midwest agency, has been granted an Interstate Commerce Commission tour-broker's license to operate bus tours for the handicapped on a national basis. Judd Jacobson, quadriplegic president of the agency, plans to charter standard tour coaches that will be modified with ramps and lifts to accommodate wheelchairs so that interstate recreational travel can be offered at a lower cost than programs by air or cruise ship.

Write to them at 143 W. Bridge Street, Owatonna, Minn. 55060.

V. 400 MILLION DISABLED

10. NEWS FROM AROUND THE WORLD

If you are a member of America's largest minority, it will interest you to know that the same ratio exists around the world: visibly or invisibly, one person in every ten of the world's population is handicapped. Whereas developed countries have made great strides in helping the handicapped, the problem is still a severe one in the Third World. Burdened by massive unemployment and poverty among the able-bodied, planners in developing countries tend to sweep the plight of the handicapped under the rug as a low-priority problem.

With over 75 percent of the world's 400 million handicapped left to their own devices and receiving no help at all, there is an enormous job to be done in this field.

A complete around-the-world report is beyond the scope of this book. Only a few highlights from here and there can be mentioned, and a listing of resources to carry on your own research, if you are so inclined.

Now known and recognized all over the world, the International Symbol of Access is not yet ten years old. Rehabilitation International approved and adopted the design in 1969, on recommendation of the International Committee on Technical Aids, Housing and Transportation (ICTA), and has made it available for use throughout the world, "so that its use might contribute to the protection of the human rights of all disabled persons and specifically to an improvement in the availability to disabled persons of the resources and facilities of the communities in which they live." *It must never be used where barriers exist.*

What are Rehabilitation International and ICTA?

Rehabilitation International, 122 E. 23rd Street, New York, N.Y. 10010, the International Society for Rehabilitation of the Disabled, is a nongovernmental federation of ninety-eight national associations, agencies and boards, governmental and voluntary, in more than sixty countries. To solve the problems of more than 300 million persons with significant physical or mental impairments who cannot obtain adequate help, Rehabilitation International has proclaimed 1970–1980 the DECADE OF REHABILITATION.

The Rehabilitation International Information Service is operated from Heidelberg, Federal Republic of Germany, by the Stiftung [Foundation] Rehabilitation.

A Spanish-language service (SIDIR) functions in Mexico with the help of the Inter-American Committee for Social Security.

The Subscribers' Information Service provides periodic mailings for selected current material in the main fields of interest ($15 per year).

The *International Rehabilitation Review,* published six times a year, gives significant international news, summaries of important trends and developments ($5 per year).

Rehabilitation International USA, 20 W. 40th Street, New York, N.Y. 10018, though affiliated with Rehabilitation International, is an independent national organization, publishing *Rehabilitation World,* the U.S. Journal of International Rehabilitation, News and Information ($7.50 per year). Membership in Rehabilitation International USA ($15 per year) includes annual subscriptions to *Rehabilitation World* and the *International Rehabilitation Review.*

More publications of interest to the internationalist:

Rehabilitation Worldwide, A Directory of International Rehabilitation Organizations. The President's Committee on Employment of the Handicapped, Washington, D.C. 20210.

Successful Disabled Persons International (Series). Committee for the Handicapped, People-to-People, Washington, D.C. 20036.

Summary of Information on Projects and Activities in the Field of Rehabilitation of the Disabled (annually). United Nations Secretariat, Social Development Division, United Nations, N.Y. 10017.

Publications of the ILO, International Labor Organization, Annual Catalog. *ILO Documentation in Vocational Rehabilitation* (English, French, Spanish), 1750 New York Avenue, N.W., Washington, D.C. 20006.

Publications, Central Council for the Disabled, 34 Eccleston Square, London SWIV IPE, England. Comprehensive bibliography, quoting prices including postage and packing. Among many: *Contact,* Official Journal of the CCD (bi-monthly); *Integrating the Disabled,* Report of the Snowdon Working Party; *Access guides* to numerous towns in England, Norway and Paris; *London for the Disabled,* excerpted in *Shopping for the Disabled in London; Who looks after you at Heathrow Airport?,* British Tourist Authority, 680 Fifth Avenue, New York, N.Y. 10019.

Ferienführer 76/77, a vacation guide for handicapped people in Dutch, English, French and German. Bundesarbeitsgemeinschaft "Hilfe für Behinderte," (Federal Working Party on Aid to the Handicapped), Kirchfeldstrasse 149, 4000 Düsseldorf, Germany. Codes hundreds of hotels, tourist attractions and railway stations throughout the country, according to their suitability for physically limited and blind persons. Prices for accommodations are included.

Welcome In(n), produced for ICTA by the Netherlands Society for Rehabilitation ICTA, Fack S-161, 25 Bromma 1, Sweden. Aimed at building owners, the brochure uses witty cartoons to point out problems and suggests solutions. Received with great interest throughout the world, the brochure is scheduled for translation into German, French and Italian by the Schweizerische Arbeitsgemeinschaft für Invalidenhilfe, Postfach 129, CH-8032 Zurich, Switzerland.

Rehabilitation Literature, "No One at Home" (January 1976). A Brief Review of Housing for Handicapped Persons in Some European Countries, Reprint, published by National Easter Seal Society, 2023 W. Ogden Avenue, Chicago, Ill. 60612.

The Council for International Urban Liaison, 1612 K Street, N.W., Washington, D.C. 20006, a federally funded organization for the "encouragement of international exchanges of practical experiences," reports some innovations of benefit for handicapped city dwellers:

In Vienna, Austria, a low-frequency "beep" sounds when a traffic light is green and it's safe for the blind person to cross. Silence means to wait. The first unit of these "talking lights" was installed opposite a school for the blind, and the city is in the process of installing more.

Sweden and Japan have attacked the problem on a national scale. Some 3,000 audio signals are currently in use at street crossings throughout Sweden. In Japan, twenty-nine of the forty-seven major metropolitan and prefectural governments, including Tokyo, Yokohama and Nagoya, use hundreds of sound signals for blind pedestrians, various musical tunes, chimes and bird calls.

In the United States, experimental programs only were reported at selected sites in Wethersfield, Conn., Portland, Ore., and Watertown, Mass.

The Swedish government has proposed new building regulations for handicapped that would require all new apartment units with more than two floors to have elevators large enough to accommodate a wheelchair. Apartments must likewise be easily accessible. The draft legislation would also apply to the renovation of old buildings.

In West Germany, public and private employers are required to hire one handicapped employee for every 16 on the payroll. Employers who cannot or do not wish to meet this obligation are required to pay DM 100 ($40) monthly into a special fund for each position that should have been reserved for a handicapped worker.

Intaglio dots on banknotes indicate the face value, for the information of blind people, on Dutch, Israeli and Swiss paper money. The U.S. Bureau of Printing and Engraving is not unaware of these issues, but considers the procedure impractical in view of the 40 billion notes in circulation. They also claim that the Bank of the Netherlands called the Dutch experiment "not a complete success," and, furthermore, the Federation of the Blind opposed the project in a resolution, arguing against the stereotype of "blindism."

LINK, a British television program by the handicapped and about the handicapped, is shown on British television in "peak viewing time" (called "prime time" in the United States). The "presenter" is Tony Northmore, a quadriplegic former RAF pilot, now a leader in an ongoing campaign to earn rights and benefits for the handicapped of Britain.

In one program Tony presented "The Adventures of the Disabled Village." It was an abbreviated version of a story by Vic Finkelstein in *Disability Rights Handbook,* published by the Disability Alliance, 96 Portland Place, London W.1, in conjunction with ATV Network Limited, on which the Sunday-morning *LINK* series is broadcast. With subtle British humor, the story forcefully makes its point:

Imagine a town full of physically impaired people, all wheelchair users. They run everything. They run shops, the factories, the schools, the television studio, the lot.

There aren't any able-bodied people, so naturally, when they built the town the community decided it was pointless to have ceilings ten feet high and doors seven feet high. "It's just a lot of wasted space that needs heating," they said. So the ceilings were built at seven feet and the doors at five feet. In every way they designed the place the way they wanted it, and these proportions are now standardized by regulation.

Everyone is happy. Years go by.

One day a few able-bodied people come to stay. One of the first things they notice is the height of the doors. And the reason they notice is because they keep hitting their heads. They come to stand out by the bruises they carry on their foreheads.

Some doctors, psychiatrists and social workers all become involved. The doctors do extensive research and conclude in their learned reports that the disabled able bodied suffer from "loss of reduction of functional ability" and the resulting handicap caused "disadvantage or restriction of activity."

Committees are formed. Many people are worried about what becomes known as the "problem of the able-bodied." Throughout the town there is a growth of real concern. Specially toughened helmets are handed out free to the able-bodied to be worn at all times. Braces are designed which give support and relief while keeping the able-bodied wearer bent to a normal height.

Getting a job is a major problem for the able-bodied. One man, for instance, applies to become a television interviewer. But first he must be examined by the doctor. There is this regulation which states that all able-bodied must be given a special medical examination when they apply for a job. And the doctor, perfectly naturally, points out in his report that it would be rather strange to have a television interviewer with a bent back who wore a helmet all the time.

He doesn't get the job.

Money, of course, becomes a major problem. Various groups of compassionate wheelchair users get together and form registered charities. Every quarter they have a collection day.

Upturned helmets are left in pubs and shops for people to drop their small change into. There is a heartening support for organizations such as "The Society for Understanding the Disabled Able-Bodied." There is talk of founding Special Homes.

But then one day it dawns on the able-bodied that there is nothing actually wrong with them, just that society excludes them. They form a union to protect themselves and to campaign against segregation. They argue that if ceilings and doors were raised, there would be no problem. But this is, of course, a foolish suggestion. You can't deny disability. After all, there are regulations which govern the height of ceilings and doors.

In the subsequent discussion, the disabled author elaborated:

What ones needs is a changed outlook, a changed attitude, a rethinking of the problems. To do this you need to question all former approaches. For example, that disabled people should adjust and accept the conditions.

Society causes disability, not the physical impairment. If able-bodied people live in a community which is designed for wheelchair living, then their physical condition becomes a disability in that society. And if society builds steps all over the place, not being able to walk becomes a disability. It's this social condition which disables people who cannot walk. Therefore, we need social solutions to these problems.

From my point of view, I think primarily we need to stop saying, you must accept and adjust to disability. We need to say "Hey, what is disability— why should we adjust to it?" Perhaps we should deny, perhaps we should change society.

The story aims at getting through to disabled people, so that they will question these former attitudes. And encourage able-bodied people to question these attitudes, to organize and to try and change society which disables us.

On these words of a disabled British citizen, I will close this book. They bring us back full circle to the opening page, citing Section 504 of the Rehabilitation Act of 1973, the American people's declared intention to change the society that handicaps their disabled citizens. All society has to do now is to make the spirit of the law come to life in the everyday lives of disabled Americans. Society's helpers in this endeavor will be those members of the disabled community who know their rights and will take ACTION to see that equal rights will apply to all Americans, in whatever racial, physical or mental condition they are spending their lives.

If this book will stimulate such "action," its purpose will be achieved.

INDEX

ABOUT THE AUTHOR

Lilly Bruck, Ph.D., developed the Division of Consumer Education with the New York City Department of Consumer Affairs. Since 1973 she has focused her attention on the education of disabled consumers. She has been named Director of an HEW project to establish a national system for consumer education of disabled Americans.

Dr. Bruck lives in New York with her husband, Sandor, and three cats.